Other books by Sean McNamara

Dewdrops of Infinity

Psychedelics, Psychic Abilities, UFOs, and

THE PUHARICH PROJECT

COLOR EDITION

Sean McNamara

SIGNAL

AND

NOISE

ADVANCED
PSYCHIC TRAINING
for Remote Viewing,
Clairvoyance, and ESP

SEAN MCNAMARA

Mind Sight

Sean McNamara

TRAINING TO SEE WITHOUT EYES
Pilot Program for Adults

DEFY YOUR LIMITS

The Telekinesis Training Method

Sean McNamara

Learn the Psi ability, then use it to empower the rest of your life.

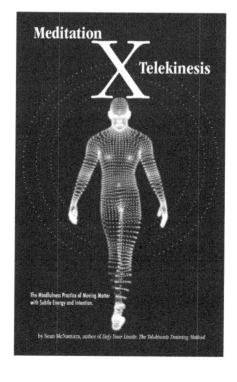

Meditation X Telekinesis

The Mindfulness Practice of Moving Matter with Subtle Energy and Intention.

by Sean McNamara, author of *Defy Your Limits: The Telekinesis Training Method*

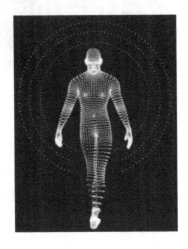

Renegade Mystic

The Pursuit of Spiritual Freedom Through Consciousness Exploration

Second Edition

SEAN MCNAMARA

Cover design, interior and photography by Sean McNamara unless
noted otherwise.

"Mind Possible" logo by Erika Wright

Other photo and image credits are listed on their selected pages.

Second Edition

Published by Mind Possible

Edited by Cierra McNamara

ISBN: 978-1-7352930-2-8

1. Self-Transformation   2. New Age and Spirituality
3. Paranormal and Supernatural   4. Psychic Development

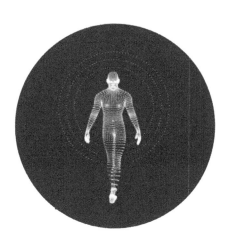

I wonder about a time after this physical life is done,
when I've returned to the other side of the veil.

"What did you discover while you were there?"
they might ask.

With a smile and a tear, I'll say,

"Us."

TABLE OF CONTENTS

DEDICATION

I dedicate this book to my dad, Marty, and my mom, Conchita. I am ever grateful for the life you've given me.

Dad, I hear the sound of your voice in my own, especially when I laugh, or cough. I think we appreciate silence and privacy the same way, which can feel lonely sometimes.

Ma, your heart burns with passion and fury. You'll always love us more than we can ever love you back. When I seek justice for myself and others, I think I got that from you.

You took Jenny and me around the whole world, opening our eyes in ways beyond compare. You are remarkable guides.

And to my sister Jenny, thanks for being my travel buddy.
Knowing you were there too is one of the few things that makes any
of it seem real.

ACKNOWLEDGMENTS

It is difficult to limit my expression of gratitude only to those who've played a proximate role in my starting, *enduring* and completing this memoir. Cierra, none of this would be possible without the guidance, love and support you've given me since the day we met. Dawn Kirkwood, not only did you review my draft and suggest helpful improvements, but you've been a dear friend for a long time, and I'm ever grateful for the times we've spent together in the meditation hall, in Moab, and various delightful coffee shops. Autumn Moran, you've listened to me kvetch about this book for years, and never stopped encouraging me. To my other meditation friends, Jill Lowy, Stacy Linrud, Kathy Bruce, Polina Rikoun and Lucie Brossard, thank you for sharing space with me over the years. You were "there" for a lot of it. I'm equally grateful to my remote viewing friends in Denver, you know who you are, and I'll mention you by name in the next book. We make a wonderful team, the best! Sandra Champlain, you were the first one to ever interview me online, and that gave me my first confidence to share my experience. Rick Nelson, you saw value in what I could teach people. By inviting me to speak at the PRF, you opened many doors for me. You have incredible tales of your own to tell, and I hope you do, if that's your wish. You've given so much, thank you. Carol Casebeer, you're a beam of light, a comrade in consciousness exploration, and quite the networker. Damon Abraham, we've been through similar trials, and I admire your ability to keep a level head when reflecting on the astonishing phenomena you and I have seen, together and apart. I look forward to making more discoveries with you. Michael Boudreaux, thanks for your ears and shoulder. Finally, to my friends, guides, and loved ones on the other side, I've heard your whispers in the dark. Thank you for showing me the way.

FOR THE ROAD

Music has the power to invoke emotion, inspiration, creativity, and memories. There are particular songs which take me back to key moments of my life. Each one touches my heart differently. I thought it would be nice to share them with you here. Listening to them from time to time as you read this book could be like two friends taking a road trip together, blasting the radio throughout the night to keep us going.

The link to the private YouTube playlist containing all these songs is available at www.RenegadeMysticBook.com/ForTheRoad

In no particular order, the playlist includes selections by Martin Sexton, U2, Led Zepellin, Waterlillies, Moby, LCD Soundsystem, Pink Floyd, Radiohead, Alanis Morissette, Sylvan Esso, and others.

ABOUT THE SECOND EDITION

Although the first edition included the detailed accounts of my out-of-body experiences, and of some of my lucid dreams, I didn't include step-by-step instructions for learning how to have these experiences. Instead, I mentioned the books and authors I relied on for my own training, hoping readers would continue their journey by seeking them out. The details of my period of striving could then serve as a valuable adjunct to the reader's development.

However, I've since decided to include some fundamental techniques in this edition, so readers can quickly begin their training, if they so desire. Instead of losing time to finding and ordering materials elsewhere, they can begin as soon as they've finished reading the book, or even from the start.

Two concise sets of instructions are found at the end of this book. First, how to have a *lucid dream*. Lucid dreaming is a powerful method for tapping into one's creativity and subconscious mind, among other things. A person can also use the lucid dream state as a launching off point for the *out of body experience*, which is the goal of the second set of instructions.

These are only a small selection of instructions found inside many books available today. Still, they're enough to get you started, and probably enough to lead you all the way to your desired experience. They worked for me. What you take away from them, is up to you. It largely comes down to steady training, unrelenting desire, and grit.

AUTHOR'S NOTE

In darkness, the realities we'd rather not see eventually shine their way into our awareness. Their light interrupts the dreamy version of our life, one we work so hard to maintain, day after day. Opening our eyes, we realize there are choices to be made, and time is running out.

This is my journey of confusion, passion, attachment, betrayal, and eventually finding the freedom to seek my own path. I'm sharing it with you so that you might learn from my mistakes, and to encourage you if you ever find yourself taking the lonely road. Let me tell you now, it's worth it, and you'll make new friends along the way.

Many readers will enjoy this book because it offers the backstory to why I decided to explore, practice, then teach other people how to use their psychic abilities. Others will appreciate the implied connection between widening one's perception and having spontaneous encounters with non-ordinary, or shall I go so far as to say, *non-human* beings. Any readers who refer to themselves as "black sheep" will be in good company here, as will the rebels.

Some readers may consider this a book about how to find one's own way through reality, how to be a *consciousness explorer*, or even how to seek out paranormal phenomena. It's a book about the attitudes, risks and demands involved in being a certain type of person.

However, this is not a "how to" book. If you'd like to learn the specific techniques for having out of body experiences, lucid dreams, for meditation, for telekinesis, or for remote viewing, try my other books and online video courses.

Nevertheless, this book *does* contain rare and valuable guidance for students and researchers of these phenomena.

Learning abilities such as these takes work, commitment, determination, and a large dose of inspiration. This book will help you along your journey by sharing my personal examples with you. This should aid you in finding your own unique answers inside yourself, within your own life.

I begin my story by discussing ordinary aspects of religion and spirituality. Mostly, you'll hear about certain things I endured as an adult student of Buddhism. I'll also make comments about other religious influences in my life. Allow me to make it clear, now, that this is *not* a book about Buddhism, Catholicism, or any other "ism."

More importantly, whenever I am critical of people, the discerning reader will see that I am discussing their individual actions, how they think, and how they affected me. I make no blanket statements about entire religions, or the groups of people who belong to them. My intention is not to attack anybody's religion.

I minimized technical references about the techniques and meditation of the Buddhist tradition I formerly belonged to, so that anybody can enjoy the reading, no matter their background. Still, there are some aspects of it which I needed to explain, mostly in the first chapter, in order to help you understand my experience. I tried to do so just enough to keep things meaningful without being overbearing.

To share my story as honestly as I have, I changed the names of some of the people who were a part of it. I am who I am today, in large part *because* of them. I suppose I'm thankful even though I'm not happy about what happened between us. Like me, they've moved on with their lives, and I don't want my story to anchor them to their past. We must all continue to grow, and learn, and hopefully become better people.

Besides, this book isn't written for them. I wrote it for you. And to be honest, I wrote it for me, too. Please remember, it's the *lessons* which matter most, not the people who suffered them.

Timelines and conversations were recorded to the best of my ability, as much as my memory allowed, and to ease storytelling. The transcripts from my dream and OBE (out of body experience) journals were lightly edited for readability.

Aside from those changes, everything I shared with you here *actually happened*. There should be no confusion regarding which events were dreams, out of body experiences, wakeful conversations with the deceased, and events where the basic laws of physics seem to have been violated.

You'll read about strange things I *saw*, some which seemed to have symbolic value. These things were also real, although there's no way to know for sure if they meant anything special when they happened. Sometimes, life stands out in particular ways for no reason at all.

This is a unique book. A strange book. Don't worry about keeping track of events as we move forward and backward in time. Just let each experience wash over you as you turn the pages. I'm not concerned with appealing to your rational, logical mind. What I really hope for is to make contact with a deeper part of you. A much deeper part.

If you're perfectly happy with how you *think* life works, or how reality functions, and if you don't want anything to threaten your status quo, then you should stop reading now. You won't be the same person afterward.

Finally, there are many important, beloved, and supportive people whom I was unable to include in this memoir. To do so would require a second, or even a third volume. If you're one of those people and happen to be reading this, please know that you have my utmost gratitude for being a part of my life. I thought of you often while writing this book.

CHAPTER 1 INNOCENCE LOST

I could feel her behind me as we lay in bed with our backs to each other. We weren't even touching. I was up to the edge of the mattress on my side, and I think she was trying to stay away from me too. My heart felt like a cold, hard, slab of concrete, the way it always did when I'd reached my limit and was unwilling to say anything else, to try again, or to give in. I felt terrible.

It was nothing compared to what was about to happen later that night.

We should have been in a better mood. We'd been at the meditation center a few days already, and finally underwent the initiation we'd come for. Regarded as an "empowerment" in Tibetan Buddhism, this was a rite of passage granting us the guru's permission to begin practicing a special, "secret" meditation connected to a "yidam," a wisdom-deity, from the Buddhist pantheon named Vajra-yogini.

The empowerment took all day to perform, partly because there were almost a hundred initiates who had arrived from all over the world to attend. The shrine room was filled with rows of low, wooden tables occupied by people sitting on cushions, just inches above the floor. Each of us had a copy of the liturgy along with various implements required to perform this complex meditation, including our traditional bell, drum, and scepter.

The centerpiece at the front of the room was an enormous shrine filled with offering bowls, statues, flowers, and burning incense and tapestries. Next to the shrine was the throne. This was an overstuffed seat decorated with beautiful silk patterns, and supported by a raised wooden platform. It was so high, the head of a person standing in front of the guru would only reach the level of his feet or torso.

While guru is a more Indian term, Tibetans refer to the head of one's lineage as "Rinpoche," which means "precious jewel." Instead of

Playing the traditional bell (ghanta) and hand drum (damaru)

using the guru's actual name, we just called him Rinpoche, the way you might refer to your university teacher as "Professor," instead of "Mr. Jones" or your doctor as "Doctor" instead of "Fred."

On the day of the empowerment, Rinpoche led the ceremony from his throne. We chanted the liturgy for hours, pausing at the appropriate times so he could perform the requisite act of consecration or purification.

At other times, we'd stand up one-by one to approach him, and he'd reach down from above to perform some gesture of anointing. We drank sacred water, had symbolic implements placed on our heads and in our hands, and performed a dozen other rituals as part of the ceremony.

Separately, Andrea and I had worked hard for years to be here, and especially hard the last few months as a couple to get to this point. When the ceremony was finished, we were elated. But that had been a couple days earlier, and the underlying stress of our relationship had risen to the surface again.

We'd gone to bed after raising the white flag and agreeing to wait until after the retreat was over to focus on mending our relationship. We had a few days left, which we'd spend learning how to do the complex visualizations, mantras and other rituals associated with Vajra-yogini. This was our top priority now. Repairing our relationship would have to wait.

I first met Andrea at a retreat in Colorado the year before. We were both students in the same Tibetan Buddhist lineage, and she had flown out from Los Angeles to attend. I could tell she was as devoted to her spiritual path as I was, which made her doubly attractive to me. She felt the same way, and during the retreat, a spark turned into a flame.

She returned to California after the retreat was over, but we were able to keep that flame burning by having regular phone conversations. We didn't really know that much about each other, but that didn't prevent our frail connection from deepening over time. Our relationship was mostly based on our mutual determination to meditate and to follow this particular path of spirituality.

We missed each other very much, but a solution to being apart from each other came one afternoon during one of our regular after-dinner phone calls.

We were working toward finishing a set of practices called "ngöndro", or *preliminaries*. After completing the ngöndro, we'd be qualified for initiation into the lineage's more advanced and *secret* meditation techniques. These practices are regarded by its followers as the *fastest way to achieve enlightenment*. For me, enlightenment symbolized no longer being afraid, and there was something I'd been afraid of for a very long time.

On the phone that evening, we talked about Rinpoche's recent announcement that he'd be giving the initiation in Vermont that

Sean McNamara

October. I told Andrea how much I wanted to attend it. She was almost finished with her ngöndro and had already planned on being there. *Oh, if only we could go together, wouldn't that be perfect?* But the only way for me to finish my ngöndro in time would be to quit my job, enter retreat, and become a full-time yogi.

I had done several solitary retreats already. Some lasted a week, some were ten days long, and one lasted a full month. I spent each one completely alone inside an isolated mountain cabin, where it was almost guaranteed I'd never see another person the entire time.

I knew finishing my ngöndro would take me several months of non-stop practice, but I knew I wasn't prepared on either the practical or psychological level to spend that much time alone in a cabin.

"Why don't you just come stay with me and finish it at my place?" I *think* she asked. I can't honestly remember which one of us came up with the idea.

Regardless, somehow we came up with the idea that I would move in with her that summer and focus all my time in L.A. finishing the ngöndro in time to join her in Vermont.

I had plenty of room left on my credit cards, and I didn't feel particularly attached to my job at a group home for developmentally disabled adults. It was a far cry from what I could've done with my degree in computer science, and I was already used to leaving one job for another to accommodate my spiritual pursuits.

I loaded up my old, red Chevy Trailblazer and headed west to be with Andrea. Two days of driving passed quickly, and I spent most of the time daydreaming about our wonderful opportunity to be together. I was about to spend four months dedicating every day to meditation while living with my new girlfriend. What more could I ask for?

The first hours of the drive were spent winding my way up, down, and through the Rocky Mountains. Eventually, the mountains appeared in my rearview mirror. Miles of monotonous desert

4

highway stretched out before me, with rocks, ochre sand and endless patches of dried shrubbery on either side. It was stark, and hauntingly beautiful.

Pristine blue spread out above in all directions. Distant mesas and buttes stood like sentinels, silently peering down to see a tiny red carriage racing along the ribbon of asphalt which stretched all the way out to the horizon. The driver inside seemed to know exactly where he was going, and what would happen once he arrived.

I was still a few hours east of L.A. when suddenly something caught my eye, causing me to quickly press down on the brake pedal. The front tires pulled to one side so strongly that I cut across a couple lanes while trying to control the vehicle. Looking around afterward, I was surprised and relieved there wasn't another car to be seen in either direction.

At first, my brain couldn't understand what it was that made me stop so suddenly. The road was moving. I knew it wasn't a mirage. Something *out there* was actually moving.

The road was crawling.

I squinted my eyes to focus better since my windshield was covered by a delicate layer of dust, accented by dozens of splattered bugs. Something long and dark appeared to be crossing the road. It was at least fifty feet wide. I gingerly pressed the gas pedal to inch the car forward.

This thing wasn't *a thing*. It was thousands of things. Locusts. Each one was at least two inches long. Their long, broad wings draped down against their sides. Spindly legs swiveled beneath their reddish-brown bodies, pulling them forward at the same speed as if they were all on a moving walkway. They looked like an army of tiny robots marching across the land.

I rolled down my window to see them better. The air was still, and everything was eerily quiet. I knew that sometimes life has a way of communicating special messages to us. This was so strange that I wondered if this was one of those times. What did this mean? Did it even mean anything? Should I slow down? Should I turn back? I felt nervous.

Where the hell are the other cars? A chill ran up my spine, a sharp contrast to the warm sweat soaking the back of my t-shirt.

You're being superstitious, just keep going. I had no idea how long it would take for the bugs to cross the road. *Why did the bugs cross the road?* I did my best to avoid squashing them as I lightly pressed on the gas pedal. I rolled up my window, not wanting to hear the crunching and crackling shells beneath my tires.

I drove slowly while repeating the mantra "namo amitabhaya hrih" under my breath. I'd heard it many times while attending several "sukhavati" ceremonies. These were done on behalf of the recently deceased to help them during their time of transition. Ideally, the ceremony would help them gain entry into one of the afterlife's Pure Lands where they could resume their spiritual development.

I used the mantra now to assuage the guilt over squashing them with my tires. I suppose I could've just waited for them to pass, avoiding their deaths altogether. But I didn't. I couldn't. Andrea, my retreat and eventual initiation were waiting for me.

Our reunion in L.A. was happy and gleeful. We were two long-distance lovers reunited under the banner of spiritual bliss. We didn't really know each other, not well anyway, but it didn't matter. I buried any worries about that unfortunate detail as deeply as I could. If she felt the same way, she must've buried her worries too. I was here to enjoy my new lover's home for the next four, happy months.

I could tell it was a very small home even before getting out of the car. But there was no way I could tell it would be some very long, and not so happy four months.

Her tiny cottage shared the block with three others of similar design, all nestled inside the cute suburban neighborhood. As I walked inside for the very first time, I noticed the bedroom and living room were really just the same room, with a small closet on the other side. Her bed was on the left. She'd transformed the right side into a meditation area, complete with a shrine. On it were bowls for burning incense and for making ritual offerings, and various pictures of Rinpoche and other teachers.

The distant closet was to the left of a short hallway, which included an adjoining bathroom. Beyond, the hallway opened to the kitchen. It was more of a kitchenette, really, and it included a dining table just big enough for two.

The clock was ticking, and we quickly established our daily routine.

We'd wake up very early each morning and prepare an extra strong brew of French-pressed coffee in the kitchen. Then, we'd take our hot mugs over to the meditation area, setting them down on the low tables we used for reading various liturgical texts and practice manuals.

We'd meditate together for a couple of hours, and then she'd quietly get up to leave for work. She was further along her ngöndro than I was, and didn't need the extra time on the meditation cushion. I stayed put, continuing the visualizations, mantra recitations and body movements which composed the ngöndro.

Lunch time often included a walk around the neighborhood to stretch my legs, and to shop for food. If there was enough time, I'd take a nap after returning to our little abode.

Rested, I'd continue meditating several more hours until Andrea returned from work. Then, it was "us" time. We'd enjoy refreshing glasses of gin and tonic and make dinner together. *This is the life*, I thought.

When I was younger, there were times when I felt drawn to becoming a Catholic priest. I was attracted to the mystery, the rituals, and sacred ambiance of church. The priests I knew as a child were smart and funny, and they seemed to care about everyone's welfare, which I admired. But I knew that would mean depriving myself of other kinds of intimacy. As I grew older, I realized I could never be a priest.

Therefore, living in L.A. as a yogi-by-day and boyfriend-at-night was idyllic, a dream come true. My spiritual and worldly aspirations were equally fulfilled, for the time being, anyway. "Perfect" situations have a way of falling apart, and this would be no exception.

One evening, I went out for a stroll. Andrea returned from work while I was out. Strangely, I didn't see her anywhere when I returned, but I knew she was back because her car was parked outside.

It only took a dozen steps to reach the kitchen, but she wasn't there either. After standing still for a few moments to wonder where she could be, I heard a whimper. Then silence. Then another whimper. My stomach sank as I made my way back to the bedroom, something odd was happening. The closet was shut, but I could tell the light was on inside since it was streaming out from beneath the door.

I opened it and there she was, hiding between the hangers of dresses, pants and jackets that filled the tiny closet. She turned her back to me as if to burrow deeper and get away somehow. But there was nowhere for her to go.

"What's wrong?" I asked. I reached for her shoulder, gently trying to turn her around. Her cheeks were wet with tears and her forehead wrinkled with anxiety.

"Please!" Her voice was pleading. She avoided my eyes. She didn't want me to see her. Or maybe she didn't want to see me.

"I just need to be alone. I need space."

"Ok, honey, I'm sorry…." I didn't know what was going on.

I felt confused. Was she angry with me? Had I embarrassed her by finding her in the closet? I knew nothing good would happen by crowding her and offering to fix whatever was wrong. I went back outside for another walk.

Later that night, she felt well enough to explain. "Every morning when I wake up, you're here. We meditate together and then I go to work, but you're still here. Then I come home and still, you're here. It's relentless."

She was right. I'd become a constant presence in her life. To make matters worse, the ngöndro had a way of making a person feel psychologically raw, exposed. My constant presence had become particularly irritating to her, even though she cared about me.

We only had a few weeks left before flying to Vermont, but I was terrified that she'd call it quits and send me packing. Not only because it would be a disaster for our relationship, but also because it would mean not being able to finish my ngöndro in time to receive the initiation.

The pressure between us grew worse. We bickered more. We started going out at night more often, to visit her friends and get some fresh air at the same time. We both needed to decompress. Those nights were her opportunity to talk to anybody else but me for a change, and I felt ignored, like an outsider.

Nevertheless, I understood her need for some distance. I needed it too. Maybe I should've done a solitary retreat instead. When you're all alone, there's no one to bother but yourself. Or, maybe I should've taken my time, a couple of years maybe, and done the ngöndro while living a regular life back in Colorado.

But I couldn't slow down. I was in a hurry, and I wasn't interested in taking the slow road. I thought I was closer than ever to finding something I'd been looking for most of my life.

Sean McNamara

One night, just a couple weeks before leaving for Vermont, I had a dream. Andrea and I had managed to keep our relationship intact, and we could see a light at the end of the tunnel.

> We stood on the rooftop of a concrete building somewhere in the city, five or six stories above ground. There was plenty of room and there were people all around, talking and laughing with each other. Cocktails, wine and hors d'oeuvres were being served. For some reason, everyone wore light-colored clothes in shades of white, cream and yellow.
> Andrea stood across the rooftop, looking at me. I looked back. She smiled, then raised her glass. I raised mine back, feeling sad and grateful at the same time. My chest felt warm. I appreciated her so much.

Then, the whole scene shifted into slow motion. My eyes looked over her shoulder, toward the horizon where the sky meets the earth.

> And it began to rise up, incredibly fast. The distant ground swelled like a gargantuan tsunami wave, and it was heading toward us.
>
> The sky grew dark as the ground rose into the sky, flinging off blocks of steel and concrete, which crumbled into rubble everywhere they landed. The wave rushed toward us at an impossible speed. A deafening roar caused an explosion of terror throughout my body.
>
> But she just stood there calmly, looking at me with love in her eyes. Did she know what was about to happen? I did. The world was ending. Why was she so calm?
>
> "Andrea..." I wanted to tell her something, but there was no more time.
>
> Suddenly, everything went dark.

I never told her about the dream.

10

Like a marathoner struggling to the finish line, we held it together long enough to make it to Vermont. I think we assumed there'd be some kind of relief once we arrived. At least we'd be happier because of the distraction.

But here we lay, inside our private room at the retreat center, silently brooding in the dark after yet another stupid argument. I couldn't tell if hours had passed, or only minutes.

Was she asleep, or was her head churning like mine? We'd probably forced something that wasn't meant to be. Had it all been a fantasy?

Maybe there's hope, if we can just hold on for a few more days, and then start over.

A knock came at the door.

I could tell by how quickly Andrea rose out of bed, she hadn't been sleeping either. I rolled over to see who knocked, but she'd already stepped out into the hallway to speak with the visitor. I couldn't hear their conversation.

Moments later, she came back in, closed the door, and turned on the lights. "What's going on?" I asked. The whole building, filled with sleeping retreatants, instructors, cooks and staff members, had been silent for hours.

"That was one of Rinpoche's attendants," she said curtly. My heart quickened. "He's invited me to come over."

"When?" I asked, nervously.

"Right now." She couldn't even look at me, for some reason.

I felt myself coming undone inside. Suddenly, I regretted our argument, wishing we could turn back the clock, if only for a few hours. Then we could move forward again, and *this time* communicate better, more tenderly, more patiently. This time, we'd fall asleep happily and securely in each other's arms. And maybe

11

Sean McNamara

nobody would come knocking on the door. But I couldn't do that, I couldn't turn back time.

"You don't have to do anything you don't want to!" I urged. It was a feeble attempt to stop her from doing exactly what would happen next.

"I know," she said. Was that restrained excitement I heard in her voice? She still wouldn't look at me.

Speechless, I watched her open a dresser drawer and pull out a pair of stockings. Then a skirt, and a blouse. Then she was gone, and the room was quiet again.

I knew what was happening, though I couldn't believe it. Then, I became angry, remembering a strange conversation we'd had a few days before.

We'd both heard rumors that Rinpoche had slept with some of his female students in the past. He wasn't a monk and he wasn't married. But still, as the absolute leader of our lineage, as the *guru*, it didn't seem right for him to do that. That's why this was a rumor, because more than a few people didn't think it was right, but they never said anything out loud. For others, though, there was something from the tradition which made it acceptable.

The concept of the guru sleeping with students is an old one in Tibetan Buddhism, and older yet in India. It's embedded in the ancient tales about the "mahasiddhas", the wild yogis famous for their non-conformity with social norms. The mahasiddhas were known for expressing their enlightened point of view by breaking accepted rules of behavior, including having sex out of wedlock or outside of one's caste, or with their disciples.

Tibetan Buddhism includes a practice called "karmamudra," which uses sex to rouse the subtle energies inside one's body for meditative purposes. Karmamudra is regarded as a *secret* practice, and strictly reserved for the most spiritually "ripened" individuals. The usual

12

explanation is that for an ordinary person, practicing karmamudra would be no different from ordinary sex, and its accompanying psychological baggage.

I think many of us privately wondered if we'd ever "get to that level." Most of the community members were middle- and upper-class westerners, mostly Caucasian. But we'd done the reading, we knew the lore.

I thought Andrea felt the same way I did about Rinpoche's dalliances. I asked her flatly, "Would you ever sleep with him if you had the chance?"

"No way!" she replied, almost like she'd been grossed out by the idea. "He's my guru, and I have devotion to him, but I don't want to *have sex* him."

Case closed, I thought, breathing a sigh of relief. But that was a few days ago.

Now, our room had become a twilight zone where reality was suddenly turned inside out, and I was alone. Now, she was inside Rinpoche's car, and his driver was whisking her away to some location miles away from the retreat center.

Was I in hell, or was this some sort of test? I wanted to throw up.

I had just taken tantric vows, called "samaya" vows, with this man. Samaya vows include a student's *promise* to regard the guru as if he or she were a fully enlightened being, in the flesh, and *incapable of doing anything "wrong."*

Samaya vows are integral to the tantric Buddhist tradition. The idea is that whether we're enlightened or not depends on how we perceive the world, or reality itself. The personal relationship between the guru and disciple becomes a training ground for our perception.

Sean McNamara

A traditional saying goes, "If you see your guru as the Buddha, then you'll receive the blessings of a Buddha. If you see your guru as a Bodhisattva (which is a lesser level of spiritual attainment), then you'll only receive the blessings of a Bodhisattva. If you see your guru as an ordinary person, then you won't receive any blessings at all, and you'll remain trapped in samsara (the perpetual cycle of suffering caused by reincarnating into states of un-enlightened existence).

Basically, criticizing one's guru is a *major* no-no.

These ideas had always seemed provocative and even made logical sense. But now, my guru was actually sleeping with my girlfriend. And apparently, he couldn't care less that she was attending the retreat with her boyfriend, me. What about me?

I spent the next couple hours sitting on the bed, trying to meditate. I recited all the liturgies and tried to imagine giving my girlfriend away to him. I tried to see that I was being selfish and confused, that this was just my unenlightened nature.

If I was enlightened, I wouldn't have a problem with this, would I? *Of course, not,* I thought at the time. What was wrong with me? I felt guilty for being a bad disciple. I felt guilty for being angry at him, and at her.

The meditation wasn't working, and I continued to implode. Physically, it was as if the years of irritable bowel syndrome I'd grown up with had been a dress rehearsal for this night.

I was going to the toilet every fifteen minutes, my guts releasing an inexhaustible stream of liquefied distress into the sewer. My whole body ached, and I couldn't stop trembling.

Every half-hour or so, I'd leave our room and stand on the porch outside. The freezing air only made the tremors worse, but I didn't care. Peering through the darkness, I searched for the headlights of the car which would inevitably bring Andrea back whenever

Rinpoche was finished with her. But I didn't know when that would be, and there were no cars to be seen.

I spent the darkest hours of the morning pacing inside our room, lying sleeplessly in bed, going to the toilet, or scanning the road from the porch outside.

Why did he choose her? As far as I knew, he'd never had a conversation with her. All I could figure was that he must've noticed her among all the other participants sitting below him on the floor. Row after row of eager students looked up at him for hours each day while he gave his talks. When did he first notice her? And why did he choose *her*? And what did he do then?

Obviously, he must've gone out of his way to find out what room she was staying in. He must've had a staffer look into it. Was it the same staffer who'd come to our door? How many people were involved? Is this something they did all the time? I wonder if any of them thought to tell Rinpoche, "By the way, maybe you should pass, she's got a boyfriend…"

My mind churned ceaselessly with these and other questions, replaying my thoughts over and over again. I couldn't stop.

Eventually sunrise began, and the whole building stirred from its slumber, ignorant of my waking nightmare.

I couldn't be alone anymore, and took a chance by knocking on the door just down the hall. I knew the director of one of this organization's main city-centers was staying there. I hoped she might be able to offer some advice.

She opened the door, and could tell by the look on my face I needed help. She closed the door behind me and asked, "What's wrong? What happened?"

"Rinpoche asked Andrea to see him last night!" My eyes were becoming wet. I watched the director's head sink in resignation. "And she went!" I continued, feeling strained. The director slowly shook her head.

Sean McNamara

"I don't know why he does these things." she said quietly, with resignation.

She didn't have any answers for me, and she didn't defend him. But she didn't criticize him either. She had taken the same vow I had, to see the guru as an enlightened being, and to never contradict him.

Not only was she his student, but she was a director of one of his centers. She was part of the business; therefore, *it was her job* to support her guru and his organization.

Still, I felt a little better after telling her what happened. It was too much to keep to myself. For a few minutes, I wasn't alone. But soon I was alone in my room again, a new emotion breached the surface.

I was furious.

I went to the administrative office where I knew some of the retreat staff worked, and demanded to know my girlfriend's whereabouts. At first, they didn't seem to know who or what I was talking about. But as I described the "invitation" at our door, the looks on their faces told me they understood exactly what was happening. They'd been through this before.

As soon as I told them I wanted to talk to Rinpoche, I could hear the alarm bells ringing inside their heads. *What did this guy really want?*

They asked me to slow down and relax. They also wanted to know, "How are you feeling right now?" I could tell they wanted to make sure I wasn't a threat. History is filled with men hurting or even killing other men for sleeping with their lover or spouse. They must've been worried that I'd do something rash.

But I wasn't interested in hurting anyone, and after answering their questions, they must've figured as much.

One of the staff went to another room to call Rinpoche's house. Minutes later, he came back and told me Andrea was still there with

16

him. He and his entourage would be coming back later that morning.

Finally, Rinpoche returned, trailing behind him a small group of attendants, assistant-teachers, and staffers. And Andrea. They were casually chatting with each other as they walked by me and the others waiting to see them in the hallway.

She didn't even notice me until I grabbed for her arm and growled under my breath, "We need to talk right now!"

Alone in our room, I demanded to know exactly what happened between them. She refused to tell me anything.

"What happened was *my experience*, and it was between me and him. It had nothing to do with you, and I don't have to tell you anything!" She was acting cold.

But then her face softened when she asked, "Can we still be together?" I couldn't believe it. She was actually asking me if we could stay together. Now, it really felt like the twilight zone.

"No," I replied, feeling strong and justified. "We're done." Andrea and I were clearly living inside two different realities, and I had no desire to enter hers.

But I wasn't done with Rinpoche, I'm embarrassed to say. I chose to remain his student and do my best to honor my samaya vow. I justified my choice to stay by telling myself I was hurting simply because I didn't share my teacher's point of view, because I wasn't enlightened yet. *Because I wasn't good enough*, is how it really felt.

Today, as I write this book, I can tell you most assuredly that his wasn't an enlightened point of view. Many years after this night in Vermont, news reports and social media posts would erupt with allegations of sexual abuse by Rinpoche, against multiple female students, often while intoxicated. These incidents spanned across *years*, and the allegations were backed by solid witness testimonies.

This was nothing unique, of course. Other rinpoches, zen roshis, priests, school teachers, CEOs, filmmakers, politicians, doctors and others in positions of power have done and continue to do the exact same thing. All they require is to be surrounded by people who allow it.

Reading these reports helped me realize that there had never been any spiritual intention behind what he did with Andrea. It also meant there really wasn't a spiritual purpose to the anguish I endured that night. I was simply collateral damage, nothing more. Nothing good came of that night, at least for me. I can't speak for Andrea, and will probably never know her perspective.

As they say, *hindsight is 20/20*. I didn't know any of this back then. I thought this was all real, and that everyone involved was earnestly trying to better themselves. I strove to be the "good student" committed to my teachers, and devoted to "the path."

I was blind, naive.

For a few years afterward, I'd feel a wave of anxiety pass through me every time I sat down to meditate. Moments would come and go during each session when I'd have to pause to shove the rising memories of Vermont back under the surface, trying to forget them again.

The meditation practice I'd been initiated into was now my daily practice. Unfortunately, I think it acted as a trigger for some kind of post-traumatic stress disorder. This happened every time I sat down to meditate, which was almost every day. For years.

Finally, but still long before the public allegations, I admitted to myself that I wasn't getting anywhere, and I left Rinpoche to train with another teacher. It was easy to do, since Rinpoche didn't know who I was anyway. He was a figurehead, a reference point, a placeholder. I was just one of the thousands of "members" who mailed in their monthly dues, attended their local meditation center, and once in a while paid thousands of dollars to attend another retreat. All I had to do was stop showing up and let everyone forget I was ever there.

When I did, no one ever contacted me to ask "Why did you leave?"

Why did I let this happen to me? Why, when hearing rumors about Rinpoche sleeping around, hadn't I ended my association with him and with everyone who supported him? Why didn't I pack my bags and call a taxi the moment Andrea walked out of our room? Or why didn't I leave as soon as she returned the next morning? Or after the retreat? There were so many times I should've left, but didn't.

This teacher, his organization, and his lineage offered a path to enlightenment, apparently, and I was willing to let myself be hurt for it. Why?

How did I get here?

CHAPTER 2 THE SEED

One night, in third grade, I couldn't fall asleep. My stomach hurt. It hurt *bad*. I tossed and turned, trying to make as little noise as possible because Jenny, my little sister, was in the other bed and I didn't want to wake her up. We shared bedrooms everywhere we lived when we were growing up. Now, we were in the Philippines, attending the International School of Manila.

For some reason, I also didn't want to disturb my parents, whose bedroom was just down the hall. I wanted to wait and see if the achy pressure in my tummy would go away on its own. Time passed, and I became tired enough to fall back asleep, ignoring the pain.

In the morning, things felt better inside, so I didn't mention it at breakfast. Jenny and I grabbed our lunch boxes and backpacks, and our driver Pepe took us to school.

In the days before cell phones and GPS, having a local driver was a very real need for foreign business people and their families. Pepe not only knew the way to school, my dad's office, and to the grocery store, he knew the whole city.

This was useful at a time when the kidnapping of foreign business people, diplomats or their families was a real threat. Pepe had military training, it seemed. I remember his biceps were as big and as hard as softballs, he was very strong. He enjoyed teasing and joking with us when we were alone in the car with him.

I always sat in the front passenger seat next to him, and he'd challenge me to punch his arm as hard as I could, like some kind of test of strength. It felt like hitting a brick wall. Then he'd reach over and squeeze my little arm and laugh, "Egg pie!" I'd laugh too. He must've been utterly bored with this job, and getting a reaction from the children provided some entertainment.

But this morning, I kept my arms crossed over my stomach. The pain kept getting worse as we got closer to school. I just stared out the window.

After he dropped us off, Jenny and I went our separate ways inside the elementary school building. Her classroom was somewhere on the ground floor. Mine was on the third.

Climbing the stairs intensified the pain. It had started off as dull, but now it felt much sharper, and I winced with every step. I moved slowly, and all the other kids were inside their classrooms by now. I was still on the stairs when a wave of hurt came over my body, forcing me down to my knees. When a teacher found me a little while later, I was still trying to crawl to my classroom.

She got me to the nurse's office, and someone called my parents. Soon, Pepe returned to take me home. I remember him lifting me up and putting me in the back of the car. A doctor came to the house, but he didn't know what was wrong with me. Another day passed without improvement, so my parents decided it was time to go to the hospital.

I remember waking up after the surgery, and finding the stitches above my right hip. I'd had an emergency appendectomy. It was a good thing we went to the hospital when we did. Someone told me that my appendix ruptured in the doctor's hand during the operation. If this had happened while I was at home, or in school, or anywhere else, I might not have survived.

That was the first time I ever thought about my own death. And it was the first time I felt real pain. That was when a seed was planted. The seed was *fear*. Fear of *the end*, to be more precise. *First comes pain, and then comes death.*

Sean McNamara

This idea became my constant companion. Over time, it became silent as it burrowed deeper and deeper into my psyche. It became a part of me.

CHAPTER 3 SEE THE WORLD

I probably thought about death more often than the other kids did. My experience with a ruptured appendix planted the idea, but living in a place like the Philippines offered other kinds of reminders.

We usually spent our holidays on the coast, swimming in crystal clear tropical waters and basking on warm stretches of pure white sand. The mountains and jungles were also idyllic, filled with mangoes, coconuts, and lush foliage.

Yet, we didn't need to wander too far outside the resort's boundaries to come face to face with the other side of this reality, one of abject poverty. Shoeless children clothed in dirty rags played in muddy street puddles. Villagers of all ages suffered from a lack of access to modern medicine.

My world was a protected world, with education, money, and healthcare. That's why, when traveling overseas, it was shocking to see a massive goiter sticking out of someone's neck, or people we ignorantly called "hunchbacks" suffering from severe scoliosis. I saw many people blinded by cataracts, something which is easily solved in wealthier parts of the world, as long as a person has enough money. These people did not. Ignored and abandoned, they sat by the road, begging.

Soon after moving to the Philippines, dad took us to see the famous Banaue Rice Terraces. For at least 2,000 years, the indigenous people of that region, the Ifugao, formed, preserved and cultivated the seemingly endless terraces stretching across many hills and

Sean McNamara

valleys. Some people call this place the "Eighth wonder of the world."

But I don't remember it at all.

Instead, what stuck in my memory from that day was the village we stopped in on our way home, to buy souvenirs. There by the road, standing in front of a broken-down shack, were two stray dogs. They both had short brown hair, and long, crusty tails. I could see their ribs pressing out against their mangy skin.

They just stood there, quietly looking around in a daze.

I barely noticed them as I scanned the rest of the street. Then, without warning, a thick, greenish-brown liquid streamed out of the anus of one of the dogs, forming a thick porridge on the dirt. The poor dog barely seemed to notice what just happened in the back side of its body.

The other dog came closer to look over the sewage. I couldn't take my eyes away as it lowered its head and began lapping up what was probably the only source of food it'd had for days. Finished with its meal, the dog licked its chops and went back to staring at nothing.

Still, the Philippines is a beautiful country. We also saw other beautiful places during those years, such as Greece and Turkey. We also visited Ireland, whose castles were built much more recently, clearly designed to protect and honor the lives of royalty.

One of my favorite trips was to Egypt, especially to see the Great Sphinx and pyramids of Giza. Their narrow, dimly lit passageways served as mysterious portals into a time on this planet we know very little about. In contrast to Ireland's castles, these structures were built to honor the dead. At least that's what they say. I wonder if they could've served other purposes instead.

Every summer, I looked forward to boarding another jumbo jet to cross the oceans and continents, landing in some strange land. At first, Jenny and I were small enough that if we were lucky, we'd find a row of empty seats to claim as our own. We'd close the armrests' built-in ashtrays, then lift all the armrests up all the way, and lie down on our makeshift beds. That was when smoking was allowed on airplanes. Even today, the smell of coffee and cigarettes provokes a feeling of adventure.

We stayed in the Philippines until I finished 7th grade, when the company my father worked for decided to transfer him to Hong Kong. Naturally, our whole family had to go. This was before the internet existed, at a time when international phone calls were too expensive for children to make. This meant that on the last day of school, I'd be saying goodbye to all the friends I ever had, all at once.

Inside the Great Pyramid

The school was filled with children of international executives, many of whom were already accustomed to being uprooted. This was my real first time. We'd moved before, when I was a toddler, but I barely remembered those times.

Sean McNamara

On the last day of school, during the final class period of the last day, it seemed like all my classmates were crying. A few of them were leaving too. I didn't cry, and I don't know why. Perhaps I thought it was better to keep the sadness inside. Or maybe, some part of me knew this wouldn't be the last time I'd leave people behind, and I'd better get used to it.

Hong Kong International School offered the opportunity for new friendships, which I made easily enough. The school offered an annual travel program called "interim," which I was able to participate in during my second year there, in 9th grade. We had the option to travel to Australia, China, India, or other parts of Asia. I chose Nepal for my trip, and joined a dozen other students, led by a couple of teachers, for a tour of the Annapurna valley.

I chose Nepal partly because I was intrigued about the idea of trekking in the Himalayas. I also chose it because of an interest in Buddhism that was fostered by summer visits to other Buddhist countries with my family. We'd been to Myanmar (it was called Burma at the time), Thailand, and Japan.

In Yangon (Rangoon when we visited), the valley was dotted with dozens, even hundreds, of pagodas spread out as far as the eye could see. Those, and the many gold-leafed statues inside the temples made it clear to me that Christianity wasn't the only significant religion on the planet. There are other ways, older ways, that humans thought about the meaning of life, and what happens afterward.

On an evening tour, there, we visited a pagoda which apparently possessed tiny strands of hair belonging to Siddhartha Gautama, commonly referred to as the Buddha, born around five hundred years before Christ.

I barely remember the building or the room where it was being displayed, although I do remember seeing gold on the walls, on the statues, everywhere. I also remember standing in front of an elaborate shrine and straining to look through some very thick glass and see the tiny, sacred strands of hair.

Cairo, Egypt[1]

---

[1] Color images of all the pictures in this book, and extras, can be found at www.RenegadeMysticBook.com/pictures

Sean McNamara

Tikal, Guatemala

Yangon, Myanmar (formerly Rangoon, Burma)

Sean McNamara

Bangkok, Thailand

Shannon, Ireland, with Grampa and Granny

Kathmandu, Nepal

Looking at them caused me to feel a spontaneous feeling of reverence. I had only a vague notion of who the Buddha was, but his impact on architecture, religion and culture was obvious. It felt like a really special event to see these tiny little pieces of his long-dead body with my own eyes.

Now on interim, I was fifteen years-old and exploring Kathmandu with my classmates. It was crowded, noisy, and absolutely beautiful.

There were temples and holy people there from Hindu, Jain and other religions. And Buddhism too, of course.

It was the first time I saw renunciants, people with no belongings and no homes, who dedicated their lives entirely to their sacred practices and beliefs. For a young boy born and bred into a modern, sterile world, these ascetic yogis seemed to possess hidden knowledge.

More than that, the look in their eyes told me they weren't afraid of anything. They didn't care about impressing anybody, or putting on airs. They had no other place they needed to be other than where they were, right then and there. They were free, and had nothing to lose. At least it seemed that way to me at the time. As an adult, I recognize how easy it is to romanticize scenes like these.

After adjusting to the altitude in Kathmandu, our group continued to the Annapurna region for several days of trekking. We passed through tiny villages where technology and modernity hadn't yet taken over, which made it easy to project an aura of peacefulness and simplicity onto them, and ignore the signs of hardship. Like the Philippines, there was poverty, sickness, and a lack of modern education.

Back home in Hong Kong, we saw the world transforming in other parts of the world from the comfort of our living room. The Berlin wall came down. In Beijing, over a million students protested in the name of greater political freedom and better education, and thousands of them were shot and killed by soldiers at Tiananmen Square.

Sean McNamara

In an incredible act of defiance, a single unidentified man stood before a column of tanks, refusing to move out of their way, thus slowing the military's squelching of the protests. He was carried away and never heard from again.

Inevitably, my dad came home one night and announced it was time to say goodbye, once again, to all my friends. This time, I'd be starting over in Brazil, attending the Escola Americana do Rio de Janeiro. It was a lot easier this time, though. The act of leaving behind another set of friends seemed simple, direct.

Our apartment in Rio was only a couple blocks from the beach in the suburb of Barra da Tijuca. I loved going to the beach after school and on weekends. After boogie boarding all afternoon, I'd lie in the warm sand while gazing out onto the vastness of the Atlantic Ocean.

We attended mass on Sundays, and I'd made a friend there, Bernardo. He was a couple years younger than me, like Jenny. Our parents were friends too, and one night they all came over for dinner. Bernardo and I decided to go to the beach and to bring my boogie board along with us.

It was dusk, and for some reason there were barely any people around. Any beach-goer in Rio knows to be wary of thieves targeting unguarded blankets and bags, but we hadn't brought anything with us. Our plan was just to wade into the shallow water to play there for a little while.

We became careless, and made our way into deeper water, where we took turns surfing on the bigger waves. We had the boogie board to hold on to whenever we got tired, now that it was too deep to stand up anymore.

A full moon had risen over the horizon, illuminating the white crests of the waves and the buildings along the shoreline. The sky was black. We had been in the water much longer than we'd planned. Now, we were farther out in the ocean. Much farther.

We were both holding on to the boogie board for rest, and I pointed to the buildings. They looked small, too small. "We need to get back to shore," I said nervously. I couldn't even tell which one of those buildings was my apartment.

We tried swimming toward the beach, and I pulled the boogie board behind me since it was strapped to my wrist by a long elastic cord. After a couple of minutes, we noticed that we were actually moving farther away from the land. We were scared. The water felt cold, but my arms and legs burned with lactic acid from fighting the ocean. We were caught in a rip tide.

Exhausted, little Bernardo rested on top of the boogie board while I struggled to drag him toward the beach. But I was too tired. The buildings were so far away, and there was nobody to wave to for help. Now, the waves were swelling up in front of us, making it hard to see the beach.

Was Bernardo crying? I wanted to cry. The sky was dark, and so was the water. Anything could've been swimming beneath us and we'd never see it until it was too late, until we actually felt its teeth piercing our ankles, or our thighs, or our bodies. I was also afraid of becoming exhausted or hypothermic, then drowning.

All we could do now was pray. And we really did, *out loud*. We both knew the "Our Father" and the "Hail Mary," so we recited them over and over again, almost shouting the prayers into the sky. We were tired and scared, and needed a miracle.

And a miracle did happen. After a few rounds of prayer, the water behind us swelled, lifting us high enough to look over the waves in front of us and see the beach. I felt a glimmer of hope. Then it rose again, and we could tell the sea was behaving differently now. Since our muscles got a chance to rest while begging Jesus and Mary to be our lifeguards, we began to swim again.

Another wave rose behind us, and we let it thrust us closer to shore. *Just a few more waves, God...please.* Soon, we were lying with backs against the warm, safe sand. Warm tears streamed across the sides

Sean McNamara

of my face. I tried to keep quiet so Bernardo wouldn't hear me crying.

We caught our breath, stood up, and took the long walk back to the apartment. Not saying anything to each other along the way, we joined our families for dinner without telling them what happened. Life was normal again.

Then, one day I watched a program about the ocean, and learned that what happened to us hadn't been, in fact, a miracle. We'd simply been caught up in a rip current. And we responded the same way so many other victims have, by trying to fight it by swimming directly toward the beach.

The program explained that with a rip tide, it was completely natural that we'd be swept out to sea, then parallel to the coast line. It was also completely normal for the tide to bring us closer to shore after a while, positioning the waves behind us again. Without the boogie board, we may have become too exhausted to last long enough. But we had one, and we did.

There had been *no* miracle.

After watching that program, I felt like a fool. I blushed at the memory of asking Bernardo to pray with me for help. I was embarrassed. *Maybe there really wasn't anybody to call for help after all*, I thought.

CHAPTER 4 LOOKING FOR A WAY OUT

The living room glowed with an eerie greenish-gray. Every few minutes, bright flashes of light would burst out from the TV screen. Iraq had invaded Kuwait a few months earlier, and America was responding with Operation Desert Storm. Airborne attacks were happening at night, so TV crews used night-vision technology to videotape the scenes of anti-aircraft artillery shells exploding over Baghdad. There were also daytime scenes of buildings exploding into rubble and dust with every missile strike. We watched as clouds of smoke filled the city, thousands of miles across the ocean.

Glued to the TV, I'd never seen anything like this before in my life. I don't think anyone else had either. For the next month and a half, our television became a virtual reality device, instantly transporting us from our peaceful sea-side apartment straight into hell, somewhere in the middle east.

Is this the start of World War III? Are they going to use nuclear bombs? I didn't fully understand what was happening, and had no idea how far it could go. I was scared. Apocalyptic thoughts looped over and over again in my mind, and I feared the worst. All the ingredients were there for me to piece together a worst-case scenario. Missiles. Bombs. Explosions. Tanks. Armies. Oil. Middle East. Christian. Muslim.

It wasn't just that the end of the world could be around the corner, I was also in love. Every summer, after visiting yet another exotic land, we'd spend our last free weeks with Grampa and Granny in Florida. They lived in a pleasant suburban area by the Manatee River reserved for retirees.

Sean McNamara

We spend our time there riding bicycles, going fishing, lounging by the pool, and playing with the other grandkids who spent their summers there too.

One of those kids was named Barbara.

Barbara was from Virginia, and her grandparents lived a couple streets away from mine. We'd met the summer before, and by the end of it, we'd developed a very heavy crush for each other.

This summer, we got to it as quickly as possible. After our first kiss, things progressed very quickly and spending every possible daytime hour together wasn't enough. So, once the rest of my family had fallen asleep, I'd sneak outside, stealthily walk the bicycle away from the house and out of hearing distance, then ride away to meet Barbara.

We'd find someplace we could be alone, so we could explore each other in privacy. Hours later, I'd quietly ride my bicycle through the sleepy neighborhood and sneak back into the house, where I'd fall asleep absorbing my newfound knowledge about girls and their bodies. I still remember how raw and tender the inside of my cheeks and lips felt from mashing my mouth, which was filled with braces that year, against hers every time we were alone.

I lost my virginity that summer, inside one of our secret make out spots. It was the equipment shed of the communal swimming pool. After that, I was more in love with Barbara than I'd ever been with anybody in my life. This made it especially painful once it was time for us to fly back to Rio at the end of the summer. On one of our last nights together, we promised ourselves to each other.

Even though it was completely out of our control, we hoped to see each other again the following summer, and the summer after that, and again after that... This was the best we could do as teenagers who lived continents apart.

We stayed connected by writing letters to each other since we still didn't have the internet. Then the Gulf War happened. I truly feared the end of the world was near. Scared and in love, I wrote a sincere and probably too dramatic letter telling her if nuclear war happened, she ought to stay in Virginia and I would make my way, by any means possible, all the way up from South America to be with her.

I never heard from her again.

Did my letter turn her off? Did she get pregnant? Or did she simply lose interest and fall in love with someone who lived a little closer than 4,600 miles away? Over time, I realized it wasn't that she stopped writing to me which upset me so much, but the fact that I didn't know the specific reason *why* she stopped.

Teenage hearts being what they are, I was forlorn. And, I still worried about the middle east. I really thought the world might end. Maybe I was watching too much footage of the war.

Luckily, I found something else to watch instead, something very different from watching cities exploding through night-vision cameras.

It was a rerun of a mini-series called "Out on a Limb," based on the book by the same title. It starred actress and singer Shirley MacLaine, also the book's author. Like many other kids my age, I had an interest in paranormal topics like ghosts and bigfoot, but "Out on a Limb" introduced me to far more interesting concepts I wasn't aware of, such as reincarnation, mediumship, and guides from other galaxies.

One scene depicted her having a spontaneous out-of-body experience while soaking in a natural hot spring during a visit to Peru. As she meditated on the glow of a candle, she felt herself rising above her own body, then out into the night sky. As she rose higher and higher, she looked down to see a long silver cord connecting her energy body to her physical body down below.

I was entranced. After finishing the whole show, I thought about that scene more than any other. I realized I wanted to do what she did,

Sean McNamara

to have MacLaine's experience for myself. I wanted to leave my body.

I don't remember how, but soon after watching the show, I got my hands on what at the time was *the* manual for leaving one's body, "Journeys Out of the Body" by Robert Monroe.

In it, Monroe described his experience of separating his consciousness from his physical body. It began spontaneously in adulthood, and in time he learned how to initiate these bedtime anomalies. It wasn't a religious book, and Monroe's experiences didn't match anything I'd heard about spirituality, consciousness, or the afterlife.

What I appreciated more than anything was that Monroe wasn't asking his readers to believe him. He simply offered a way for people to try it for themselves, and he didn't make any promises.

If I could *do it*, if I could actually separate myself from my physical body and still exist somehow, then I wouldn't need to be afraid of dying anymore. It would be proof I had a soul, or at least something like a soul. It also meant that everyone else had one too, and goodbyes wouldn't have to be forever.

The couple of techniques he offers in "Journeys Out of the Body" require establishing two preliminary conditions. First is a deep state of relaxation, in which one lingers on the border of sleep and wakefulness. This was easy for me to understand, even as a teenager.

The second step, however, wasn't. It was the production of something called the "vibrational state." He instructs the reader to imagine a point in space several feet in front of one's face, then to direct that point upward at a ninety-degree angle on a line parallel to the body, so that the imagined point in space is moving further up past one's head.

At just the right distance, one would encounter some energetic vibrations, then pull them into one's own head and body. If you, the reader, find it difficult to understand these instructions, you're not alone. In that chapter, even Monroe acknowledges the vagueness of the description. But it's the crucial element for his technique. According to his book, until this step is accomplished, one can't go further towards separating from their physical body.

Night after night, and filled with hope, I'd allow my body to drift toward sleep without crossing over into the blackness. Then, I'd reach out into the darkness in front of my eyes with my mind. But nothing would happen.

I'd search the space around me, behind and above me, looking anywhere I could for the elusive vibrations. They were the key to discovering my own immortality. Yet the only thing in my bedroom was the ocean breeze drifting in through the window. I always ended up falling asleep before anything else happened.

I decided to get experimental, and see if I could use music to stimulate the vibrational state. I made a mix-tape of two songs which played over and over again, Pink Floyd's "Comfortably Numb" and "Learning to Fly." There was something about the trill of the guitar, and the way all the instruments would reach a crescendo together. Then, with a barrage of drums, the sounds would drop into a deep, humming valley of what felt to me like emotional surrender.

A blissful tingle would course through my body as I drifted to sleep during these parts of the songs, but I don't think it was the particular vibration I was looking for.

The only remarkable effect from my nighttime experiments was an increased ability to remember the previous night's dreams. One night, for better or worse, it seems that I experienced a special kind of dream, warning me of something about to happen.

My new girlfriend (teenage hearts heal quickly) was a senior, a year ahead of me. I was a bit amazed that she accepted me as a boyfriend even though I was only a junior. More than that, though, I just wasn't as sophisticated as her other friends.

Sean McNamara

One particular weekend, she'd gone away on an overnight school trip with the other seniors. While she was gone, I had a dream in which she was making out with one of the other seniors. He was one of the "cool" kids, and he definitely seemed more sophisticated than me. I spent the rest of the weekend feeling irritated and worried by the dream. I had to get it off my chest as soon as I could. When I saw her in school the following Monday, I pulled her aside and described it to her.

Her eyes darted from side to side as she searched for words. And then, she admitted it. She *had* been sexual with him that weekend! I couldn't believe it; my dream had actually warned me of something that really happened somewhere far away. Of course, this realization was soon eclipsed by the anger and disappointment at her betrayal. First Barbara, now this, on top of the fact that my experiment at leaving my body had failed. I just didn't know where I fit in life, or who I was supposed to be.

Not too long after that incident, my dad came home from work and told us it was time to say goodbye again. We were going far away, to Colorado.

Good. Get me the hell out of here. I was ready to leave this place behind and start over somewhere else.

CHAPTER 5 ALONE IN THE DARK

Moving to Denver was different from our other moves because I was already familiar with America from visiting Grampa and Granny in Florida every summer. Still, it had its own challenges. I attended a large public high school with over four hundred kids in my grade alone. This was my senior year, and it seemed like everyone else in my class had grown up together.

Just get through it. All I really knew about American high school kids was what I'd seen in the movies "The Breakfast Club" and "Sixteen Candles." And it turned out that American high schoolers really were divided into cliques. You had your jocks, your nerds, your stoners and the rest, just like in the movies. I tried not to let it bother me. *One year is nothing, and you can start over in college.*

In Manila, Hong Kong and even Rio, there was a real sense of inclusion, largely because the kids came from everywhere on the planet. We were *all* different. It was *normal* to hear many different accents, to see many different shades of skin, to taste food from different countries, to learn about various religions, and to be *accepting* of it. How could we not? That would be like asking the whole world to be something different from what it really is. Besides, having friends from around the world was fun and interesting.

In Denver, my classmates seemed to have much less exposure to people from outside the United States. I wonder if that had something to do with why the school was so cliquey.

Sean McNamara

Luckily, I found myself in a small circle of friends who were open minded. In fact, most of them were part of an official club whose mission was to welcome newcomers into the school. But I knew from the beginning that they were a social lifeboat more than anything else. I was simply holding my breath, waiting to exhale once I graduated and moved on again. I'd learned not to trust that wherever I was could be called "home," or that my new "friends" would be anything more than a memory a couple years from now.

The school year moved along at a nice pace, and I actually looked forward to moving on and starting over in college. But then something happened, and time slowed down for a little while.

A tender area beneath my nipple had formed into a hard, palpable lump over a couple of months. It became noticeable enough to worry me, so I showed it to a doctor. He said that it would be a simple out-patient procedure to cut it out of me and biopsy it to figure out what it was.

I wasn't nervous about the procedure so much as what the biopsy would reveal afterward. Only one question filled my mind. Did I have cancer? After lying down on the table, the doctor undraped my chest and numbed the area by poking a needle into and around my nipple to inject the area with anesthetic. Once it was numb, he began to slice it open with a scalpel.

Lying there, I could feel a tugging sensation as the doctor worked to incise the unwanted tissue. He used some type of electric tool to cauterize the miniscule tendrils which kept the lump rooted inside my chest. I could smell my flesh burning as thin wisps of smoke floated up toward the overhead lamp. Then he sewed the incision closed and taped some gauze over it to absorb whatever fluids seeped out.

"We'll get it tested and have the results back in a week or two," said the doctor. The physical soreness didn't bother me nearly as much as *the waiting*. Was this little lump benign, or malignant? Less than one percent of breast cancer cases happen to men, but knowing that did little to assuage my fear.

44

One day, I received a phone call telling me the test came back negative. I was relieved, and the clock began moving forward at a steady pace. Beneath the relief, though, was the reminder that one day *the end* would come, and I still didn't know what happened afterward.

After finishing high school, it was my turn to decide where to live. I could apply to colleges anywhere in the United States if I wanted to. But the mere idea of moving again was exhausting. I chose to stay put in Denver, and enrolled at Regis University, a relatively small private college with Jesuit roots. I looked forward to being a stranger among strangers, where we'd all be "new," and the playing field would be level.

Things were off to a great start. I made friends and had a lot of fun living the college life. But one day, I noticed that my chest felt sore again. Over a couple of months, a nodule grew underneath the scar tissue marking where the previous lump had grown. Eventually, I admitted to myself that I needed to return to the doctor.

There I was, lying down on the same table we used last time, inhaling the familiar odor of burning flesh as he cauterized the lump's tiny roots. Like the time before, I lost a lot of sleep waiting for the results. And again, it was nothing. "But if it happens a third time, we should run some tests," warned the doctor.

It felt like something or someone was haunting me, refusing to let me ignore my mortality. As if that wasn't enough, I began to struggle with the longer periods of darkness in the wintertime, and became depressed.

I started spending my nights contemplating what it would be like to be dead as I fell asleep in bed. I'd visualize myself as my future corpse, lying inside a casket, and being lowered down into the earth.

Then I'd rest my mind in a kind of black nothingness, trying to imagine what it was like to be dead and non-conscious, as if I didn't have a soul or anything else that might continue after death. I'd linger in this stark visualization as long as I could, trying to come to

Sean McNamara

terms with absolute annihilation before falling asleep. The cold, anxious sweat dripping off the back of my neck and soaking my pillow made it easier to stay awake longer than usual.

Then I'd do it again the following night, and the night after that. I wanted to experience some semblance of non-existence, because *what if I didn't have a soul after all?*

I still attended church on most Sundays, but I remained skeptical. I never forgot the lesson from that night in Brazil when Bernardo and I prayed to the heavens for help. Rip currents always pull you back to shore as long as you don't struggle. It's natural. There was *no* miracle that night, and nobody answered our prayers.

Eventually, springtime returned, the sun was staying out later, and my seasonal affective disorder went away. I stopped my nightly attempts to experience non-existence, but was left with the pleasant after-effect of having better dream recollection. In Rio, the same thing happened, as a side-effect of trying to follow Robert Monroe's instructions.

And just like in Rio, a night came when I dreamt of my current girlfriend messing around with another guy. In this dream, that guy was my closest college buddy, the only person I'd ever thought of as my "best friend." The dream was so vivid that I confronted her, asking if my suspicions were accurate.

I was shocked to hear her admit that yes, she and my best friend had been intimate recently. It was just once, and it was unplanned, but it had happened.

Both of them responded to my outrage as if I was taking the whole thing too seriously, and like they hadn't really done anything wrong. Suddenly, I felt like the joke was on me, and old feelings of not fitting with everybody else returned. It was like something was wrong with my version of reality, and everybody else knew what was really going on. I was back in the twilight zone.

The only person I could really talk to about what happened was Charlie. Charlie was a psychology professor, and also a Jesuit priest. We'd become something like friends since we were usually in the gym lifting weights at the same time. He was around twenty years older than me, but we shared the same sense of humor and got along quite easily.

After the incident, I went to see him, crying in frustration. He was supportive, and helped me feel like it was perfectly normal to feel hurt by what happened. I think he appreciated that I'd let him into my personal life this way, and he reciprocated by telling me about his personal struggles. On one level, he was a man of the cloth, and a professor, and he also worked as a psychiatrist. But on another, he was lonely, didn't fit in with his peers, and had other struggles I won't go into here. I think for some reason I don't understand, I may have been one of only a few people he trusted enough to share his problems with.

Later that semester, Grampa died. I was sad, but not surprised. He'd lived with dementia for several years, and was in his eighties.

I remembered being a lot smaller and sitting on Grampa's lap, many years before his mind started to go. He had a big lump on the side of his belly from an old hernia, but it never seemed to bother him. He sometimes left his shirt unbuttoned because of the Florida heat, and I'd stare at the long, purple scar running down the center of his chest from the heart surgeries he'd undergone.

I liked rubbing the skin in front of his ears, just below his sideburns, because it was so exquisitely smooth. He said it was because of years and years of shaving. I remember him teaching me how to fish. After helping me put a worm on the hook and cast the line out into the Manatee river, we'd stand side by side and enjoy the silence, waiting for a fish to come and nibble on the bait. But now, he was gone forever.

Somehow, Grampa's death made it easier for me to let go of my worries and focus on getting college over with. I became more distant from my friends, and focused more on my schoolwork

instead. This was only my third year in college, but it already felt like I'd been in the same place too long. I was ready to leave again.
I decided to live at home with my parents during my senior year and commute to school. I spent even less time with my peers, and after graduating, the only person I stayed in touch with was Charlie.

But even that relationship had its limits. A couple of years after graduating from college, I became seriously interested in Buddhism and stopped going to church altogether. Since we were friends, I didn't mind telling Charlie about this part of my life. But more often than not, usually toward the end of one of our regular lunches, he'd find some way to insinuate I was only having a philosophical dalliance which would eventually pass. "You're a seeker," he'd say. "You just need to find your own way back to God."

His comments sounded respectful on the outside, but on the inside they felt insulting and disrespectful. I knew that he truly cared about me as a friend, but it was clear that he was unable to accept the idea that I was choosing a different spiritual path. After a while, I couldn't tell if he was my friend first and priest second, or if it was the other way around.

We had lunch less often, and I eventually stopped calling him altogether. One day I realized I'd let our friendship lapse. Even after realizing it, I didn't do anything to reconnect with him. I let go of Charlie the same way I'd let go of every other friend I'd made, which was something I'd come to regret many years later, after his death.

A few months later, the meditation center I'd been going to put on a special ceremony in which new members could take a "loyalty vow" to deepen their connection with it. Just before the ceremony began, I felt a strong urge to be included, and I told my meditation instructor at the time that I wanted to take the vow. The opportunity came once a year and suddenly I didn't want to wait.

Her response surprised me as she looked me right in the eyes and said, "You don't have to do anything you don't want to."

Was she trying to protect me? Did she think I was feeling pressured to do this? Or did she think I was too swept up by the exotic scene of the shrine, the incense, or the exotic imagery of deities and the Buddha?

Like most Buddhist lineages from Tibet, it claimed to offer a "fast path" to Buddhahood for anyone dedicated enough to do the required meditations. *Other paths take many lifetimes, our way offers enlightenment in just one, this one.* That was the clincher for me. I had questions about life and especially death, and these people claimed that I would find all the answers here if I worked hard enough at it.

So, against my instructor's suggestion that I wait, I took the loyalty vow to mark my fledgling commitment. This was just the first of many vows, such as the Refuge and Bodhisattva vow, I would take over the years, each one marking a progression along this "fast path."

The idea of a path that had been passed down over millennia, from enlightened teacher to enlightened disciple, gave me something concrete to focus on. As a child, I'd seen the temples in Asia, the pyramids in Egypt and Guatemala, and the Acropolis in Greece. The power and majesty of those places emitted a sense of significance and power. However, they now stood empty, unused, and mysterious mostly because there is still so much we didn't know about them.

But here, in this little meditation center, I had access to teachings that have been kept *alive* for two thousand five hundred years, and that was a tremendous draw for me.

Later that year, I had the opportunity to attend my first month-long retreat. I'd been recruited away from the company I'd joined after college, and my start date at the new firm gave me the necessary time off to attend. This would be my first chance to really explore meditation in a powerful way.

CHAPTER 6 A CERTAIN KIND OF DHARMA

A sharp crunching sound broke the pre-dawn silence that enveloped the pine and aspen trees through the night. Snow had fallen again, but now the sky was clear. Looking up, I could still see stars above. The sun wouldn't even start rising until our first period of sitting meditation was over.

I'd slept through my alarm, and needed to hurry. My dormitory, a 1900's school house filled with bunk beds, was normally a ten-minute walk from the meditation hall, but I was already more than ten minutes late. I walked briskly, careful not to lose my footing on the icy path which was already packed down from the other retreatants boots. This was in the mountains of northern Colorado, close to the Wyoming border.

Minutes later, I could see the meditation hall up ahead. Seeing the orange glare from the porch light had the effect of increasing my anxiety. I was late. For the past three weeks of the month-long program, I'd shown up on time, every time, for each lecture and meditation period. But not today. I was deaf to the noise of dozen roommates putting on their jackets and boots, then heading out into the cold.

Now my perfect attendance record was broken. There would be around one hundred meditators sitting row after row inside, with the teacher sitting next to the Buddhist shrine in the front of the hall, watching everyone as they quietly meditated. Would anyone notice my empty meditation cushion? The good Catholic boy inside of me felt guilty for not showing up on time.

There was a flat area of land just downhill from the meditation hall, which was used for outdoor dining in the summer. Since it was free of trees and rocks, I decided to pick up my pace and jog across it.

Suddenly, as I raised my right leg to lunge forward, it stopped in mid-air. I was too confused and sleepy to react in the moment, and gravity won. I landed right on my chest and face, slamming flatly against the frozen dirt. I reflexively let out a strange sound, something between a cough and a shout.

I sat up quickly and looked around. *Did anybody see me?* No, everyone was inside meditating. I looked down at my feet to figure out why they'd failed me. One of the bunny ears from the lace of my right boot had caught itself on the lacing hooks of the left boot. I untangled myself, then carefully made my way to the hall to join the others.

Steve, the retreat leader, usually gave some type of a lecture or teaching after breakfast and before dinner. Aside from the question and answer period that followed every talk, and periodic discussions with breakout groups, the rest of the program was done in complete silence. No talking. So, I didn't even have the chance to tell anyone what had happened on my way to the hall that morning, which is why my jaw hit the floor as soon as Steve began his morning lecture.

"If you're going to follow the path of dharma, you have to be willing to fall on your face," he said.

Had he somehow seen what happened outside? Or did someone tell him? It felt like he was talking specifically to me. Were we having a psychic moment from across the room? Or was this just a curious moment of synchronicity?

His talk that morning was about how practitioners seek to become a better version of themselves, and strive to reach some type of perfection while ignoring the realities of being human. We had to acknowledge our starting point, he said, by including all of our limitations, foibles and confusion.

If we couldn't do that, then we'd just be fooling ourselves into thinking we'd become something *more*, or that we'd finally discarded all the unwanted qualities of our own minds, and of our lives. But it was by going deeper and taking a closer look at ourselves, that we'd eventually understand why we hurt so much. And with that understanding, we could then experience compassion, wisdom and perhaps, freedom.

Steve gave teachings like these almost every day of the retreat, which lasted a full thirty days. Each one was a gem in its own right. He brought the dharma[2] to life in a way that no book was capable of doing, and he often included personal examples of his own.

His talks had a secondary benefit, in the form of relief from nearly eight hours we'd spend in strict meditation each day. During meditation, we had to sit perfectly still for forty-five minutes at a time, then spend fifteen minutes doing walking-meditation. After the walk, we'd sit down again for another 45 minutes, simply following our breath in and out watching as our minds did whatever minds do when there's nothing around to distract.

By the end of the month, every meditator in that hall felt some kind personal bond with Steve. His comment about falling flat on your face had cinched it for me like some kind of magical bond. He was my teacher.

A large part of the retreat revolved around the theme of death and "letting go." Steve would lead us in different types of visualization practices to contemplate not only our coming death, but the demise of our friends, family, enemies, and every creature that has ever been born in this universe.

He led us into a meditation in which we'd all lie down on the floor and imagine descending down into the ground, into the earth, lower and lower, until we felt a profound sense of groundlessness. This

---

[2] Here, "dharma" is defined as the Buddhist teachings. In other contexts, it can mean "truth" or "reality."

practice was meant to help us understand what "letting go" meant, not as a cliché, but as a *felt experience.*

If we could get comfortable with groundlessness by using it as a meditation technique, then we'd be able to accommodate the very groundlessness of everyday struggles, as well as the ultimate struggle at the end of all our lives.

This felt familiar to me, and when I realized why, I felt even more connected to Steve. I'd done this years before, as a mildly depressed college kid lying on a sweat-soaked pillow, imagining himself being lowered into the ground while peering into his inevitable non-existence. I didn't know it at the time, but I'd been producing my own type of groundlessness. The problem was that without the proper context, it had become an exercise in torturing myself with fear.

At the retreat, it made sense to think of letting go as a constant requirement of being alive, and that death was something that would touch us all one day. Day after day, Steve's talks seemed to involve death and groundlessness to one degree or another. There were nights when every meditator in the meditation hall had tears running down their face as we acknowledge our fear and sadness about this topic. It seemed cathartic, and mourning life's vicissitudes with each other did a lot to produce a feeling of deep relief, at least for me. It also did a lot to create a bond between us and the teacher.

Curiously, Steve never gave a talk about what it's like after you die. In Buddhism, reincarnation is the standard model for understanding what happens afterward. The tradition even includes descriptions of the in-between state, referred to it by its Tibetan name, "bardo." But Steve never discussed it in any significant way, that I can recall, and I never asked him about it.

His teachings focused on helping us as we were in the present, alive, and dealing with the groundlessness of *this* life.

But that was alright at the time because his teachings were so captivating. He would have the whole meditation hall brimming

Sean McNamara

with emotion as he guided us in meditations designed to help us come to terms with the difficult aspects of life.

The idea was for us to delve into the thoughts and feelings we usually avoided. We would also visualize experiences, such as sinking into the unknown depths of the earth, in order to cause us to release our false sense of control over reality.

There was no small talk here, and this seemed like deep stuff. His observations about life sounded unique, honest, and certainly dramatic. He made the things ordinary people chatted about seem artificial, mundane, which only made him seem more interesting.

After four weeks of meditating, eating, and walking in silence, it was time to return to the ordinary world. But the experience only deepened my interest in a spiritual life, and I wanted to do more retreats like this in the future.

But alas, it was back to the ordinary world for now. I moved into my new cubicle, learned new software, attended weekly team meetings and did all the usual stuff that happens inside corporate America.

At the same time, I felt a hangover from the retreat, and it wouldn't go away. I could feel whatever peace and insight I'd cultivated that month leaving me as I dealt with my day-to-day responsibilities, which frustrated me. I was earning a lot more money at this company, and I had a lot of opportunities to climb the corporate ladder, but none of that interested me as much as my spiritual path did.

I was also frustrated because by starting over at a new company, I only had two weeks of vacation available to me that year. It would be at least two or three more years before I could take a whole month off to do another long retreat, and there was no guarantee that I'd be allowed to take it all at once.

So, until then, all I could do was continue meditating at home and at the local center. During the week, I'd sit in my tiny cubicle tapping away on a keyboard. I didn't love it, but I was content.

54

It seemed that the undercurrent of fear I'd grown up with was gone. Everything was going smoothly, except for one thing.

CHAPTER 7 LOOKING FOR THE LIGHT

My fear of death wasn't the only thing that had accompanied me from childhood. On the physical level, I regularly experienced an onset of heart palpitations. They were more sporadic when I was younger, but now in my mid-twenties, they occurred often enough to worry me.

During an episode, my heart would spontaneously start beating at an abnormally high rate. It wasn't just beating though. More like *pounding*. Sometimes they started after I coughed, or while I was exercising, and sometimes they would start just as I was waking up in the morning. There was no rhyme or reason to what brought them on. During a typical episode, I could lift up my shirt in front of the mirror, look at the spot just below my sternum, and watch the flesh there pulse with every beat.

A normal heart beat sounds and feels like paired beats, da-Dum, da-Dum, da-Dum. But when the palpitations came, they changed to a single, rapid-fire striking in my chest, THUMP THUMP THUMP THUMP THUMP.

At the same time, I'd become just a little bit woozy, indicating my blood pressure was being affected. It could last a few seconds, or several minutes. And then my heart would stop beating.

A few moments later, it would restart with a normal, steady da-Dum, da-Dum, da-Dum.

As a teen, I figured out that if I held my breath and focused on my heart a certain way, I could stop the palpitations altogether. I could stop my own heart, then wait a couple moments, and feel it restart again.

The palpitations were happening more often now. Sometimes they came multiple times in a day. There wasn't anything strenuous happening in my life. I spent most of the day sitting in front of a computer, and got a fair amount of exercise at the gym after work.

I decided to see a doctor about it. The first one I saw, a general practitioner, couldn't tell what was going on because my heart decided to be well-behaved during my visit, so there was nothing for him to see. He referred me to a heart specialist.

This doctor set me up with a holter monitor. This was a small computer which hung by a strap which was slung around my neck. Wires ran from the box to the places around my chest where they were taped against my skin. I was to wear it non-stop for the next few days in order to capture some readings next time the palpitations came. Fortunately, it was a success and the monitor captured some readings for the doctor to analyze.

"You have Wolff-Parkinson-Wright syndrome," he told me. "You've basically got an extra nerve to your heart which randomly sends improper signals to your heart."

"Is that bad?" I wasn't nervous since I'd lived with this all my life, but I had to ask.

"Well, the thing is that, as people with this get older, sometimes heart issues can happen. You know how it stops for a second before it goes back to normal?"

"Yeah?" I replied. When I'd told him that earlier, he replied that it was common for people with WPW to figure out how to do that on their own.

"Well, it's possible that it won't start again after the pause. It's rare for that to happen, but you're getting older now, so we should do something to take care of this now."

57

He said there was medication I could take, but that I really wouldn't like the side effects. There was also a surgical option.

"We'd put you under anesthesia, and go in through the veins in your upper thighs, near your groin. We'd send some wires through, all the way into your heart, and locate the unwanted nerve. Then, we'd cauterize it, pull the wires out, and we'd be done."

It seemed simple, but I began to feel anxious. As minor as it seemed, it was still heart surgery nonetheless.

"You're lucky," he said, watching me fidget in my seat. "Ten or twenty years ago, we'd have to crack your chest open to do this, but thanks to technology we don't have to do it that way anymore."

We scheduled the surgery.

The odds of dying on the surgical table were miniscule, but reading the hospital's liability-release forms reminded me that it was a very real possibility. And just like that, my old fear of death came back, front and center.

But this time, I saw an opportunity. I was going to be put under anesthesia, and then remain "out" until the procedure was finished.

Even though I was still a novice meditator, I was training regularly and reading anything I could get my hands on about the "advanced" Tibetan practices. Many of these were gathered together over time into a cohesive set called the Six Yogas of Naropa.

These teachings include *inner heat,* in which yogis learn to raise the temperature of their bodies and stimulate the flow of subtle energy through special visualizations, postures, and breathing techniques. Another of these yogas is called *illusory body,* in which one meditates upon every experience having the nature of a dream in order to help with "letting go." Then there is *bardo yoga,* designed to prepare a yogi for the in-between state after dying but before being reborn.

Dream yoga is another, in which the yogi achieves lucid dreaming, then meditates within the dream state with full awareness. Another is *transference of consciousness at death*, in which the yogi projects their consciousness out of the top of their head in their final moments, with the intention of transporting their consciousness to a "pure land". Pure lands are places where inhabitants are either enlightened or nearly enlightened, and those fortunate enough to be reborn there can finish their spiritual evolution with their help.

The practice which interested me now was the *clear light meditation*.

The first step of this practice is for the yogi's body to settle into physical sleep. Then, the coarse levels of consciousness which everybody experiences would dissolve away. If the yogi is able to maintain focus on his or her heart-center during this phase of sleep, he or she could eventually experience their own "clear light." These teachings say the clear light is none other than our most fundamental nature, and something that is beyond impermanence. It's something beyond time, beyond birth and death, and something that can never experience suffering.

For me, the clear light represented a possible solution to my fear of death. If I could experience it for myself, then that would solve my problem. I'd know that some part of me would go on after I died. I'd know this not just by faith, but by experience.

I didn't have years to prepare for this meditation since I was having surgery in just a few days. But if there was any chance I could experience my own clear light, as tiny wires were threaded up through the veins of my thighs into the waiting chambers of my heart, then I would have found what I'd been looking for all my life.

The big day was quickly approaching. The Six Yogas of Naropa were secret practices, given only to the most advanced meditators after years of preparation and only with the guru's blessing. I didn't care about that though. I didn't have specific instructions for how to do this, and definitely didn't have any guru's blessing, but if I could

Sean McNamara

just figure it out on my own and even just a glimpse of this "clear light awareness," I'd be free.

I meditated as much as I could when I wasn't at the office. I even meditated while I walked, and while running errands. Most of all, I practiced keeping my awareness in the center of my chest as I allowed my body to fall asleep each night, hoping I was doing the right thing.

Finally, surgery arrived. My parents took me to the hospital, understandably nervous. It wasn't the first time they'd taken their little boy in for surgery.

After undressing and putting on the hospital gown, the nurse had me lie down on a gurney in a waiting area outside the operating room. Dad and Ma sat just a few feet away, waiting for me to be wheeled in for surgery. I knew the precious few minutes I had to myself were ticking away, and I needed to prepare myself.

I drew the privacy curtain around me so that I was instantly in my own little dark meditation room. Instead of lying down to wait, I sat up, using the pillow as meditation cushion, and began by following my breath as it moved in and out, trying to steady my mind.

Outside, I could hear footsteps approaching. A nurse had come to check on me. Then I heard my father's voice say "He's o.k., he's just meditating. Please let him be." She walked away without even drawing the curtains open. I was touched to hear my dad protect those last minutes I had to myself.

I was also surprised to hear him use the word meditation. By then, my family knew about my separation from Catholicism and my new commitment to Buddhism, and they weren't happy about it. Whenever I tried to share what I was learning during family dinners at their house, my dad would quickly change the conversation, or remain silent. Actually, nobody at the table looked comfortable at all when I talked about Buddhism. I knew better than to try to force him or the rest of my family to accept it, so we'd talk about something else instead.

60

However, today, minutes before going under the knife, he was on my side. He might not have known why I was trying to meditate before surgery, but he knew it was important to me.

But meditation, it seemed, was not on my side that day. I had barely managed to stabilize my attention on my breath when the nurse came to wheel me into surgery.

Now I was lying on the operating table, and people moved around the room getting everything ready. The anesthesiologist was the next person to speak to me.

"As the anesthesia enters your system," he said calmly, "I'd like you to count backwards, down from one hundred."

This was it. This was my big opportunity. If I could just hold on to my consciousness while my body blacked out, and while the doctor guided tiny electrical filaments through my veins up into my heart, I'd come face to face with my true, undying self.

Ninety nine…
Ninety eight…
Ninety se---

I opened my eyes. I felt groggy, but I was awake enough to realize that I'd survived the surgery. And then I realized I'd passed out only seconds after receiving the anesthetic, unable to retain my awareness in the process. I'd failed to see the light.

Shit.

CHAPTER 8 EL CÓNDOR PASA

Recovery was fast and I was back to work a couple days later. The palpitations were gone, so the surgery was a success.

I'd only been back at the office a few weeks when my friend and co-worker, Phil, mentioned that he and his brother Pete were planning a trip to Peru. They were going to fly to the capital, Lima, then take a short flight to Cusco, which at one time was the capital of the Incan empire.

At an altitude of over eleven thousand feet above sea level, they'd stay a couple nights to acclimate themselves before spending several days trekking the Inca trail and sleeping in tents each night. At certain points, the Andean path would pass through dense and humid jungle foliage, then climb above the clouds to elevations surpassing thirteen thousand feet, passing a variety of archeological sites along the way.

Their final destination was the legendary Machu Picchu.

"Do you want to come with us?" Phil asked. "We're going next month."

I'd just undergone a heart procedure and felt a little bit nervous about pushing it. Strapping on a backpack and hiking at altitudes where I'd only get 75% of the amount of oxygen I was used to in Denver might not be the best idea. I told him I needed to think it over.

But I didn't need to think for very long. Something felt *off* at the office ever since the surgery. The work was the same, and nothing else at the office had changed. It was life as usual. It was me, *I* was off. I was glad to be alive, but it really bothered me that my experiment with meditation-under-anesthesia had failed. As much as I tried to ignore the irritation, it was there and I knew it. I needed something big to distract me from it.

"I'm in!" I told Phil the next day.

I'd seen many beautiful photos of the mysterious stone city high atop a mountain plateau. It included temples, houses, and large structures oriented to mark the equinoxes. Mysteries still surround it since no one really knows what it's true purpose was, why it was built at that particular location, or how the Inca people were able to construct it with their level of technology.

Reports by many tourists over the years gave Machu Picchu an aura of spiritual power. "It had a special energy," is what people usually said after returning.

And maybe that's what I needed, something with "special energy." Something out of the ordinary. Something with real meaning. An adventure.

We flew from Denver to Miami. There, we had several hours before our flight departed to Lima. The beach wasn't too far away, so we left our luggage at the airport and took a cab. I hadn't packed a swimsuit, so I took off my blue jeans and waded into the ocean.

Tasting the sea water, a tingly feeling spread over my skin and a flood of memories entered my mind. At least a decade had passed since leaving Rio de Janeiro for the center of the North American continent, which is about as far from the ocean as any person can get. In the Philippines, we'd drive from Manila out to the coast to spend holidays at the beach. In Rio, a moist ocean breeze would blow into my bedroom every night. In Hong Kong, our apartment overlooked Tai Tam Bay, so the ocean was a constant presence there as well.

Sean McNamara

The ocean reminded me of home, yet I never had a place to truly call "home." The roots that were torn the first time, when we left Manila, never really grew back. The ocean, then, signified leaving my known world, and the people in it, behind. But, it also meant new friends and new challenges.

I tasted the saltwater again and wondered, was a big change coming again?

I dried myself off with my shirt, put my jeans on over my wet underwear and we headed back to the airport to continue our flight to Peru.

I spoke Spanish, so once we landed in Lima, I secured our flight to Cusco. I sat next to a woman from Australia named Lynda who was traveling by herself on holiday. She was also on her way to Machu Picchu but didn't speak the language, which seemed very courageous to me. We got along very well during the flight, so by the time we landed, I invited her to join our little band of travelers.

Nothing had been planned ahead of time, we had no itinerary. I asked the taxi driver for some lodging ideas, and he dropped us off on a cobblestone street which was lined on both sides with old Spanish-era homes. We knocked on the thick wooden door and were welcomed in after a few moments. The ground floor was comprised of several simple tables where breakfast would be served, and the bedrooms were upstairs.

Each room came with an attached bathroom, and something I'd never seen before. In the bath, the hot water would be supplied by a small electric heater attached to the shower head, through which cold water would be routed. From the device, a long cord extended out of the shower and plugged into a wall outlet.

I was more afraid of getting electrocuted than I was of the tepid water. But this was my first chance to wash the Floridian sand out of all my nooks and crannies, and I was happy to be clean again.

64

Afterward, a local woman knocked on our door and asked if we were going to be visiting Machu Picchu. Obviously, she had a relationship with our hosts, and they'd probably alerted her to our arrival. We hadn't yet figured out the details of how we'd actually get to our final destination, so I was happy to hear that she could add us to her trekking company's group and take care of all the details. We settled on a price, and she told us to be ready the morning after next.

Until then, we passed the time visiting churches, museums, and the nearby Inca ruins Coricancha and Sacsayhuaman. We ate in open air cafes by the railroad tracks, and drank coca tea while our bodies adjusted to the high altitude. It was important to take our time and give our bodies the time they needed because soon we'd be going a lot higher.

Finally, it was time for the next part of our trip. We boarded our bus, and I saw we were joining a group of about ten other travelers from around the world. I felt like I was back in school again. Several hours later, we arrived at the trailhead for the *Camino Inca*, and began several days of hiking through some of the most beautiful scenery on planet Earth.

We climbed up steep and narrow paths, at times shivering under a cold drizzle of Andean rain. At other times, the sun would shine down to burn off the surrounding fog, revealing endless mountain vistas beneath the rarefied dark blue atmosphere. I felt like I could almost touch outer space. I saw a condor once, and llamas made regular appearances along the trail.

My body loved being exposed to the elements. I hadn't realized how much sitting in a cubicle for the last few years had robbed me of natural feelings like these. At the office, it was always the same air-conditioned temperature, the floor was always flat beneath my feet, and I never felt anything. But here on the trail, I was often tired, sweaty, sometimes too hot or sometimes chilled to my bones, and my lungs burned on the steeper trails. *This is what being alive should feel like*, I thought. I was happy.

The tour group operator the day of our departure.

Lynda, Peter, Phil, and me on our way to the "Camino Inca,"
the Inca trail.[3]

---

[3] Color images of all the pictures in this book can be found at
www.RenegadeMysticBook.com/pictures

Cooling off in the mountain mist.

At the Sun Gate the final morning on the trail.

Our whole trekking group, at Machu Picchu

The main complex of Machu Picchu

At the railroad tracks at Aguas Calientes

Everyone in the group paired up to share tents. Phil and Peter shared one, and since Lynda and I didn't know anyone else, and because we felt very comfortable with each other by now, we decided to share a tent as well. Our instant friendship, begun on the flight from Lima to Cusco, quickly evolved into a passionate connection.

My heart was already physically healed, but now it was receiving another kind of medicine. I felt even more alive, connected, and tender in the best of ways.

On the final night of the trek, we arrived at a large hostel, oddly out of place along a high-altitude trail in the Andean mountains. It was basically a massive room lined with rows of bunk beds. Dozens of travelers from all over the world slept there every night, preparing for their grand finale the following day.

Our plan was to wake up in the early morning darkness and complete the final stretch of the Inca trail, racing against the sunrise. If we arrived at the *Sun Gate*, a vantage point high above Machu Picchu, in time, we'd be able to photograph the ancient complex down below before the gates were opened to let in the other tourists, the ones who'd arrived by train. Once they entered the complex, it would be impossible to take a decent picture.

I barely slept that night. Not because of anticipation, but because of the lice which lived inside the sweat-stained pillow that came with the worn-out mattress on my bunk. The fiery itchiness on my scalp made it impossible to stop scratching long enough to fall asleep.

I was ready to leave as soon as the others had stirred from their exhausted slumber. I knew that after visiting Machu Picchu, we'd soak in the hot springs of the nearby town aptly named Aguas Calientes. All I really wanted to do was dunk my stinging head in the water to either drown or cook the bugs living inside my skin. I hiked as fast as I could, scratching my head so much that by the time we reached the Sun Gate, my fingernails were embedded with dried blood and sweat.

Sean McNamara

After taking our photos, we made our way down to enter the complex and explore what remained of the mysterious complex. Visually, it was magnificent. I made a point to linger at the spots associated with ritual and astronomical significance, and tried to feel any special energy that might be there.

But, as much as I wanted to feel it, there was none as far as I could tell. But either the lice had me so distracted that I wouldn't be able to feel an elephant if one was stepping on my foot, or whatever energy had been there at one time was now long gone.

Still, I was ecstatic to be in Machu Picchu instead of inside a plastic holding cell, pecking away at a keyboard beneath the incandescent zombie light. Here, I felt truly alive.

After treating our aching bodies to the hot springs, we boarded the train back to Cusco. We didn't speak to each other very much. We were tired, and I think, introspective. Night fell as the train continued alongside the Urubamba river, back to where we started.

There were two little boys on the train, brothers perhaps. One was a couple years younger than the other, and it was obvious they were poor. They walked through each car, entertaining the passengers by playing "El Condor Pasa" on tiny pan flutes in the traditional manner. We'd all heard "Flight of the Condor" about a thousand times since landing in Peru, but I didn't mind hearing it from these children.

The lights inside the car were turned off, and the overcast sky outside permitted only a bit of moonlight to enter through the windows. I couldn't see the boys' faces. Their small silhouettes stood out as they played their music for these strangers. *Where were their parents? Did they even have parents*, I wondered? They finished their performance and stretched out their hands, and we thanked them with some money.

They seemed so innocent, harmless, and defenseless. Perhaps that was what made their music sound so sweet. Here they stood, together alone, surviving one day at a time in a world that might easily forget they ever existed. They were alive, just like me, but their experience was a world apart from mine. Maybe it was the altitude, or that I already felt a coming nostalgia about our trip, but my heart broke just by looking at these two little boys.

Our vacation was now over and the next day, Phil and Peter boarded their plane back to America. But Lynda was looking for a way to get to Lake Titicaca, the next phase of her travels, and I didn't want to leave. I wasn't ready to go back. I knew I'd see Phil again back at the office, but I knew I'd probably never see Lynda or Peru again.

So, after rescheduling my flight, I rejoined Lynda and settled in for a full day's bus ride to Puno, on the north-western coast of Lake Titicaca. I was thankful for how long the bus ride took, and for the periodic stops in small villages along the way. I wanted, or needed, rather, time to slow down. Even though I'd extended my vacation by a few more days, I could already feel it coming to an end, and I didn't want to say goodbye. For some reason, this was really hard for me.

We arrived late that evening and found a hotel, and went to sleep. Only a couple of hours later, I was awake and sitting on the toilet and cradling a trash can between my knees at the same time. It was food poisoning. "Bouts of diarrhea and vomiting" were the last item I'd put on my list of "How to make the most of your final days on your trip," but here it was, there was no choice in the matter.

In the morning, I was able to pull myself together enough to walk through town toward the docks. We wanted to take a boat on the lake. I wasn't too excited about the prospect of bouncing up and down on the waves while vibrating to the motion of the boat's outboard motor, but I wanted to make the most of the day instead of lying in bed all day.

On the way to the docks, we passed an old, earthen walled church along an empty street. It looked abandoned, dirty and in need of repair. In front of the massive, dilapidated wooden doors, I saw a brown dog lying on her side.

At Lake Titicaca at Puno, floating Uros islands, fishing boat

Residents of Taquile Island

Sean McNamara

I could tell by her enlarged nipples that she'd had puppies, but probably a long time ago. Her eyes stared out into nothingness, and her breathing was the only sign that she was still alive. Standing next to her was another mutt, perhaps her mate or brother. He stayed close to her, watching her carefully. As Lynda and I turned the corner at the end of the street, I looked back at them one last time, and caught a glimpse of him lowering his head to sniff her pelt.

We found our way to the boats, and hired a tour guide to take us first to the island of Taquile. Afterward, we'd continue on to visit the Uros people, who lived on tiny floating islands constructed of hollow reeds layered on top of each other.

Returning to shore later that afternoon, we walked through town, passing the same church we'd seen that morning. Mother dog was still there. I peered at her ribs and belly for signs of breathing. But there were none, and her companion was nowhere to be seen. Black flies buzzed over her lonely corpse.

I'd spent all day taking in beautiful scenery, having wonderful encounters with the local people, and these experiences with Lynda. I didn't want to say goodbye to any of them, especially because I knew I'd never see them again.

But at that moment, it was as if something or someone invisible, in the background of my awareness, was quietly nudging me on. *It's time to let go.* I wondered how long the other dog had lingered over her corpse before deciding to leave. How did he feel, now that he was alone? And why did I care so much?

It's time to let go.

CHAPTER 9 OUT OF THE BOX

A couple days later, I was back at my desk, in my little box tucked into a row of other boxes filled with other people sitting at their desks. Everything looked especially drab inside the office. Although I had only been gone for a week and a half, returning to this environment took a lot of adjusting. I could smell the gray paint on the walls. I could almost feel my lungs inhaling whatever toxic chemicals were used to produce the endless gray carpet running between the gray, plastic cubicles.

On the surface, everyone seemed to be working hard to accomplish whatever "action items" had been assigned to them. Meeting room conversations had a tone to them as if our work really mattered. Underneath, I could tell that everyone was scared. Tech stocks were beginning to crumble ahead of what would eventually become a small market crash. Budgets were being slashed, people were being let go, and nobody felt stable in their position.

There were smiles on people's faces, but their eyes betrayed their underlying anxiety. I pretended to be happy too, and acted like I was glad to be back after my vacation. I tried to seem grateful to them for letting me take the time off. But I wasn't happy at all.

One end of the office had panoramic windows which looked out toward the western side of Colorado. There, in the distance, were the Rocky Mountains, stretching from north to south for many miles. They reminded me of Peru. I felt a yearning inside, and every time I stopped to look at the mountains, it grew a little bit more.

Months passed like this, and the yearning turned into anxiety. Almost every day, I'd find myself calculating how much my stocks were worth, and with compound interest, how many years it would take to retire. How soon would I be able to leave my cubicle for good? How soon before I could have a more meaningful life? I didn't have that much money saved, so even if the stock market was up or down, my retirement date always came out to thirty-or-so years in the future. *Thirty years* before I'd be free!

Day after day, I sat at my gray, plastic desk, and breathed the gray, plastic air while conforming to a gray, plastic culture for what were most likely to be the best years of my life.

One day, I saw that another month-long meditation retreat was going to be held that December. I'd already used most of my vacation time for Peru, and asking for more time off so soon after returning would have been out of the question. But meditating inside a beautiful meditation hall, smelling the incense and taking afternoon walks through the trees was a stark contrast to sitting in my cubicle, and I felt frustrated that I couldn't go because of my job.

If I couldn't go now, then when? Would I have to wait another year or two? And afterward, how long would it be before I could do it again? At such a stunted pace, would I ever find the spiritual answers I'd been seeking? And even if I could go on retreat every year, I wasn't sure if it was acceptable to me anymore to spend the rest of the year inside my cubicle, a tiny cog in the wheel of corporate America.

Was the money worth it? They were paying me a very nice salary, especially for a bachelor in his twenties. This was a golden prison, but the door to the cell had always been open, and nobody was forcing me to stay.

My heart wanted earth, and wind, and real connections with real people, and to not be afraid of dying anymore. And for that, what I needed most was *time*. But with each passing day, time passed through the hourglass just a little bit faster than the day before. I looked at the mountains in the distance. They seemed to beckon me with a silent promise. Another kind of life was possible, if I was willing to take a chance. *It's time to let go.*

So, I quit.

CHAPTER 10 A GOOD TEACHER

I attended the retreat that winter, and many others after that. In between, I sought jobs that were more humane and meaningful to me, and which also offered the flexibility I needed to attend teachings and other programs which supported my spiritual pursuit.

My first job after that retreat was in a group home for developmentally disabled people, where I fed and bathed the residents, and also gave them their medication. Alas, the ridiculously low pay made it difficult to justify staying there for more than a couple of years. The company gave me the flexibility to go on retreat as often as I wanted, but ironically, I couldn't afford to go since I got paid so little.

Next, I tried selling cars. I had a friend who made a lot of money doing it, and he suggested I join him at his dealership. I figured this line of work would give me a chance to be of genuine service to people and to also earn a decent living. It turned out that the reason my friend did so well was because he happened to have very thick skin and didn't mind taking advantage of people when it came time to negotiate on price. I wasn't built the same way, and as long as I tried to live up to my Buddhist ideals in this environment, there was no way for me to succeed.

Eventually, I found a happy medium by studying at the Boulder College of Massage Therapy, then opening my own business inside of a chiropractic office in Denver.

By this point in my life, I'd already ended my association with Rinpoche and his organization. To be honest, I hadn't immediately "left" him after returning from Vermont and Los Angeles. I spent a very long time trying to reconcile what he had done with how I thought a guru was supposed to behave. Was I being unfair? Was I shooting myself in the karmic foot by thinking he was just a regular human, making human mistakes? For some strange reason, I doubted myself just as much as I doubted him and what happened with Andrea.

But every time I sat down at my meditation table to practice the tantric liturgy he'd empowered me to use, adrenalin would flow through me as memories from that terrible night flooded my mind. A lump would fill my throat while I chanted the long liturgy. Clearing my mind for meditation was often difficult, if not impossible.

Eventually, I realized my self-imposed re-traumatization I went through every time I tried to do the practice wasn't worth it. I got tired of pretending that I felt any kind of positive connection to this guru, and that he felt any kind of connection with me. By this point in time, he probably wouldn't know who I was if I were to pass him on the sidewalk. He was a figurehead, and I was just one of thousands of his "students," and one of thousands of dues-paying members of his organization.

So, I turned my devotion to Steve who, at just around the same time, decided to start his own lineage. For years, he had been a senior teacher in another organization, also headed by a Rinpoche. As that group's spiritual leader, the Rinpoche was the only one allowed to give initiations and empowerments. Like my former guru, this Rinpoche was the figurehead in Steve's organization, and this was also how he retained his authority.

But after several years of leading annual retreats and teaching classes on behalf of Rinpoche, Steve had developed truly personal relationships with many of his students. He had extensive knowledge of the Buddhist teachings and more importantly, his profound experience on the meditation cushion was undeniable. He was a scholar as well as a strong meditator, but most of all, he was charismatic. This made it easy to bond with him.

Eventually, students who hadn't already received the "advanced" practices but who were ready to do so, asked to receive them from Steve instead of the Rinpoche.

Steve often spoke about trusting oneself and being honest with how one felt, and these students took it to heart by asking him to give them the empowerments. They were honest by saying they felt no real connection with the organization's figurehead, and that they wanted to receive them from the teacher they felt truly connected with, which was Steve.

Besides, Steve was clearly more than qualified for the task since he'd been doing these practices for decades. But it just wouldn't be allowed, he said. There could only be a single source of these teachings, and that source was the Rinpoche. Needless to say, the organization was just as much an income-producing business as it was a spiritual lineage, and this business belonged to the Rinpoche.

Privately, Steve felt the same way his students did, although he initially reserved his comments for his most loyal students, the ones he could trust the most. But after some time and significant encouragement from his growing body of personal students, Steve left the organization and started his own.

I imagine that this was a tremendous spiritual offense to that Rinpoche, a betrayal of sorts. Practically speaking, it must've been a significant loss of income for the organization, now that these students would be spending their money elsewhere. A single student typically paid several thousand dollars to enjoy a full month at the feet of the teacher. A retreat could hold nearly a hundred students. Doing the math, anyone could see this was a lot of money.

Next, Steve did something truly unheard of. He *appointed himself* as a Vajra Master. This title is reserved for lineage holders of the Vajrayana tradition, more commonly referred to as the tantric Buddhist tradition of Tibet.

This was unheard of because traditionally, Vajra masters were recognized as reincarnations of enlightened masters and trained from birth to be the future leaders of their respective lineage. Rarely, an adult, typically a yogi who'd spent their life meditating alone in a cave somewhere or someone raised in a monastery, either one exhibiting extraordinary spiritual qualities, would be publicly recognized and authorized by another lineage holder to take on this role.

All that is to say, to *crown oneself* as a Vajra master was unthinkable.

But Steve did it. There wasn't any kind of ceremony, though. It was just something he announced in due course, and we didn't really think twice about it. Although a few of his students chose to stay with the other organization, most of them left in order to dedicate themselves solely to Steve's teachings. I left my Rinpoche (the one who slept with Andrea), and was just happy to continue my practices with Steve.

At the time, we (his new body of committed students) celebrated this courageous act of rebellion in the name of "authenticity." It was a bold and sacrificial act on his behalf, because by committing it, he burned every bridge he'd ever built with his prior community. Teaching programs for the other organization had been a substantial part of his own income as well, so he was starting over on various levels.

It was just him and us now. He had nothing left to lose, and we had everything to gain. It seemed he'd done what was necessary for his own evolution, as well as ours.

Not only was he our new guru, but he was also our meditation instructor. This meant that we could meet with him privately to discuss our meditative experiences, frustrations, as well as other things that were happening in our ordinary lives.

Steve often talked about how, centuries ago, lineages were often between a teacher and only one, two, or a handful of students at the most. This was the ideal situation, he often said. And even though there were nearly fifty of us when he started his new lineage, I think we felt we were doing something that truly resembled the ancient way.

Eventually, he created liturgies and rituals for his new lineage, and we were more than happy to start using them instead of those belonging to the other organization. Bit by bit, he created something new, all his own, and he shared it with all of us.

By empowering himself, we felt like we'd been empowered too. Truth, confidence and self-trust were the main themes of his talks at the time, understandably. And it seemed like each one of us was hearing something we'd needed to hear for a long time. At the very least, it justified my leaving my career in corporate America to make my own way in the world. *This*, I thought, must be why I'd left my gray, plastic career, and why I'd attended every retreat possible.

The other community members became my closest friends, since we were bound by a feeling of "we're all in this together." We shared an overt understanding that *this was it*. This was a real lineage, and this was the most important thing we could be doing with our lives.

The retreat environment also became the place where romantic relationships were made. Many of Steve's talks were centered around the idea that one's partner or spouse was a spokesperson for "reality," because it was the person closest to you who would inevitably point out where your ego was causing you problems.

Steve was married at the time, and he spoke openly about how they challenged each other, and how there was a spiritual meaning to it. We admired how open he was about his personal life, and didn't mind the sometimes-shocking level of self-disclosure he used during some of his teachings. Soon enough, many of us began to look for "the one," who could help us with our spiritual growth in the context of a love relationship.

Retreats always included a couple of special banquets. One occurred after the first two weeks, and the second was on the final night. For many of us, these banquets were a time to let the pressure out a bit and just have fun. After dinner, we'd play music over the loudspeakers, refill our cups with the wine we'd been served during the banquet, and dance for hours.

After spending weeks in silence and sitting still in meditation, this was a fantastic opportunity to socialize and feel our bodies move. It always seemed like by the end of the night, several of the unused rooms became secret make out spots for new couples who'd only first met at the start of the retreat and barely had a chance to talk since then, but now had the opportunity to really connect.

None of us were monastics, after all, and it seemed like an accepted part of the culture. Of course, after the half-way banquet, it would be another two weeks of silence and meditation before these romances could continue, at least for those meditators who followed the rules.

Something happened after one particular banquet which inspired me to think about becoming a teacher myself. It was about a different kind of intimacy.

I was one of the retreat's meditation instructors, and decided to do some cleaning inside the hotel the morning after the banquet. There was an unused dry sauna in one of the hallways, and on a whim, I decided to take a look inside while on my way to another part of the hotel. On the floor, I saw a very large, but empty, bottle of alcohol. Next to it was a dried-up puddle of vomit.

I was angry. By all appearances, one of the participants had stolen the alcohol for their private use, thrown up, and left without doing the courtesy of cleaning up the evidence.

As I walked down the corridor to find some cleaning supplies, I saw one of the participants, Paul. He seemed to be in an aimless daze, or was he pacing? When I approached him, he appeared to be on edge. He was in his twenties, and though he was normally sweet and deferential, there was something a little bit off about him at this moment.

"I just found a saké bottle and some puke in the sauna," I stated flatly. He looked away suddenly, which made me suspicious. "Was it you?" I asked.

"No, I don't know what you're talking about!" he assured me, his eyes wide and defensive now.

I wanted to trust him, so I let it go and went to find some cleaning supplies in another part of the hotel.

When I returned to the sauna five minutes later, I found Paul there on his hands and knees, vigorously scrubbing and rinsing the floor with a hand towel and a bowl of water.

He was trying to erase his mistake before anybody else found it, and he probably didn't expect me to show up. He looked up at me with guilty eyes, and nodded in surrender when I told him, "We need to go talk to Steve."

I felt upset at Paul, but looking back, I'm not sure why. Was it because he'd lied to me the first time I asked him about what I'd found? Or was it because I bore the title of "meditation instructor" and felt some sense of ownership and defensiveness regarding everything that happened at these programs? Deep down inside, did I think I was superior to him in some way?

It was still early in the morning, and Steve answered his door wearing nothing more than his boxers and a white, sleeveless undershirt. I may have woken him up, and I felt terribly awkward, albeit justified.

He noticed Paul coyly hovering a few feet behind me. He resembled a kid waiting to meet with his school's principal. I asked Steve if I could chat privately first, and he invited me in. I told him what happened, feeling a bit like a "tattletale," but also enjoying the opportunity to speak with him alone. It felt like we were working on some problem together, or like this was something we could bond over.

"Do you want me to tell him to pack up and leave?" I suggested.

There have been countless times since then, especially whenever I've been in a difficult situation with a student, when I remembered the next words that came out of his mouth.

"Maybe what he needs is for us to accept him. Maybe he needs more love."

Steve dismissed me, and invited Paul to come in next. They must have chatted for twenty minutes or so while I waited outside the door. When Paul came out, the look on his face was priceless. He was glowing. He stayed for the remainder of the program, without another incident.

Remembering that morning, I can't decide what struck me more. Was it Steve's kind and insightful response to a student's distress, or the fact that he was willing to see him without delay, still in his underwear?

Steve had put me and others through his official "meditation instructor training" program, but it was life's random, intimate moments like these which offered the richest learning opportunities. In those years, I watched, and learned, as Steve spoke to students kindly, patiently, and while seeing only the best in them. He encouraged them to trust themselves as he trusted them.

In time, it seemed that Steve really loved us, and we loved him back.

With Steve's encouragement, I started a local group of my own in Denver. Offering guided meditation sessions every weekend, along with one-on-one guidance, I began to put everything I'd learned from Steve into action. I strove to see the best in each person, to be humble and transparent, and to teach in a way which related to real life instead of repeating what was written in dusty old books.

I soon discovered that being a teacher was another way of learning, and the stakes were higher than before. Nothing brings out the worst in people than *other people*, and my students often helped me see my own limitations. As much as I found fulfillment in leading my group, I also often felt frustration, impatience, and other such feelings while working with them. They showed me where I needed to improve myself, and years of meditation helped me keep my self-awareness when working through difficult feelings with them.

But Steve's examples weren't all lovey-dovey. There were also times when he needed to be stern. I remember a one-on-one meeting in which I told him about my new girlfriend. This was a relationship I initiated very soon after breaking up with my previous girlfriend. I wasn't good at saying "goodbye" in any form, to anyone, and that included breaking up. The excuse I gave my previous girlfriend was that I felt I needed some time alone, to be by myself. I thought it was kinder than saying I just didn't like her anymore.

To make matters worse, our community was relatively small, and the pool of available singles was quite limited. Because of this, my new girlfriend was also a member of the community, which made it even more painful for my ex-girlfriend. Naturally, she felt hurt when she found out I'd started up with someone else several weeks later. I suspected she'd taken her woes to Steve, probably in the context of a private "meditation instruction" meeting.
The look that came over his face when I started explaining myself confirmed that she had indeed already told him. I think she must've really made me out to be the "bad guy," which was understandable. Nobody likes getting dumped.

Using as few words as possible, he made his point that I needed to treat people better. As if to put me in my place and make sure I heard him, he asked pointedly, "What are you going to do about it?"

"I guess I need to meditate more?" I suggested, although I sounded more like I was asking a question.

"No!" he slammed back, his voice raised. I held his gaze nervously. Was that frustration in his eyes, or contempt? "You need to look at your life!"

It was difficult to see this side of him, and it was rare at the time. He was right, even though I didn't like the way he delivered the message. If he had spoken to me gently or sweetly, I may not have gotten it. It was another learning opportunity for me as a fledgling teacher.

Later on, things would happen in Steve's life to change him, and more and more people would talk about receiving harsh feedback from Steve. Oftentimes, it would seem completely off-base and unfair. But in this instance, and at this stage of our relationship, I was grateful for it.

With every retreat, more new people attended his programs and wanted to stay connected with Steve afterward. Naturally, he needed to form an organization of his own to manage the influx, and that would require a staff. In the beginning, these were all volunteer positions. But over time, and because of the demands of the organization, they became paid, full-time positions. Steve's teachings had become his main occupation. He was a full-time guru now, and this was his sole source of income.

Once in a while during a retreat, a participant, usually a first-timer, would pack up their bags while everyone was asleep and drive away without letting anybody know, as if escaping. Sometimes, they'd let their meditation instructor know their plans ahead of time. Often, the participant would be asked to meet with Steve before leaving. Sometimes they did, sometimes they chose not to.

In response to these sudden absences, Steve would give a brief talk to the whole group the following day, explaining the single, empty meditation cushion in the room. One explanation I recall hearing Steve use more than once was that the participant's ego just couldn't take it anymore.

But, Steve usually suggested, we should all regard that person's choice to leave as a gift. After all, he explained, some part of each one of us had wanted to leave the program, or perhaps their entire spiritual path, at one point or another. Therefore, that person's departure was a symbolic way of giving us all some mental breathing room.

After hearing this, we paid no more attention to the odd absence and continued on with the retreat. I don't think any of us wondered if there was a good reason why that person left, or if they saw or experienced anything we should be concerned about.

Instead, I think we felt even more loyal to each other and to Steve for being the ones who stayed, who'd completed yet another retreat together, and who were a part of the overall growth and success of this lineage.

Those were the good years.

CHAPTER 11 FRICTION

In time, it became clear that renting a space every time Steve wanted to lead a retreat wouldn't work anymore. He wanted and needed to teach more often, and needed more space to host his growing number of students. The organization was beginning to feel growing pains, and they decided they needed to either buy or build their own permanent retreat center.

As stressful as the search for a new retreat center was, it wasn't the only thing Steve was struggling with. It seemed that his marriage was on the rocks. His wife was usually present at these retreats, and because many of us had known each other for years, they made very little effort to keep their frustrations with each other private. In some ways, this took on a parent-child dynamic. Steve and his wife were "mom and dad," and those of us who comprised his closest students were the "kids" in the family.

In time, everything changed. First, Steve, through his organization, obtained sufficient donations to buy mountain land and build a brand-new retreat center.

Second, he'd fallen in love with someone new, and his wife was no longer present during the programs. He eventually divorced her, though it's unclear to me whether he'd begun his new relationship before their separation. The rumors were that he'd met the new woman when she was a participant at one of his retreats. She'd been his student. Curiously, it turned out that she was quite wealthy and had joined the organization' elite circle of wealthy donors.

Sean McNamara

Since Steve was our leader and his new girlfriend was somewhere past middle-age like him, few people seemed to bat an eye, at least publicly, at what was going on with his personal life. He seemed quite happy, which was reflected in the many teachings about love, passion and compassion he gave during retreats at this point in time. Many of us felt badly for his wife, though. She'd been cast aside, and everyone kept their eyes forward, focused on Steve's direction.

Those changes must have been highly uncomfortable for him since he was already in the spotlight as the head of our lineage and our personal teacher. He couldn't tell us absolutely everything that happened in his personal life, which was understandable, yet he still shared enough to maintain the level of intimacy he'd established from the very beginning.

Even with the support of the wealthy donors, the organization would need to rely on steady monthly donations and the income from retreat attendance to cover the long-term operation of the center and the organization. The business had to keep growing in order to cover its costs.

Fortunately for Steve, he'd attracted students at various levels of training so that he could offer retreats at every season to meet their needs.

The most "advanced" students were interested in traditional tantric Buddhist practice, and Steve began to give the same empowerment to them that I'd received from Rinpoche so many years before. Most of those students had urged him to leave his former organization, so that they could receive these practices from him instead of the Rinpoche, who was only a distant figurehead for them.

But it seemed that the majority of his new students had no interest in the traditional Tibetan methods. This wasn't a problem for Steve though, because over the years, he focused more on teaching other styles of meditation, styles which didn't resemble Tibetan Buddhism at all.

There were the retreats when we spent a considerable amount of time meditating while lying on our backs. Looking back, these techniques were no different from the *savasana* technique common in hatha yoga, or the increasingly popular *yoga nidra*, but he never used those labels, as if these were his own creation. Then there was a phase when the sole focus of his retreats was on the Zen technique of "just-sitting."

There were other phases too, including pseudo-aboriginal rituals and ancestor worship.

Every year or two, it seemed, Steve sent us on a new training path, and we followed eagerly. He wrote new kinds of vows and liturgies to accompany the newest direction of his teachings. Usually, an email would be sent to the whole community urging us to attend the next retreat if at all possible, so that everyone in the community could stay up-to-date on his newest revelations.

Obviously, the more people who attended each program, the more income there was to pay for the organization's staff and office costs, the retreat center's operating expenses, and Steve's salary as well.

Those of us who'd received the advanced Tibetan practices continued using them.

A not uncommon complaint from a student was that once they'd finally landed on a practice they felt comfortable using, Steve would announce a completely new course of practice and study. Should they abandon their old way of meditating? Or follow Steve's lead and adopt his shiny new practice?

Steve's catalogue of teachings and meditation techniques was growing. Yet he didn't seem to like it when a student asked if they could also receive training from another teacher, or to experiment with other methods.

In one case, a long-time community member named Walter had become interested in exploring the use of entheogens in his spiritual

Sean McNamara

life, much like traditional shamans do all over the world. It seemed like a fair question for him to ask Steve.

All I remember is that one day Walter was there, then gone the day after, never to be seen again. No one, as far as I knew, heard from him afterward. For reasons I would understand only too late, I didn't bother to contact him myself to ask if he was doing alright now that he'd left our community.

Steve gave a brief talk about Walter's departure, which I vaguely remember. Walter was a well-liked member of the community and Steve needed to put the issue to rest. In so many words, Steve explained that this was a *good thing* for Walter, and it was all part of the *reality's* enlightened way of setting us on our appropriate paths. But he also stressed the idea that it wasn't good for a student to be distracted by other spiritual techniques. If we wanted to get anywhere on our path, we needed to have a singular commitment to Steve and Steve's techniques.

I think for many of us, the increased demand for loyalty had an attractive quality, and it made it seem like this lineage really had something special, unique, and powerful to offer. But his demand was also matched with a kind of pressure, or a friction of sorts, which was steadily increasing particularly between him and his closest students.

I remember one afternoon, in the middle of a retreat. I was chatting with a couple of instructors and administrators when suddenly Liz, one of the senior teachers, barged into the office.

Tightly gripping her phone, her eyes flashed with anger. She released a growl of frustration, then threw the phone across the room. We stared at her in shock. One could hear a pin drop at that moment. Then, she looked up at the ceiling and drooped her shoulders in a gesture of surrender.

Somebody asked "What's wrong Liz?"

Her single-word response told us all we needed to hear.

94

"Steve!"

She didn't need to tell us the details of the argument she'd just had with him because by a certain point, accounts of personal conflict with him were becoming more common.

While the newer community members saw a wise, kind and gentle teacher on the pedestal at the front of the meditation hall, his closest and most senior students were getting to know an increasingly different version of the same man.

I wasn't privy to many of the details, but from the outside it seemed like the staff were dealing with more and more impractical or at least difficult requests from Steve. Whispered conversations about who Steve was angry with become more frequent, eventually followed by a story of how he'd generously made amends with that person, making everything ok again.

He was also becoming more severe with his team of meditation instructors. If they'd responded to a participant's spiritual question in a way too apart from how Steve would have responded, he was quick to correct them. Often, the correction happened in a group setting so that the others got the same message, since his view was that this was all part of his teaching process. These situations could feel quite embarrassing for the instructor being corrected, as well as those watching.

Simply put, it felt like over time, more and more of the community's energy was being focused on monitoring Steve's personal life and working to keep him happy, which was becoming more difficult to achieve, it seemed.

But we'd all signed up for this, particularly in the context of how he presented his tantric lineage. If this was about the guru-disciple relationship, then the more a teacher could locate, hunt and crush a student's ego, the faster that student would mature on his or her path.

Sean McNamara

The apparent mood swings were interesting to watch from a distance. An afternoon of drama between him and some student, the details of which we'd hear about through the grapevine, would put everyone on edge. But, by that evening, or the next day at the latest, he'd be in good spirits, and whatever rift he'd had with the student was forgiven. Then we could all relax.

It was inevitable for someone in Steve's position to hurt someone's feelings without him even knowing it. One weekend, he scheduled a weekend of public teaching near downtown Denver.

Given that I'd been leading a meditation in group in Denver as a representative of Steve's lineage, I thought it would be fitting to place a stack of flyers on the registration table for people to take. This way, they could join our little satellite community and continue practicing what they'd learned from him that weekend.

Strangely, Steve had an assistant remove the flyers, saying something about "not wanting to confuse the situation." I didn't understand it. Everything I'd been doing with my group was in support of him, his teachings, and his organization.

What was he afraid of?

I felt hurt, but tried to couch it as some sort of spiritual lesson. Perhaps he was trying to dissolve my pride, or something like that.

Conflicts weren't restricted to staff members and meditation instructors, though.

Steve offered question-and-answer sessions after many of his long talks, and participants would stand at a microphone at the front of the room. Once in a while, their back-and-forth ended awkwardly, with the participant walking away from the microphone feeling ashamed or embarrassed. This usually happened when they challenged Steve on something he'd said, or when they had a perspective that veered too far from where Steve was trying to lead the room.

Worse than that, Steve would sometimes kick a participant or staff member out of the retreat, and this was also something that began to happen more often as time went on.

One summer, one of the meditation instructors had apparently upset his own student somehow, and Steve decided the instructor had to leave immediately. I volunteered to drive the instructor back to Denver so that he could catch a flight home the next day.

I didn't know the details of what happened to force his departure, but I felt bad for him. He was a good person. As we pulled up to his hotel near the airport, I said "Don't feel bad, it could happen to anyone. We all take our turns. Next year, I could be the one getting kicked out."

I tried to encourage him, knowing that it was probably another case of Steve overreacting. What I didn't know was that at that moment, I'd unconsciously foretold my own future.

CHAPTER 12 A FORK IN THE ROAD

It was time for yet another month-long retreat. By this time, there had already been several programs inside the meditation hall, but it still felt new to us. My role for that retreat was as one of the program staff's coordinators. One of my duties was to manage a team of volunteers who arrived several days before the retreat began to help clean, organize and decorate the building before the rest of the participants arrived.

That's when I met Trish. She'd flown in from the west coast and it was her first time at one of our programs. She was nearly a decade older than me, had a kind smile, and we worked in similar fields back in the "real world." The moment we met, there was a strong attraction. It felt like we already knew each other on a much deeper level.

The setup crew spent their time vacuuming, making beds, stocking bathrooms, and doing other chores. Everyone was having a good time and bonding with each other and with the other staff members who'd arrived early.

Trish would check in with me when she was done with a task so that I could give her another task. Every time we chatted, I felt a spark, and it was clear that she felt it too. It would have been obvious to anyone watching us talk to each other.

On the second or third night, I was walking into my room when I noticed my neighbor's door opening. I lingered on the threshold, waiting to see who the occupant was since I had no idea who'd been assigned to that room, and they'd be my neighbor for the next thirty days. Lo and behold, it was Trish.

I figured this was either a kind gesture from the universe, or it was some kind of cosmic setup.

From the look on her face, she must've been thinking along the same lines.

We were on our best behavior, though. I focused on my work as a coordinator, and I was also one of the program's meditation instructors. Looking over the group assignments, I was happy to see that Trish hadn't been assigned to me. If she had been, I would not have been able to allow our sense of connection to grow. Again, I wondered whether some greater force was at play by assigning her to another instructor.

Several nights, following the day's final meditation session, Trish and I would find a private corner so we could talk to each other. Romance was brewing between us, and we acknowledged it verbally. She wanted to take it to the next level, physically, but I refused, at least in the beginning.

I was well aware of how quickly rumors spread during these programs. Our community wasn't just a rumor mill; it was a rumor *factory*. Endless days of silence and meditation only added to people's temptation to talk about each other's dirt after hours. I'm a private person, and I hated the idea of people knowing my business, even if many of them had been my friends for years.

This is why when Nicholas, a senior teacher and Steve's second-in-command at the program, asked me if anything was going on between me and Trish halfway through the program, I lied. I just didn't think it was any of his *darn business*, and I knew that if *he* knew, soon *everyone* would know.

Besides, it's not like we'd slept with each other.

But after several more nights of kissing and groping as the rest of the participants slept, Trish asked me to have sex with her.

It felt like too much, too risky, and like a line that I shouldn't cross. We were falling in love, and very quickly, but something inside told me to hold off. It wasn't an easy feeling, because there was something very special here, and we both felt it. Could she be the one I'd been looking for? Could she be my spiritual companion?

Steve's talks frequently reflected his newfound joy at having met his new girlfriend. More than ever, he stressed the idea that full spiritual development required a partner. I didn't realize at the time how much his example influenced my own decisions.

Trish seemed to connect with Steve, these teachings, and the rest of the community, and I was already fantasizing about combining our romantic and spiritual aspirations.

But I said "no." I just couldn't go there with her, even though we were already emotionally "there." The next night, she asked again. Once more, I pulled myself away, using all my available willpower to do so.

The following evening, we found ourselves sitting on her bed after she invited me to her room to talk, and kiss. And then she asked again.

This time, I surrendered.

Just before we started I uttered some words, words which should've signaled me to stop, but didn't. "Please don't tell anyone." My conscience was still operating, and knew I shouldn't do this, but I was long past the point of obeying.

Happily, and hastily, she agreed. "I promise, I won't."

But she ended up breaking her promise, which changed the course of my life.

That next morning, I went to check in with Nicholas about the day's schedule as usual. But the first words out of his mouth told me this would not be a usual kind of day.

"We have a problem," he said, and I could see the disappointment in his eyes.

I asked him what it was, hoping I was wrong and this problem was about something, *anything* else, but what had happened the night before.

"You had sex with Trish."

My face must've turned ashen, and my legs felt like rubber. Nausea came over me as blood rushed out of my stomach as if preparing me to run. I could feel the adrenaline begin to course through my veins.

Nicholas had found out about us through Trish's own meditation instructor. Apparently, Trish had lost a lot of sleep and was experiencing a lot of intense emotions. Early that morning, she broke her promise to me and told her instructor everything. She told her only after making her promise not to tell anyone else. Her instructor agreed, but decided this was too much, so she went and told Nicholas.

"Do you want me to tell Steve, or do you want to tell him yourself?" he asked me. I suppose he'd been generous to give me the option. I decided to fall on my sword.

I wanted to be the first to hear his reaction, and to get the whole nightmare over with as quickly as possible. Technically, I hadn't broken any rules, but I knew he'd have something to say about it.

Recently, the senior members of the community came to understand that eventually, Steve would find a reason to come down hard on each one of them, one by one, for one reason or another. No one knew when it would happen, but we all expected it to come eventually. The idea was something between an inside joke and a very real word of caution.

Now it was my turn to experience his wrath.

His very first response was not what I expected, though. "Don't you realize that you've put everything at risk?" He was angry, but not exactly for the reason I expected. He continued, "You barely know this woman, what if she was crazy? She could sue us and take everything we have! We have these buildings now, and she could use you as an excuse to take them away from us!"

I could see his logic right away, and he was right. I had taken a big risk. Meditation retreats have a way of inflating what were normally passing fancies. Hours of sitting on a meditation cushion often leads to an overactive imagination, and people often fall in love when they normally wouldn't if they'd met under ordinary circumstances. Maybe that's all this was, and I had made a foolish decision to follow my heart.

"You're one of our senior teachers, and you should've known better!" He was right.

"Obviously, you have to leave. I can't let you stay."

There it was, the banishment. Steve's concern was about legal risk, and he had to do some cleanup work. Allowing me to stay at the program could be interpreted as gross negligence if, for some reason Trish decided that I was a bad guy.

I needed some fresh air after meeting with Steve, and went outside to sit in the smoking area next to the parking lot. Everyone else was inside the building, quietly meditating. No doubt, they'd soon notice that my cushion was empty.

Then Trish came outside to look for me. She'd just had her own meeting with Steve.

The night before, we'd said goodnight beaming with happiness and joyful anticipation of the next time we could be alone together. Now, she looked at me with guilt and sadness on her face. She knew that

I'd been kicked out of the retreat. I tried to restrain the anger and disappointment I felt.

She felt bad for getting me in trouble, and said she hadn't intended for any of this to happen. All she'd done was talk to her meditation instructor because she had no one else to talk with. She just wanted to share her intense feelings with somebody else, and none of what she'd told that other instructor was meant as a complaint against me.

I had to be careful with how I responded to her. Steve made it clear that she was a participant, a customer, and a possible threat against the organization. I wasn't even allowed to talk to her, but she had come looking for me, so I had no choice.

I was polite, and coolly explained that Steve was right. I was in a position of authority as a senior member of the community. Even though I wasn't *her* meditation instructor, I still shouldn't have done it. I'd put my personal interests above hers, and that was wrong. Now I had to leave.

She said that she'd asked Steve to let me stay. But it was too late, steps had to be taken. I still had to learn the lesson, even if she didn't feel like I'd done anything wrong. I said goodbye and went to pack.

I loaded my car and began an agonizingly long drive back to Denver. I felt embarrassed. I felt sad that our budding relationship had been terminated against our will. I was mostly worried about what Steve thought of me.

Perhaps this was a special opportunity for us to bond as teacher and student. Ancient lore from India and Tibet is filled with tales of conflict between gurus and their disciples, whose common theme being that conflict was necessary to spiritual growth. Was this what they were talking about?

If you're going to follow the path of dharma, you have to be willing to fall on your face.

Foolishly, I hoped the whole matter was over with now that I'd left the program. Trish wasn't upset with me, and I knew she wasn't crazy or interested in suing anybody. I'd been sent home as punishment.

But Steve seemed to grow angrier with every new email he sent me in the days and weeks following the incident. He said I'd broken my instructor's vow, so I could no longer serve as meditation instructor to any of my year-round students or during any of the organization's programs. I was on the organization's board of directors, but he told me that I was no longer a member.

He said I had deep "issues" I needed to work on, and that if I ever wanted to return as an instructor, that I had to commit to undergoing professional therapy.

With every email, his comments felt angrier to me, spiteful even.

On the bright side, but oddly too, he was completely fine with me continuing to lead my group in Denver. I figured that he didn't really care about them anyway. He'd never done anything to support our group over the years, materially or otherwise. Once in a while, I'd invite him to come and teach in person, but for some reason, he declined every time.

I was good at taking my lumps, though. No one could make me feel worse about myself than me, and I felt terrible. I didn't know what he was telling other people behind my back, so that added a feeling of paranoia. I was dejected.

I wanted to do everything necessary to be welcomed back as an instructor, so I started seeing a therapist right away. In our first meeting, he asked my reason for seeking therapy and I explained what I'd done on retreat and the fact that this was mandated by my teacher. Oddly, my therapist didn't make a big deal about any of it, and we focused my therapy on more general "life stuff."

He began his work by asking me, "Think back to your earliest memories, and the first time you were hurt by a parent or someone close to you. Were you hurt? Or were you abandoned? Or were you….." I don't remember the other questions, but it was clear that he was getting to the root of something without wasting any time.

He explained that everyone has an experience of hurt which led to them developing survival strategies which could influence the rest of their life. I suppose this was one way of helping me understand my decision-making with Trish and probably every other woman I'd had a relationship with. Maybe it affected my relationship with my teachers, too.

Over time, I became pleasantly surprised to realize these therapy sessions had boosted my level of self-understanding far more than many years of devoted meditation had. Repeating endless mantras, visualizing myself as a deity, burning incense and playing my tantric bell and drum for years and years... none of this increased my level of true, practical insight the way receiving therapy from a trained counselor did.

Some of Steve's meditations had a quality that resembled the insights one could gain from therapy, particularly with what he called "opening the heart." I recall times when people would be crying or depressed on retreat after recalling deeply painful memories during Steve's guided meditations. He was really skilled at opening old wounds for a room full of people. Retreatants often bonded over their shared pain, which had a certain kind of attraction to it.

But that's where we'd finish, at simply acknowledging our reawakened pain, as if acknowledgment was enough. There didn't seem to be a meditation or any kind of process in place to help with healing and integration, though. Looking back, I see that it was a big problem for a lot of us.

Still, I wanted to get back on Steve's good side and rejoin the community since by now, they were my oldest and most stable set of friends. And I still wanted to serve other people as a meditation instructor. Meditation has its own benefits, such as access to

Sean McNamara

profound experiences of peace and deeper levels of awareness, which are not particularly available through talk-therapy.

I wouldn't have to wait long to return, though. Just a few months after being stripped of all my duties, I was welcomed back in. Steve said he could tell that I was really doing "the work." The timing of his decision was good and not too surprising because I was scheduled to lead a two-week retreat that very summer. Only two or three senior students were leading programs of any length at that time, and the additional income was important to the organization.

After I came back, many people told me privately, *always* privately, they thought Steve's reaction had been too harsh. Some implied that he'd used me to set an example for everyone else. We didn't even have any written policies in place, and my punishment had sent a message to the other instructors and staff members. Some of them had done the same thing I'd done, but they'd done it in the days before Steve had his own retreat center, before he had anything to lose.

My penance was complete and I was fully entrusted with my previous roles. On the surface, I was happy. But over time, I realized deep down inside I felt differently. The more I thought about the whole thing, the angrier I became.

After all, Steve had become romantic with one of his own students, and she was now his current girlfriend. He was the leader, the lineage holder, and the senior-most teacher. There couldn't be a more obvious example of a "power differential." On top of that, she was a significant source of financial support for the whole organization. If her feelings about Steve were to change for any reason at all, she'd be infinitely more damaging than Trish could ever be.

I also remembered Bill and Marcy, the instructor-student couple whom Steve had literally walked in on. He didn't seem to mind their situation at the time

106

The whole situation started to feel unfair and hypocritical, and I started to reconsider everything.

When Steve first left his old organization, he criticized them for being an impersonal dharma-machine which made money by creating "levels" of training, hoops for students to jump through in order to feel like they were developing spiritually. By this point, Steve and his organization were doing the exact same thing. There were levels, vows, prerequisite retreats, and other ways student's development was measured by.

His other criticism was that the other organization's leader was only a figurehead, much the same way Rinpoche was for me years before, when I was with Andrea. Steve was committed to maintaining an authentic relationship with each of his students in the beginning. But by now, his focus on growing the size of his organization made it impossible to do that, and many students only had limited contact with him. He'd become a figurehead himself.

I also developed second thoughts about what he was teaching. He still offered the Tibetan Buddhist teachings many of us had followed him for. But mostly, it seemed that every couple of years he'd reinvent a meditation technique from some other tradition and make it the "main thing" for everyone to focus on. After a while, he'd change directions entirely and have us make some other technique our main focus. I think he was looking for something he hadn't found yet for himself, dragging us behind him in the process.

I realized that I probably wasn't practicing real Buddhism anymore, even though that's what he called it. In fact, he told us this was a different kind of dharma, something rare and special, and much better than anything else out there. And we believed him. That's the kind of power he had. And power, I realized was what this had become all about.

Every once in a while, I'd hear of yet another member of the community who experienced a private conflict with Steve. It usually happened when someone appeared to question or challenge something he said, either in a lecture, a staff meeting, or some other kind of gathering. Steve seemed to perceive their innocent questions as some kind of dissent, and he sometimes responded aggressively. This happened mostly to senior students, meditation instructors, and staff members as well, usually leaving them feeling embarrassed, hurt, and confused.

Newer students, the ones attending a retreat for the first or second time, or who hadn't yet taken the more "advanced" vows, seemed to be shielded from this side of his personality. It seemed that only his closest and most dedicated students wore the invisible target on their backs.

At a certain point, I began to ask myself, "What am I doing here?"

I realized that so much of my energy over the years had been spent supporting Steve and his organization while my own spiritual development had stalled.

Of course, on the surface, it felt like I was getting somewhere, what with the title of "senior teacher" and "meditation instructor" and "retreat leader" to my name. But was I? Was I getting anywhere? Or was my energy being used to promote someone else's growth instead of mine?

Fortunately, one afternoon during yet another of Steve's retreats, something happened that would change the direction of my life.

CHAPTER 13 UTTER PEACE

For those who've never attended a meditation retreat, the idea of sitting calmly all day long without talking to anybody can sound relaxing and peaceful. In actuality, it can be quite exhausting because of two things. First, it takes considerable discipline to sit completely still for forty-five minutes to an hour at a time, without constantly changing one's posture, stretching, or scratching the random itch.

Second, the stillness forces one to become fully aware of every thought and emotion the mind produces, second after second, which is a severe contrast to the distracted way we go through a typical day. Rather than sitting in blissful stillness, meditation becomes an unending psychological roller coaster, at least until one is sufficiently trained to reduce one's reactivity to the constant change, or to reduce the level of mental activity itself.

Retreat participants were always happy to take a break from meditation during meals, the mid-afternoon break, and in the evenings. However, staff members and instructors filled those times with group meetings, individual instruction sessions, or simple things like chopping wood for the fireplace. It was nonstop. Retreat practice had a way of wearing a person down mentally, emotionally, and physically as well.

On this particular day, I felt especially tired. Fortunately, there weren't any afternoon meetings, which meant that I could go to my room after lunch and lie down for a nap. Outside my door, the sounds of people's footsteps and a passing vacuum cleaner faded into the background as I let go into much-needed sleep.

Sean McNamara

I don't know how long I'd been asleep, but suddenly, I became aware. My body was still asleep, and my eyes still closed, but I was awake *on the inside*. I felt a peculiar sensation swimming up and down my spine, from my pelvis to the back of my neck, up to the base of my skull.

It didn't hurt at all, but the sensation became more powerful the longer I paid attention to it. It felt like a stream of electricity vibrating through empty space. In fact, I had no sense of the rest of my body at all. I couldn't feel my muscles, my bones, or anything else. I felt absolutely weightless, like I was floating in outer space, and comfortably numb.

The experience shifted as I felt myself slowly curling up like a little black roly-poly bug. It wasn't so much that the "me" was curling up, though. It felt like my spine, or rather the electrified wave coursing through the place where my spine should be, was curling into a spiral. It also felt like I was peeling forward, down, and away from my torso.

I'd never felt anything like it before, and I was captivated by it. Then, without warning, it stopped.

After I opened my eyes, the electrified buzzing sound which had filled my being seemed to dissipate into the deepest recesses at the back of my skull.

Then, there was only peace.

I rolled from my side onto my back, and looked up at the ceiling. Everything seemed different. But not a thing in the world had changed. It was me. I was different.

To put it more precisely, something was missing, something which had been inside of me. It was the usual stream of mental noise that I'd lived with my entire life. The mind garbage. The analysis. The planning ahead. The hesitation. The anxiety. The hoping. The fantasizing. Those, and many other permanent (or so I thought) fixtures of my sense of "me" were simply gone, and replaced by ... nothing.

But I was aware, and fully functional. I decided to leave my room and go for a walk through the building. As I approached the dining room, one of the cooks popped out of the kitchen and headed straight for me with a sense of urgency in his eyes.

"Hey Sean! The dishwasher is messed up. I think it's the garbage disposal. Can you take a look?" On a large retreat like this one, a broken dishwasher can have a significant cascading effect on the staff. One way or the other, those dishes need to get cleaned in time for the next meal. A mechanical breakdown meant an immense inconvenience for the overworked kitchen staff.

I'd spent enough time at the center to know how to fix a lot of the issues that came up from time to time, so it wasn't out of the ordinary for someone to ask me for help, even though I was there as a meditation instructor.

Normally, I would have become concerned right away, just by looking at the cook's face. I tend to be overly-empathic, which is a quality I probably learned from my mom. On retreat, and in a Buddhist context, my over-caring reflex was inflated even more.

At this moment, though, "Mr. Nice Guy" wasn't home. The overly inflated empathy wasn't home. Anxiety wasn't home. Inside my mind, there was only the understanding that something was broken and perhaps I might be able to fix it. I calmly followed the cook back into the kitchen and looked over the commercial-grade stainless steel dishwasher. I pushed a few buttons and the machine promptly returned to normal working order.

The cooks expressed their gratitude at not having to hand-wash a hundred sets of plates, bowls, cups and silverware, and I calmly left the kitchen.

And still, my mind was empty of unnecessary thinking and emotions. The cooks didn't seem to notice anything different about me. More importantly, the part of me that would have noticed and cared whether or not they noticed anything different about me just wasn't there anymore.

I walked around outside and viewed the world through quiet eyes. Everything around me seemed "just as it should be," for lack of better description. The quietness inside my mind remained effortlessly, without me having to do anything extra to keep it that way.

Yet, I had the wherewithal to understand that this was an unusual experience, perhaps a valuable one. As a meditation instructor, I knew this experience could be helpful for others to know about. It was new for me, and I wondered if Steve could shed some light on it. At the very least, I thought he should know that these kinds of things were happening to at least one of his students.

Minutes later, I entered Steve's office. He and his girlfriend were sitting across from each other at a small round table, and I took a seat in between them. I remember sounding plain and direct as I explained what happened during my afternoon nap, and what the inside of my mind felt like. It still felt empty of its usual activity while I spoke to him.

After I finished, he glanced over at his girlfriend, then back to me. "Is there anything else you notice, anything different?"

"Yes, colors look more vivid, especially the color red." I'd spotted a red flower as part of a decorative arrangement in another part of the building, and the color had an aliveness to it that I'd never noticed before. It was as if an entire, albeit non-essential section of my brain had gone off-line, and that made room for another part to shine a little brighter.

The three of us just glanced at each other. After realizing Steve didn't have anything to say, I made my leave, explaining "I just thought you'd want to know in case it's helpful for you, or if it's happening to your other students." Then I walked out.

I had been completely earnest, and didn't expect any particular kind of response from Steve. In the past, there'd been times when I shared some new personal insight with him, and a part of me felt proud about it, or like I wanted to impress him with it. But during this conversation, even that part of my personality didn't seem to be present. I was at peace.

It came time to return to the main hall to begin the late afternoon meditation session with the whole group. I sat down on my cushion and, well, *I just sat there*. I instinctively knew any attempt to meditate *on purpose* would be superficial and unnecessary, like adding water to water to make it more wet. The room was filled with dozens of meditators *straining* to be present, *trying* to let go, and being pulled along the emotional roller coasters inside their heads. But what I felt in that room was far more natural and effortless than any meditation session I'd experienced before.

Was I one step closer to whatever it was we were aiming for on this path? I didn't know what we were going after anymore, though, and I certainly wasn't expecting this.

Steve didn't have anything helpful to say about it. I had entered, sat down, described my internal mental atmosphere, then left after realizing he wasn't going to say anything helpful to me. Was it because he didn't know what this was, or hadn't ever experienced it himself? Or did he think I was just fine and didn't require any additional commentary from him?

It didn't matter at the time. But the clock kept moving forward and by dinner, I noticed my mind filling up little by little with the old mental noise. There was a new feeling too, of wanting to hold on to this extraordinary level of inner peace. The "holding on" had a texture of its own, subtle at first, but quickly becoming coarse. Any attempt to let go back into peacefulness failed since the *effort* of letting go only produced more tension, clouding the water.

When I woke up the next morning, I was the same old me again, with the familiar and constant flow of opinions, emotions and social vigilance churning non-stop inside my head.

All that remained were questions which would only grow with time. How, or why, did I have that experience? It wasn't part of any of Steve's teachings, and none of our meditation techniques seemed particularly geared to produce that effect. Was this something apart from what he and his teachings were about? If it was, then he'd probably see it simply as a kind of distraction, or something the ego could cling to.

Was this leading anywhere? The Zen people did zazen. Theravadins cultivate the jhanas. Vajrayanists had their visualizations, mantras, inner yogas and formless practice. Each tradition offered its own map, passed on from one generation to the next, ostensibly supported by accounts of people who eventually reached their particular interpretation of the word "enlightenment."

Yet, Steve's map appeared to be, at least partially, blank. And now I'd had a profound experience of my own, which seemed to come from somewhere else entirely. This had two effects. First, I realized new possibilities were possible outside of my current path, and beyond Steve's influence. Second, I started to realize somewhere along the line, I had set my original, personal questions as a spiritual seeker aside, and didn't know where I was headed anymore.

The fact that I was still angry and resentful about how he'd treated me after the retreat with Trish only helped me to feel myself beginning to separate myself from the whole situation. Many people knew me as a loyal and committed student and member of the organization. But that was beginning to crumble now, and I privately began to question whether I was still getting anything valuable from my involvement with them or not.

CHAPTER 14 CUSHIONS FOR SALE

At this point in my life, I'd become a real estate agent. Before then, I had loved being a massage therapist. But, overworking my hands led to the beginnings of arthritis, making my job too painful to continue. I was also bored, and felt pessimistic about my financial prospects. I could only do so many massage sessions per week before the fire in my joints became intolerable. Someone suggested real estate as an alternative line of work, because I could still help people, just in a different way.

I was still leading my local meditation group, and had rented a yoga studio in a popular area called Platte Park. We met every Sunday night for a couple of hours, during which I'd guide them by faithfully using Steve's meditation techniques. Once in a while, I'd offer a half-day or full-day retreat so they could really immerse themselves in the practice. The room was big and spacious like most yoga studios, with bare walls and a wide bamboo floor, without any furniture blocking the way.

One day, I received an email from a woman named Cierra who was selling meditation cushions. She had a shop just a few blocks down the street from the yoga studio. She was doing some grassroots marketing, and contacting every meditation teacher in the area to let them know about her cushions.

After reading her email, I decided to visit her store since it was nearby. When I opened her website to find the address, I was struck by the small black and white headshot next to her name. Her smile projected kindness and humor, and her eyes expressed determination. This woman looked strong and soft at the same time.

Realizing that I was staring at her photo a little too long, I stopped. I couldn't allow my imagination to get carried away because I had a girlfriend at the time. Our relationship was in shambles and we were going through couples-therapy to try to save it, and I had to honor that. Still, I thought it would be fine to visit Cierra's shop and learn about her cushions since my students would naturally appreciate a local source for meditation supplies.

I remember walking down the street and finally making my way up a sloping walkway toward the back of an old, single story brick building. It only took about twenty steps to make it to the shop door. But with every step, the atmosphere seemed to become denser, and time felt like it was slowing down. I suppose it could've been my imagination, but something was happening to get my attention. Something was about to change.

I walked through the door and entered the tiny, one-room shop. I didn't notice the stacks of cushions on the large side wall, or the semi-private meditation area on the opposite side of the room. All I saw was Cierra standing just to my left, minding the cash register and talking to another woman who worked there.

I introduced myself, and she gave me a brief tour of her store. On the surface, everything felt completely normal. I saw a professional opportunity here because I'd developed an idea for a customizable meditation seat, one which she would be able to sell out of her store. She liked the idea, and soon we were working together to get the seat built and sold. We behaved professionally with each other, which became easier to do after I found out she had a boyfriend. But just beneath the surface, I think we both felt something.

Months passed by, and our business relationship softened into friendship, although we never spent time together outside of her shop. She was a few years older than me and was also a massage therapist. I asked if I could rent her shop for classes and retreats, and she was excited to have more people meditating there.

So, I moved my group out of the yoga studio and into the shop, which she'd named "Mayu Sanctuary." The word "mayu" means "cocoon" in Japanese. She wanted to design an environment which expressed the same nurturing and transformative qualities her clients felt during her massages. Mayu Sanctuary was the result, a little one-room shop offering cushions and just enough floor space for a few people to meditate together. I thought Cierra was brave for trying to build a contemplative business in a world where people focused almost entirely on ways to distract and entertain themselves. I also thought she was one of the most grounded people I'd ever met, and I felt tremendous respect for her.

Eventually, my relationship with my girlfriend came to an end. I remember standing in the middle of the parking lot outside of our therapist's office, watching her get into her car after declaring that she was finished with me, and there was no point in prolonging the inevitable. We were both exhausted from keeping our relationship on life support, so I couldn't argue with her.

Single again, and available, I invited Cierra out to lunch. I wanted to dip my toe in the water and see how things were going with her. Curiously, it was during that lunch when she told me she'd ended her relationship too. After that, everything sped up for us, and a few months later, I moved into her apartment.

Everything was going well between us overall, but there was one thing that kept bothering me.

Cierra had learned meditation from various teachers, but wasn't formally part of any lineage. I was still a senior teacher of Steve's lineage at the time. I loved that Cierra and I were both meditators, and could talk about our experiences with each other. But, I was concerned that she wasn't officially part of any lineage or tradition.

She never even expressed an interest in joining my group or attending one of Steve's retreats. My complete devotion to my lineage, my teacher and my own students was clear as day to her. But she was content to support my spiritual journey from a respectful distance while doing her own thing.

The truth was that I'd developed a fantasy about reaching enlightenment, whatever that meant, hand-in-hand with a romantic partner. This came partly from Steve's seemingly endless lectures about needing a "spiritual consort" to "go all the way" on the path. But Cierra was an independently-minded practitioner, which didn't fit in with what I'd hoped for.

I began to wonder if I needed to choose between my relationship with Cierra and my spiritual path. Looking back, I think some part of me was threatened by her independence and self-confidence. I still believed I needed a guru or a teacher to help me with my spiritual growth.

Writing this now, I cringe to remember telling her how bothered I was that she didn't have a path or a main teacher like I did. She seemed to take it in stride, and simply told me that I had to figure it out for myself. But I think I hurt her feelings. She wasn't going to change for me, of course, and I didn't expect her to.

Soon after, I went away for a nine-day retreat. This particular retreat was called a fire puja. In tantric Buddhism, a fire puja is a special ceremony in which food and other symbolic items are ritually offered to a fire deity with the intention of quickly purifying our negative karma. The ritual itself continues from morning to night, with the practitioners seated around a specially designed fire pit. In our case, the puja was in the context of the meditation on our main deity, Vajrayogini.

Symbolically, Vajrayogini represents wisdom, strength, compassion, and also a sense of wildness. The ultimate purpose of the puja was to realize we had those same qualities in ourselves, and all we had to do was look beneath the surface of our egos.

One night, I was sitting quietly by the fire, exhausted as usual. Doubts about Steve, the way his behavior had changed over the years, and whether or not it was still worth it for me to be there rumbled in the back of my mind. The puja was part of an ancient set of practices from Tibet, and it had taken years of work to become "qualified" to attend it. But to me, the whole thing felt like a charade.

Suddenly, I realized that back home in Denver, somebody *real* was waiting for me, someone who *really was* strong, wise, compassionate, and very independent. Someone who could help me realize those qualities in myself. At that moment, the puja, its endless rituals, and the pseudo-worship of a symbolic goddess became pointless to me.

The retreat finished, and I returned to Denver. Cierra came down the stairs to welcome me back, and I saw she had tears in her eyes. She'd been crying because she feared I'd return only to announce my decision to leave to find a partner better suited for my spiritual growth. I kissed her, and said I wasn't going anywhere. I finally realized what an arrogant ass I'd been.

Three months later, on the fourth of July, I proposed to her as fireworks exploded high above the front lawn of the Stanley Hotel in Estes Park. I wanted to make a real life with her, and I couldn't wait any longer.

She said "yes."

CHAPTER 15 LEAVING MY BODY FOR THE FIRST TIME

On a deeper level, making such a commitment to Cierra signified that I wasn't afraid of putting down roots anymore. Dad wasn't going to come home for dinner one night and tell us it was time to move again. Also, neither my relationship with Cierra nor my work as a real estate agent had anything to do with Steve or his organization. Inside, I began to feel a sense of freedom I didn't know I'd missed.

It had been a few years since that strange afternoon when waves of electricity coursed up and down my spine as my body slept, leaving me in a profound state of peace afterward. But the memory of it had lingered in the back of my mind all this time, and for some reason, it was at this point in my life when I made an important connection.

I realized those electric waves could be what Robert Monroe wrote about in "Journeys Out of the Body." Was this what I'd attempted to produce as a teenager back in Rio, lying in bed, feeling the ocean air while listening to Pink Floyd?

Pages from Monroe's book rushed back into my memory. I recalled how excited I'd been at the thought of having Shirley MacLaine's Peruvian hot spring experience, flying high above her body, out into space.

I wondered if I should try again, after all I'd been through.

The simple act of asking myself that question was enough to make me realize something so painful that I could barely admit it to myself.

That day, many years ago when I walked into that Buddhist center in Denver and adopted their path, I had unknowingly abandoned my own.

Before that day, all I wanted was an answer to the question, "What happens when we die?" But after that day, my attention was rerouted toward following "the dharma," which included learning a well-established philosophy and practicing a fixed set of meditations to one end. To achieve liberation from suffering and become a Buddha, and "awakened one."

But after years of studying and practicing Buddhism, first in Rinpoche's tradition then in Steve's version, *I was still afraid of dying*, and I still didn't know for sure what happens after death. Learning their philosophies of reincarnation and karma didn't satisfy me. Those were just words repeated generation after generation.

I wanted to see reality for myself. I wanted a *real experience*.

Meditation was presented as a great way to "sit with uncertainty" and to be present with all kinds of emotions and painful psychological states. Years of practice had certainly yielded results, and I had grown more open hearted, more patient, and better at being with "not knowing," to some degree. I think the dharma had made me a better person in some ways.

However, none of it helped me answer my original question, the one that had haunted me all my life, "Is death the end?"

So, I gave myself permission to start exploring on my own again. I decided once more to learn how to have an out of body experience. I wasn't willing to discontinue my Buddhist practice or leave my community quite yet, but I knew having an out of body experience was something I needed to do.

I knew from the way Steve reacted whenever a student asked about working with other teachers or trying other techniques that he wouldn't support me in this. I also knew that none of my peers in the community would be interested either. I'd be doing this on my own.

121

Sean McNamara

It was the end of 2013, and over twenty years had passed since my first, brief attempts to leave my body. I'd only had one book to refer to at the time. But now, thanks to the internet, every book in the world was available to me with just a few keystrokes.

I was overjoyed to find many books had been written in the years since Robert Monroe had published his. One book, "Adventures Beyond the Body" by William Buhlman, advertised "easy to use techniques," and looked particularly interesting to me, and so I ordered it. I knew this time in my life could be my second chance.

I tried not to kick myself when I saw that it had first been published in 1996. This was the year I graduated from college, and not too long before I began my journey with Buddhism. Why didn't I think about finding these kinds of books *then*? If only, if only! But it's useless to dwell on it now.

Buhlman's book was more than I could've hoped for. Not only did he offer a variety of techniques to choose from, but he shared his personal story too. He didn't belong to any esoteric lineage, and he definitely wasn't a "woo woo" kind of guy. From his writing, he seemed, (and still does, though I've never met him) down to earth, curious, determined, and pragmatic.

His book is based on real experiences rather than theories and "ancient" techniques. In that same spirit, he invites his readers to transcend their limiting belief systems by having real experiences of their own. He offers a variety of techniques with the understanding that every person is different, and that some techniques work better for some than others.

Just like Monroe, Buhlman shares his techniques openly, with "no strings attached." These techniques didn't require a guru's blessing, going through various "levels," or any other kind of esoteric qualification. He doesn't demand or require anybody's commitment to him. He plainly shares his experiences, as profound as they are, in a way anybody can relate to.

After years of taking vows, going on retreats, going through initiations, and not finding answers to my fundamental questions

122

about life and death, reading "Adventures Beyond the Body" was a breath of fresh air. Actually, it was more than that. It felt liberating.

I began my training as soon as the book arrived. I learned that keeping a journal was an important part of the training process. Today, I'm extra glad that I did because many of those journal entries comprise a large portion of this book, as you'll see below. From the beginning, I had an inkling that I might someday share my experiences with you, the reader. This will be apparent from time to time, in the way I wrote things down.

I tried to record everything here just as I wrote it down originally, which sometimes meant in shortened, rough sentences. This is what it's like to record one's thoughts in the middle of the night or first thing in the morning, just after waking up. In some cases, though, I found it necessary and easier to rewrite an entry for ease of understanding.

Many of the journal entries will be followed by a paragraph beginning with "Commentary." I added these commentaries in the course of writing this book, not at the time of writing the journal entry. My aim is to help the reader understand my interpretation of what I experienced. In some cases, the meaning will be self-evident, or I may not know what to say about it at all, and so these will have no commentary attached to them.

Most importantly, if you analyze my journal entries one by one, they won't make very much sense and you'll find yourself asking "Why did he include *this* entry?" Think of it the following way. I'm taking you into deeper states of awareness with me, night after night. I never knew what would happen as I lay down to sleep. It only made sense afterward. You might feel the same way, so hopefully you don't mind taking this journey with me.

If you happen to be training to have an OBE right now, reading these entries will support you and help you understand your own experience. Sometimes, the things we dream about and feel in our bodies are more important than they seem at first. Although I mention my use of various techniques here, there isn't room to go into detail about them. For that, I recommend either my online Lucid Dream & OBE training course[4], William Buhlman's books and audio programs[5], and of course any other widely available resources by other out-of-body experiencers.[6]

December 10, 2013

Last night - made affirmations as I fell asleep, "I am now out of my body." I drifted in and out of the dream state as I fell asleep. A couple times, I heard "mind" sounds, which I believe mark a shift in consciousness. Tossed and turned a lot through the night, tough to relax deeply, too excited now that I'm engaging the process.

Commentary: Making "affirmations" while one falls asleep is a technique a person can apply for inducing both lucid dreams and OBEs. It's a way to send an intention to the subconscious mind, which I found out over time was key. None of the techniques you'll read about here ever led to an instant result. Instead, I applied them regularly, night after night, until I got a result.

December 12, 2013

Again, remembered my dreams later in the morning. One was of being stuck on a snowy precipice, feeling scared of sliding off.

Commentary: This was only the first of many similar dreams I'd have in the future, in which I seemed to be moving in an out-of-control way, accompanied by a sense of fear and danger. It's possible the movement was an indication that I was getting closer to separating myself from my body, and that the fear meant my conscious and subconscious minds needed to get more comfortable with the idea of having a voluntary OBE.

---

[4] See MindPossible.com

[5] See AstralInfo.org

[6] See the "Recommended Resources" section of this book

December 15, 2013

Last night, I woke up to a sense of shifting energy and the feeling of something about to happen. Lots of subtle waves through the body, not quite a full-on vibrational state. But it lasted for quite a while and I attempted separation by visualizing another location. But I couldn't separate. Still, I was very happy to feel something new!

Commentary: The significant sensations in my body were a sign that I was getting even closer to having my first OBE. I made an attempt to leave my body by doing something Buhlman and others call the "target technique," in which I imagine myself being at a completely different location, including picking up objects I'm familiar with and "feeling" them in my imagination.

This is about using visualization to *mobilize* one's intention to leave the body. Pretending to be somewhere else with this technique is like a special kind of language. This exercise is like telling the subconscious mind "I don't want to be here, let me go somewhere else now."

December 18, 2013

No wine last night, but I ate late. I did an OBE visualization before my regular meditation. Around 3-4 am I became aware of a dream that repeated itself, as if to get my attention. I don't remember the details, but I do recall feeling strongly that I had either just "been out" or that I was close to leaving. I waited for the vibrations - but none came. I went to the couch and did the OBE visualization. There was fear for some reason, I tried to let it be, but I know I need to relax a lot more.

Commentary: It's difficult to explain why I thought I'd been "out." It was an unusual feeling in my mind, as if I had amnesia after going for a walk but had the lingering sense that I'd just been somewhere else. This is one value to journaling whenever waking up at night, to

Sean McNamara

record the many strange sensations and ideas we would most likely forget by the time the sun rose.

December 24, 2013, Christmas Eve

> Did an OBE visualization in the afternoon before my normal meditation practice. Went to bed, realized the iPod was in the other room, so I did the visualization on my own. It felt like my skullcap was trying to lift off or open up, and I relaxed with it, trusting that my body is slowly adjusting over time in preparation for an OBE.

> Had a couple of dreams. In one I was preparing to do a video feed of my meditation class. All my regular students were there, but we were in a different state, some place tropical or down south like Texas or Florida.

> In the other dream, I had to spend time cleaning a public toilet before I could use it. Three guys showed up to use it before I had my chance, but I defended it for myself and told them to wait their turn. They left peacefully after I stood my ground.

Commentary: As I became more familiar with the various techniques, I began to increase my rate of practice. Since I was in real estate, much of my work was in the evening and on weekends, leaving me a lot of free time in the afternoons. That's usually when I did my regular meditation practices, and now I was adding my OBE training to my schedule. So, I'd practice the technique of my choice while lying on the couch in the living room in the afternoon, and then apply the same technique while falling asleep at night. If you work at an office or somewhere away from home, you might consider going to your car during your lunch break, tilting the seat back, and spending 20-30 minutes practicing your chosen technique as a way of reinforcing your intention to have an OBE.

As for the dream about cleaning the toilet, the symbolism indicates I had some psychological cleanup work to do before I could progress, and also that I had to stake my private territory and not let anyone get in the way.

126

December 25, 2013, Christmas

Yesterday, I did three different OBE techniques while doing a footbath at Mayu Sanctuary. Last night, I had several dreams. In the first, I was in a subway-like place, and [the woman I dated before Cierra] was breaking up with me. I felt alone and abandoned, and had no recollection that in real life I am happily with Cierra.

At some point in the night, I had an energy movement - very brief - 1 or 2 seconds - rough electrical vibration.

Commentary: A "footbath" is a specialty at Cierra's meditation center. Basically, you soak your feet and calves in hot, herb-infused water while relaxing in a dark, private booth. Once in a while I'd go there to practice my techniques in what is an inviting and safe setting. The "energy movement" was another odd sensation, which I took as another small sign that I was changing in a positive way, toward my intended goal of leaving my body. Recording these small, positive signs is important for keeping one's motivation high. I had no idea how long it would take before I had my first OBE, so I know that maintaining a high level of motivation and a focused intention was crucial.

December 26, 2013

Dreamt that Cierra was having an OBE and melting through the floor, and freaking out a little. I reassured her and was happy for her. When I woke up, I told her the dream, and she said "Of course, that was you," which was interesting - and she's right. Is my mind slowly easing me into the OBE through using other people in my dreams?

Commentary: Cierra's observation was astute. When we have a dream of other people, everyone in the dream is a projection of *us*, the dreamer. Perhaps my mind was using dreams like this one as baby steps, so that it became more of an *acceptable* idea that I could safely leave my body.

Sean McNamara

December 27, 2013

Dreamt of a girl on fire, bravely screaming at Death, saying "I'll get you on the other side!" before throwing herself off a structure to her death. She was totally fearless; she really knew that something continues even after death.

Commentary: "Death" appeared as the classical figure, in black robes holding a scythe. I don't know who the girl was, or if she represented anyone else. But the theme of overcoming fear is important.

December 28, 2013

Can't remember the dream. But I think I heard someone say "hello" from the other side, a man's voice.

Commentary: Hearing voices as one is falling asleep (the hypnagogic stage) or as one is first waking up (the hypnopompic stage) is a well-known form of hallucination during those stages. To experience these strange kinds of phenomena near the borderline of sleep is a good sign that one is staying consciously aware during deeper levels of relaxation. Being able to stay mentally awake while the body is physically asleep is almost universally held to be a prerequisite to having an OBE.

January 1, 2014

Dreamt I was at a big party, not just with people but with animals, like a bear or camel or other large creatures. Everyone was eating a lot of meat, and I ended up throwing up massive amounts of meat. It felt almost like ground beef being squeezed out of its plastic wrapping as it exited my throat. Other people, about college age, had also puked and blocked up the sink.

The dream breaks into another dream, and I'm walking past a house that had been listed for sale by a rude woman with a bird or some pet. I walked past it with a knowing sense that

I'd have a chance to own it. The backyard and side yard were very pretty, with lots of decking for tables and chairs. It was a neighborhood similar to ours.

This afternoon I practiced the cloud technique. Felt a slight sideways jerk, as if I was trying to come out sideways. It was quick and soft, but noticeable. This was after visualizing the cloud swinging left and right. I think I also heard a voice, but the words were indecipherable.

Commentary: In the "cloud" technique, you visualize yourself lying on a cloud and feeling its movement as it rises higher and higher through the air. Like the target technique, it's another way of telling your deeper mind that you'd like to have an OBE. I was wide awake but very relaxed that afternoon during the practice, and it was a new experience to feel like some part of me was trying to scoot out the side of my body.

January 2, 2014

Three dreams last night. In one, I was previewing a house for two clients and knew they'd love it. It was big, with a guest house featuring its own fireplace. In real life, my clients are under contract on a different house, hopefully they close on it!

Second dream - gathering with some folks who I don't know in a different house for some sort of program, but don't know what.

Third - very interesting - I was in a huge enclosure that had two or three staircases leading to a platform in the center. I was floating around (no sense of body shape) and discovering how sensitive to thought my movement was. I would "flicker" to other areas of the house in an instant, or change direction when my attention wasn't 100% focused. It seemed like a training ground for moving around in the OBE state.

Did two different OBE techniques this afternoon, felt that same jerk from yesterday - twice this time, once was in the right leg, the other in the left abdomen. My lower body feels more relaxed and loose than my chest and face.

Commentary: It's important to notice that memories and concerns from the daytime can leak into one's dream state. The third dream was very important because it showed me that I was able to discern between a dream and an OBE, and know that they're not the same thing.

Also, a dream can be more than a random display of thoughts, feeling and images. In this case, my dream state served a very important purpose. Interestingly, I didn't know I'd have this kind of dream, which indicates that a deeper part of me is actively involved in my process.

January 4, 2014

Today I practiced two techniques. I realized that I need to let myself get lost more in the dreaming stage in order to relax better, and not try so hard to remain "mind awake, body asleep." Too much effort. Maybe I'll try doing the technique, then shutting it off and really letting myself fall asleep without rules and see how that goes.

Commentary: This was one of the most important realizations I would ever have, not only for OBEs but other psychic abilities I'll write about later in this book. Trying too hard, or staying too alert is a surefire way to prevent anything from happening. Letting go and giving up control at certain stages of the process are crucial for success.

January 7, 2014

Last night, I had several dreams. One was again focused on finding properties for people. In another, I was at a big table having dinner with a bunch of people, Steve was there, and we were all in a good mood.

This afternoon, I did Buhlman's orb practice. This time, I visualized it from a perspective outside my body, above it, looking at the orb in front of me, floating over my physical head. It felt different and possibly more helpful. Also, when the instruction was done, I turned off the iPod and really tried to fall asleep and enter the dream state freely.

This produced more energy events than usual, and new ones I haven't felt before. My face is starting to "separate" more, and felt for a split second a sideways (to the left) separation of just an inch. But as soon as I noticed it, that part of me quickly returned to the body.

I think I'm starting to understand what Buhlman means by "letting go of the body." I need to relax my own judgement about dissociating from the body, and almost sort of push it away mentally so I'm not magnetized to subtle physical sensations. This includes letting go of the expectation of an astral body emerging right away. If I imagine departing, it must be without any conditioned ideas, like a particular form or shape. There's too much limitation in that thought for me.

Commentary: I made the last note realizing that whenever I paid too much attention to the odd sensations which occurred while using a technique, any progress would come to a stop. I realized I needed to basically ignore the sensations because all they did was steer my mind back toward a physical experience instead of remaining with whatever visualization I was using at the time.

January 10, 2014

First dream - Got attacked by a dark, smoky, unformed figure. I stayed present to it and it became a tall, pale man in dark clothes with pale skin. He seemed sad and depressed. When he transformed, he stopped attacking me and just seemed lonely.

Second dream - I was hanging out with the 16th Karmapa [the head of one of the main lineages of Tibetan Buddhism,

Kagyu. He passed away in 1981.], getting ready to travel with him through the mountains. There were Tibetan lamas and Indian sadhus sitting on a platform nearby. The sadhus' skin was dyed red and they were holding tridents, which made them look like a red version of Shiva (a Hindu god). Third dream - A guy at a bus stop tried to start a fight with me, I ended up giving him a hug and diffusing the situation with compassion.

This afternoon, I did one of Buhlman's techniques and also the "Estes Park slide." No energy events, I had a difficult time relaxing.

Commentary: Estes Park, a popular town in the Rocky Mountains, has a fun-park on one end of town featuring a "rainbow slide." People climb a metal staircase to get to the top, climb into potato sacks, and slide down, feeling slightly lifted up, off the slide, whenever it dropped down at a steeper angle. I'd ridden it enough times that I decided to use the memory of it as my own kind of OBE visualization. The key was to remember the feeling of sliding down and lifting off.

You might have a similar kind of memory which you can use to create your own visualization. If you can easily remember the *sensation of movement*, then you have everything you need.

January 12, 2014

On a mysterious, beautiful island at night. One side is sloped, the other is made up of dramatic cliffs. One of my childhood friends from the Philippines was there, we met near the top of a cliff. He said something interesting, "You know, when you're given something like that, it should be shared." I knew he was referring to my unfinished book. Interesting that my book is finding itself in my dreams.

Commentary: The book you're reading now is something I started many years ago. Back then, it was a completely different story, since most of what I recorded here hadn't happened yet. I thought it would be nice to include this dream here since I've finally finished it, even though it's not at all what I expected it would be back then.

January 16, 2014

Me and two guys are taking a ski lift through a gorge or canyon at very high altitude - no snow. We can fly, but not well, as shown by the fear we expressed when the more experienced guy began adjusting the way the chair was attached to the line so that it would be more secure for us.

This guy was making the adjustments while levitating in the air, and I could only levitate a little bit before starting to fall. The distance below was terrifying. As the dream deteriorates, the other less experienced guy tells me he's nervous about a real estate client I have in waking life, that she might want to cancel the contract on a house she's about to close on. I respond, saying that I'm also nervous about it.

This afternoon, I did a couple of practices while taking a foot bath at Mayu Sanctuary. I fell asleep, and could swear that I became conscious during re-entry. It felt like I was moving down a few inches to sit in my own lap.

Commentary: Levitating in my dreams is a sign that I'm getting closer to having an OBE. Another interpretation I've heard, and which I'm open to, is that I was actually having an OBE but my conscious mind was only able to perceive it through dream imagery. Something any OBE explorer needs to get used to is never being 100% sure what is actually happening during a dream. Besides, it's how you feel about it afterward, how it *changes* you, which matters the most.

January 17, 2014

First dream - Standing up to a female teacher who is being verbally abusive to me in a classroom. I felt empowered afterward.

Second dream - For some reason, I was trying to see if I could make out with another woman without it being a problem for Cierra. Well, it was a problem for her. I'd hurt her feelings and ended up feeling guilty.

Commentary: These dreams seem to indicate I'm exploring personal boundaries. There would be times later on, in the OBE state, when other beings would be present. Could it be that learning about boundaries on this level is an important preparation for future interactions?

January 18, 2014

Had a fuzzy dream that included conversations with two ex-girlfriends. Then I dreamt of living in a big house that was also like a store. Oddly, Cierra was there hosting a party and I saw her kissing a couple of guys. I found myself getting jealous.

Had the vibrational state tonight. It felt feminine and rich with a warmth or presence to it. This evening, Cierra did some energy work on me before we went to bed, is that why? At one point, my vision was of space before me being like golden chainmail, like what medieval knights wore for protection (without the gold). I thought it resembled descriptions of the "visionary state" taught in the Tibetan practice called Togal, which includes descriptions of countless spheres of light filling space.

January 19, 2014 - PARTIAL SEPARATION

I took the advice of two women in the OBE online forum and tried the interrupted sleep method. I got up to pee in the middle of the night, and then went to the couch. I read some Buhlman until I got sleepy again, then did some affirmations and fell asleep. Had a dream, then woke up in a vibrational state.

I didn't rush it, waiting until I felt a sense of separation away from my body. Then, I willed myself down onto the floor. It felt just like sliding down, but it seemed like my legs were still attached. I also couldn't see anything. After a few moments, I was back in my body, bobbing around like on a water bed, then totally reconnecting.

I reported this on the forum and the ladies suggested that I get really far from my body as soon as possible in order to separate fully, stay out longer, and help with being able to see. I'll try the next chance I get.

When I separated, I felt quite shapeless, kind of like an ovoid form, but definitely not human. Weightless and free. Words can't really describe it, but it seems very simple - awareness with soft borders moving through space.

Commentary: The "interrupted sleep" methods, referred to as the "wake, back to bed method" by lucid dreamers, entails waking up after the first four hours of sleep, then practicing a specific technique (visualization, writing down affirmations, meditating, etc.) for a period of time, then allowing oneself to fall back to sleep again while trying to stay conscious as long as possible. Looking back at my experiences over the years, I can say with confidence this is a highly effective "auxiliary" technique.

January 21, 2014 - FIRST FULL OBE

Woo hoo! This morning it finally happened. A couple of days ago, I had a partial separation and couldn't see anything when I got out. And yesterday I tried, filled with hope and anticipation, and nothing happened, not even in my dreams. I was bummed. But this morning, I had a chance to do the interrupted sleep method since I had to get up to pee. I went to my couch, listened to Buhlman's portal method recording, then mentally recited affirmations as I fell asleep.

Had a dream, then woke to the vibrational state. After some moments, I could tell I was separate-able, and remembered

Claudia and Lynn's tips from the forum - particularly to get far away from the body as soon as possible to avoid getting sucked back in.

I thought "Kitchen now!" and suddenly felt like I was whooshing away, feet first, horizontally, but it felt like I went much further away than my own kitchen. At this point I was pivoting into a standing position and "landing" in a room. I said "Clarity now!" and then I could see.

I kept repeating "Clarity now!" while I looked around, and it definitely was not my kitchen. I'm not sure if it was the astral parallel to my kitchen, because it was way too different (cupboards and appliances in different locations) although it was about the same size, and the window was in the same place as it was in waking life. So, was I in someone else's kitchen? Or a future kitchen (my fiancé and I talk about someday buying a place in our neighborhood)?

I'd estimate that I was in that kitchen maybe five seconds, but oh boy, were those five seconds amazing! Then I was back in my body - no feeling of movement, no jerking, just peacefully opening my physical eyes and being back. And super happy. It's so true, just apply the techniques every day (journaling, doing the visualizations, and reading about OBEs in books) and it will happen in its own time. And encouragement from others too - I think that's what helped me the most these last two days.

Commentary: In this account, I used commands such as "Kitchen now!" and "Clarity now!" The use of commands is something William Buhlman teaches for taking control of one's experience during an OBE. Once I began to have OBEs more often, commands became an essential part of my process.

After I opened my eyes and realized I was back in my body, I had two important feelings. First, my lifelong fear of death was gone. Absolutely gone. The experience was such that I had no doubt I'd experienced existence apart from my physical being, and an automatic knowing that this aspect of "me" could continue after my body died.

Second, I felt a sense of "wholeness" I'd never experienced before. Perhaps for the first time in my life, I felt *complete*. I don't know much about shamanism, but I've heard the phrase "soul retrieval," and I wonder if this is something similar to that. It felt like I'd reconnected with the deepest part of my being, and reconnection remained even after I'd returned to my body.

Over time, I realized this feeling of wholeness could fade away as I focused on the day-to-day concerns of ordinary life. But with each OBE, came a renewed sense of wholeness. I suppose the key is to lead a lifestyle which supports the wholeness rather instead of a lifestyle which quickly wears it away with stress.

From the dates in my journal entries, it looks like it took me 6 weeks before I had my first full separation. But that isn't true. I'd already spent 7 weeks before the first journal entry was made reading about and practicing the techniques. First, I focused on William Buhlman's books, and then kept reading more by other authors.

Reading about OBEs at bedtime is a technique in itself because it decreases fear by building confidence, conditions your deeper mind into accepting that you want to have this experience, and offers helpful knowledge. In fact, I even had an unplanned, unintended OBE during the several days I spent transcribing my journal into the first draft of this book.

In actuality then, it took me around 13 weeks of consistently applying the techniques, sometimes twice a day, often getting up in the middle of the night as part of the "interrupted sleep" method before I got what I'd been looking for. I share this so that you don't get discouraged if you don't have instantaneous results. Everybody is different. As I began telling people later on, after learning how to move objects with my mind, "All you have to do is *not* give up!"

CHAPTER 16 CHARLIE

On January 23rd, just two days after my first full separation, my sister Jenny forwarded me an email announcing that Charlie, my Jesuit friend from college, had died of a stroke on the morning of the 20th. He was 63. Apparently, he'd been struggling with his health for months following some kind of event. I think it was a heart attack, but I never got the full details. I wouldn't have known them when it happened, of course, since I'd allowed our relationship to fade away. Now I regret it.

Nevertheless, I was happy to be able to attend the funeral service, which was held inside the campus church. There, in the foyer, lay Charlie. The casket was open so we could all see his face and body one final time. He was tall and lean, with a broad forehead and pointed, angular face. He was dressed in white priest's robes, and his hands were folded over his body with a rosary tucked beneath them.

It was difficult to see him. My OBE had conquered my fear of death, but that did nothing to prevent the feeling of loss. The fact that some non-physical aspect of him continued on some non-physical realm somewhere didn't change the fact that the Charlie I knew was no longer here, in this life, in this body. I was very sad to say goodbye. I thought I'd never hear from him again.

I was wrong.

The day after his service, I had the following experience.

January 26, 2014

Dreamt I was at an exclusive mountain resort, and was a hotel employee while a reality TV show with some type of contestants took place. It was like a talent show, and I watched as each person crossed the stage, acting in various roles and being really "big," really projecting their personas. Then, my awareness shifted to a point of view "backstage." I saw them behind the curtains, taking off their costumes and witnessing each other's ordinariness. Everyone was equal. No one was any better, or any worse, than anyone else.

Then the show was done filming, it was the end of the season, and the contestants were leaving this place. I understood it would be a long trip "home" for each of them. It was my time to leave too. As I walked through the lobby, I started singing and drumming my hands on my suitcase. Then, an overwhelming feeling of gratitude came over me. I was grateful *just to have been alive*, to have had a chance to have had *a life*.

As I came to the lobby doors, I raised my hands to the ceiling, then started clapping, exclaiming "Thank you! Thank you!" to the heavens. Walking out to the lobby, there were many others leaving too, and we all found ourselves on a huge snowy mountain. I let myself slide down the mountainside, and it transformed into a massive ocean. I melted into the waves. This was with a knowing that it might be a very long time before I got to live again.

I woke up filled with gratitude, and a humming type of energy coursed through my body. I instinctively knew that this particular type of humming represented, or actually was, the energetic signature of gratitude itself.

Though I described this as a "dream" in my journal, I don't think it was. It felt different, not even like a lucid dream or an out of body

Sean McNamara

experience. I hadn't yet learned the term "shared death experience." I probably learned the term from a book or online. Today, I think that is what this was.

This felt different because the whole time, it felt like I was watching the scenes through someone else's eyes. The realization that this is all just a "show," that we are all actors on a stage, the joy of having had the chance to play a role, and the immeasurable gratitude for having had a life - I felt it all through someone else's being, and that someone else was Charlie. I just *knew* it was him.

Had Charlie accessed my sleeping mind in order to share what he was going through after his time on physical Earth ended? Though I didn't record it in my journal, the sense was Charlie had now merged with the deepest waters of an ocean somewhere in a different kind of existence, and he was taking a very, very long rest. He'd given so much of himself to so many people as a priest, a professor, a counselor, and a friend. I'm certain he had more challenges to overcome than I was aware of, the way we all have our own challenges that we never tell anyone about.

I think he earned an eternity of comforting rest, this was a good thing. Was he now transformed into a drop of water inside the deepest ocean of some kind of heaven, far beneath the movement and noise of the waves above?

Of course, I don't think what I saw and felt during the night was meant to be taken literally. These were symbolic images. These scenes merely represented what Charlie experienced after dying, and what he was experiencing now in another form of existence. Perhaps he saw the very same scenes himself after crossing over. After all, to be conscious is to have an experience of mind, and everything in the mind including words, sounds, images, names, etc. is a symbol.

After all, you, the reader, are *not actually seeing* the pages of this book. As you look around the room you're inhabiting right now, do you really think you're seeing the objects beyond your reach? The cup on the table, the window on the far wall, the ceiling and floor ... all

140

of these images are created in your brain after receiving the electrical signals through your optic nerves. Your brain pulls all the information together into a single version of whatever is *out there*, in the space beyond your eyeballs. Finally, your mind uses the information to help it experience this physical world.

One final note on this shared death experience. If Charlie is resting now, in the depths of a still and silent space within eternity, then was it really he (his soul, his spirit, his consciousness, I don't know which word is best anymore...) who initiated my experience? Or was it someone or something else who granted me access to Charlie's afterlife experience so that I could know it too? If so, who? Or what?

Regardless of how or why I'd been given this experience, I think it was a clue about what we're all doing here on Earth. We're born into physical bodies, play a role in this drama we call "life," then leave the stage in celebration and gratitude for having had the opportunity to do something which, perhaps, can't be done anywhere else in this universe. Or at least in quite the same way, perhaps.

I'm sure it's becoming obvious the more experiences I have, the less sure I am about what's really going on, and the less interested I am about thinking I have any final answers.

CHAPTER 17 MORE OUT OF BODY EXPERIENCES

February 6, 2014

Got up at 4:30 am to pee after having a dream about being in a bar fight with people, and walking around and looking at the dart boards. I almost went back to bed out of tiredness but for some reason, I decided to stick to my routine of going to the couch. I did some reading for 5-10 minutes, then moved to the massage table.

I decided to listen to some relaxing music, thinking when the song ended I'd listen to a guided technique. I did the target technique while listening, and played the track twice.

Then, I rolled onto my side, pulled out the ear buds, but kept the eye mask on since more light was coming in through the window.

I woke up to subtle vibrations. I stayed with it calmly, and they grew more intense over a couple of minutes. They grew to peak levels, and I chose a moment to imagine lifting out. With that thought, I rose up, and it felt just like it did the first time. I fully surrendered out of fear of messing up the experience by trying too hard.

I felt my astral body turn perpendicular to my physical body. Then it righted itself into a standing position next to my physical body, but facing away, toward the window. I had a moment of doubt about whether this was really happening, so, I reached out and crossed my arms, then squeezed my forearms. They felt physical!

I started slumping down on the floor against my will, and realized I needed to bring more energy into my astral body (I knew this from all the reading I'd done).

I shouted out "Awareness now!" and "Clarity now!" as if I was really using my physical voice - strange! I stood up, then was floating, and I could see the room. I was careful not to look at my physical body.

I knew I had to stay focused, but I wanted to see stuff. I said "Hallway now!" and floated to the hallway. It looked just like it did in waking life. Then "Kitchen now!" and saw a feast "torma," a ritual cake from the tantric Buddhist tradition, on the kitchen table. I decided to fly out the window, and remembered that various OBE authors said windows and doors could act as portals.

As I flew through the window, I seemed to get caught up in lots of tree branches (checking outside as I write this journal entry, I see that there really are lots of branches right where I flew) I decided to rise higher and higher, then flew over a mountain village of three or four really nice houses with dark red wood construction. It was still dark, but I saw an extremely beautiful rose bush down below. The houses were in a broad cul-de-sac surrounding the rose bush. I couldn't smell them, only see them. There were mountains in the background, and the clouds shone in the night sky.

Then I felt someone's hands and fingers loosely interlacing with mine, and the skin felt so rough. I thought "Whose hands are these?" With that thought, I started dropping slowly - I knew I accidentally initiated a return to my physical body - those were my own hands that I'd felt.

I landed outside a house, approached a side door and started walking in ... then I opened my physical eyes. I was back.

Sean McNamara

So, what worked?

- Written affirmations
- Consistent journaling
- Afternoon practice
- Sleep interruption
- Reading about OBEs at bedtime
- Listening to inspiring and relaxing music while doing the visualizations
- After doing a technique, rolling over on the massage table to lie on my side, and really letting myself drift to sleep

I know it was an OBE, but a little doubt arises in my waking mind - the OBE consciousness and the waking consciousness experience life so differently that there's really no easy continuity of reality. But I was as fully awake and alert as I am right now … it really happened.

Commentary: Although I had gone to my couch after waking up to do some reading, I decided to transfer to a massage table I'd set up in the same room. For a time, that massage table became a regular part of my "sleep interruption" technique. The couch was good, but after a while it was just as easy for me to fall fast asleep on it, just as if it was my bed. Too comfy!

As Buhlman teaches, going to another room to initiate OBEs is helpful because we're so conditioned to fall fast asleep in our own beds. Since my massage table offered a firm surface, it made it difficult to fall asleep while lying on my back. This gave me much more time to practice my visualization before giving in to the darkness.

Similarly, many people experience OBEs or other nighttime events while staying in hotels or sleeping in unusual situations, simply because they're more alert at night due to the foreignness of the situation.

As for the *torma* on the kitchen table, I think that was an example of a "thought form" occurring in an OBE. It was something created from my memories, which my subconscious mind projected into the environment I'd found myself in. After years of doing Tibetan Buddhist "feast practices," I'd associated tormas with celebration, initiation, and a sense of sacredness. I should also note, tormas can also be symbolic representations of the tantric deity, which in my case would be Vajrayogini.

February 14, 2014 - Purification dream

Dreamt that I was with two women who are like guides or assistants, and we're in some type of office or clinic. I'm holding a large, gray sack, roughly the size and shape of my head and torso. Somehow, I know it's filled with my blood, and we're dropping it off here so it can be purified by some type of external process. It's not just some of my blood, it's *all* of my blood, so apparently, I'm walking around in a completely drained body, which is strange. I was awakened before the dream could go further. Purification?

This afternoon, I was very tired, and I fell asleep half-way through the technique. Before I dozed off, I felt a strong tug on my solar plexus. Energy adjustment?

Woke myself snoring. I tried to stay relaxed and did the target technique. Definitely felt a "pull" away from my body a couple of times. No movement, but rather a sense of gravity toward the target. But I wasn't able to stay relaxed enough to keep going.

February 16, 2014 - A Feminine Presence

Up at 2:30 - went to the massage table, listened to two songs and did the target technique. I felt *so* ready for an OBE. I also felt a strong, feminine presence in the room. But nothing happened, and I couldn't relax. I moved to the couch to try again, and just slept instead. Then I had a dream.

Sean McNamara

It had to do with a woman who wanted to be physical with me. I felt bad about turning her down. We parted ways with a hug, and she discreetly grabbed my crotch, making me very aroused. Waking up, I saw that I was also physically aroused.

February 17, 2014 - Getting Closer Again

5:00 pm, afternoon practice - lying down on the massage table. This time, no music, but I did turn on the fan for some white noise, which helped once the recording of the guided visualization stopped playing. I fell asleep somewhere half-way into the recording. When it was over, I woke up and did the target technique. I felt my legs floating up a little. Also, had some nice overall energy flow in the torso, and a little pressure at the top of my head. I tried to lift out a couple times, but I know my body was too awake.

The energetic pull out the front of my body was strong, though. I may try to bring it back before bedtime, then go to sleep as usual in bed and see what that does.

February 20, 2014 - OBE or Lucid Dream?

The night before last, nothing happened. I had a dream that seemed like pure randomness, so I didn't write it down. This morning at 4:30 I got up to pee and realized there was a subtle, yet interesting feeling of energy in me, and there was also a strange ringing sound in my ear.

I moved to the massage table. Instead of listening to music or guided techniques, I opted to just do some affirmations, some of my slide technique, and the target technique. The slide technique was to *turn on* (stimulate) my energy, the target technique was to rouse the astral body. After a while, I could tell I had to relax more, so I turned onto my left side to fall asleep. At this point, there wasn't much energy flow overall, but there was a distinct feeling coming out the back of my sacrum. It felt like a slow bubbling out, or a slow trickle, like energy was blooming out from the chakra at that location.

My lower back, just above the sacrum, had a little flowy feeling happening in it too, but I couldn't get it to expand to other parts of my body.

I fell asleep like this: The affirmation I used the night before and this morning was a new one, "I consciously separate from my body." But it didn't happen. Instead, I became conscious that I was sitting on a bench in a park-like setting. I found a pair of sunglasses on the ground. The lenses were tinted with deep purple. Then a woman appeared, she looked like a Dutch girl I knew in high school in Rio de Janeiro. She was a punk fan, enjoyed listening to the Cure and things like that. She was looking for her glasses. I offered mine to her. Then, she came closer like she was going to kiss me.

At that point, I "woke up" to find myself standing in a large, empty classroom. I could feel a strong, but invisible, feminine presence. I've felt her before, was she my guide?

There was a surge of energy in the atmosphere, and in my body. I could float and fly around. It seemed my purpose for being there was to learn something about *how to move through space* [the space of the room, not outer-space].

The experience of looking around the room was as vivid as being physically awake. After a minute or so, it seemed time to finish, and the energy faded. I instinctively bowed in gratitude to the invisible guide.

This room had a door, and I opened it knowing that it might lead to another reality. But outside was only a hallway, an extension of the room's reality. It was empty, long, and it had doors to other rooms running alongside it.

As I approached the end of the hallway, I saw a friend and fellow student of Steve coming my way. I wanted to show him what I could do, so I jumped up, trying to fly. But all I could do was slow down my descent a tiny bit. I wonder if

Sean McNamara

this was a sign my energy was returning to my physical body at that point?

It ended, but instead of opening my eyes and fully waking up, my consciousness shifted to the dream state. When I woke up I was sure, very sure, that I'd remember it well enough to write it down later (I'm making this journal entry too late, at 1:30 pm), but alas, the memory has faded. Something about a house, a group of people, a sexy woman in a nice summer dress, perhaps purple.

I try to be consistent about writing down my dreams, but I was so tired and confident after the OBE. It was interesting, and reaffirming.

Because there were no vibrations, and because I didn't experience floating out and seeing my local environment (my living room), I wasn't sure if this wasn't a lucid dream instead of an OBE.

I checked it out with the online forum. Claudia says it sounds like an OBE. At a certain point, she stopped having vibrations at the start of her OBEs, and would just become aware that she was in a new place.

Also, the classroom setting makes me wonder if I was in one of those "night schools" that someone else had mentioned in the forum.

March 4, 2014 - Changing my training regimen

This morning around 10:00 am, I decided to change things around with my practice. I laid on the floor instead of on the massage table, and that made me feel less "exposed." This meant feeling less fear. I didn't put a bolster under my knees, and that felt fine. I did a visualization technique, remembering that I needed to focus strongly enough to separate the mind from the body. When the focus is strong, that's when I feel the energy adjustments in my body - arms,

148

legs, solar plexus, and crown of the head. If I'm too gentle, nothing happens.

Then, I continued with a combination of the rope and target techniques in which I imagine pulling myself with a rope down the sidewalk from our apartment toward Mayu Sanctuary a few blocks south. Once I imagine arriving, I focused on picking up various items, feeling their weight in my hand and noticing other details about them. The sense of *really being there* had to be strong, undistracted, and undivided. I did this for almost an hour. Being late in the morning, it was difficult to fully relax the body since it was fully rested and ready for the day.

Regardless, I felt a deeper response to the practice than usual, and a new level of focus. Spending a whole hour on the practice helped too. There were even a few moments when I thought I'd really be able to leave my body right then.

Commentary: The "rope technique" is a classic. Typically, a person does it while lying down, and imagines that a rope is dangling down from high up above. As you fall asleep, you simply imagine grasping the rope, hand-over-hand, and pulling yourself higher and higher. For some, this initiates a lucid dream. For others, it can initiate an OBE. The difference? Your *intention*, what you desire to happen.

In this case, I modified the rope technique. Instead of pulling myself up into the sky, I imagined one end of rope was inside of Mayu Sanctuary, a few blocks down from our apartment. I imagined pulling on the rope as I walked on the sidewalk, the idea being this could enhance my focus and concentration, and strengthen the effect of my intention. This is an example of how you can be creative and experiment with these techniques. There is no dogma here, no rules. If there were one rule, though, I think it would be "do what works best for YOU."

Sean McNamara

March 8, 2014

I went to sleep last night while mentally reciting these three different affirmations:

"Now I'm out of body."
"I remember everything."
"I'm awake during separation."

I felt myself drifting into sleep, then my body jerked the way it does sometimes, in a way not at all related to OBE training - just the natural full-body jerk that many people experience, called "hypnic myoclonia." Oddly, Cierra, who was already fast asleep, did a full-body jerk at the exact same time as me.

Later that night, I became conscious of the vibrations. I spent the next few minutes experimenting with them. I found that I could modulate the vibrations by holding my thoughts and emotions in different ways and, of course, through changing my level of relaxation. The most important thing I realized was that I could *take my time* feeling the vibrations without needing to rush out of the body as soon as possible.

I was even able to maintain the vibrations as Cierra shifted around in bed, and even though parts of her body were touching mine. Being able to experience the vibrations while in bed with Cierra, and even while making contact with her, was encouraging.

Commentary: Somewhere along the way, I'd developed the belief that I couldn't have any kind of experience if someone else was in bed with me. Luckily, this experience served to deconstruct that belief. Please be careful about turning any idea or experience into a blanket rule. It could accidentally keep you trapped at a certain level of development for a long time.

The note about Cierra jerking her body at the same time as me is interesting. A similar thing began to happen more often after I'd begun my OBE journey. Cierra usually falls asleep very quickly, leaving me awake for a long time afterward, and then slowly drifting off. I began to notice just as the first moment of a dream entered my awareness, Cierra's body would do one of those "full body jerks."

Again, and again, and still to this day, as soon as I start to dream, she physically jerks her body in response. Every time I wake her up to ask if she knew what had happened, she says she had no idea, and had been in deep, dreamless sleep herself. Is it possible that some kind of signal is being transmitted from my mind to hers, specifically when I enter the REM stage[7]?

March 13, 2014

I had a series of dreams tonight, all of them taking place in a different part of my life. In the final dream, Steve was greeting me happily, and made a move to embrace me. I was wearing glasses [though in waking life, I stopped wearing glasses many years ago]. Before he got too close, I quickly took my glasses off. It seemed important to me that he saw *me*, and that he saw my eyes without any kind of obstruction. Was this a mark of self-confidence? Was this about honesty? Or about some kind of personal disclosure?

After the dreams, I had a strange knowing that I had also been to a "duplicate Earth." The mental image I had was of another Earth, directly opposite to us on the other side of the sun.

I also remember a source-less communication either asking or telling me that I could have the ability to always travel like this between worlds. My response to whoever was sending me this message was a sort of weak "I don't know." I can't quite tell if I was expressing fear or a lack of interest.

---

[7] REM, or <u>r</u>andom <u>e</u>ye <u>m</u>ovement, occurs while dreaming.

Sean McNamara

March 15, 2014 - Cierra's OBE

I woke up, maybe around 1:00 am, and Cierra was awake too for some reason. She asked me if I heard the conversation she'd been having in her sleep. I told her that I hadn't, although it could've been what woke me up. Then I went back to sleep.

Around 2:00, I awoke with vibrations, but my body was too awake to do anything with them since I had to pee. After going to the bathroom, I went to the couch instead of the bedroom. My body felt *so ready*, the vibrations were right there under the surface. But I tossed and turned for a really long time - I couldn't relax on the couch. I knew I had to fall asleep to let the vibrations take over. And eventually I did.

The vibrations were strong enough now. I waited for them to peak, then I thought of lifting out. As I rose up, my feet rose higher than the rest of my body, and I soon found myself upside down in space. I had the thought to go down to the first floor of our building, and I dropped through the floor, landing right side up.

I had to repeat "Clarity now! Awareness now!" to help center myself and be able to see. My first thought was that this was my chance to see other people, specifically my downstairs neighbors. Would I see them sleeping, perhaps?

But as I walked around, going from room to room, it was clear that I wasn't in my apartment building. This floor plan was a little bigger, the rooms were empty, and there was a strand of Christmas lights hanging above one wall in the front room. It seemed there was nothing here for me to see, so I decided to fly out through the front window.

I rose in the air and held out my arms like Superman, gliding toward the window. I knew this was an opportunity to really feel what it was like to move through an object. I felt the window pane through my fingertips, my hands, arms, head, and the rest of my body. It felt like a 3-dimensional hardness, but hollow. There wasn't any kind of vibrational sensation, just a gentle resistance as I pushed through.

My awareness seemed to have shifted gears after I moved all the way through the window, because everything that happened afterward resembled a dream more than an OBE. I flew to a land similar to a nearby suburban area I knew, with low hills and houses being built upon them. I was suddenly in a situation where I was helping some people to find a place to stay in. Then, the scene shifted to another dream [which isn't necessary to include here].

I opened my eyes after the last dream, stood up from the couch and went back to the bedroom. Cierra was awake and waiting to tell me something. She'd had her first OBE sometime during the night! She remembered sitting up, partway out of her body, and that I was there, in front of her, telling her to stay focused on my hand. I was holding it in front of her, helping to keep her focus forward, and encouraging her at the same time. The rest of what happened is hers to record.

Yet, I don't remember this happening! I think it was either her higher self, her subconscious mind, or perhaps even one of her guides using the image of me as a tool to help her leave her body.

Or what if it *was* me, and I just don't remember? She never expressed an ambition to have her own out of body experience. From December of the previous year to now, Cierra had supported me, and cheered me on, knowing how badly I wanted to do this. But as far as I know, she never felt the desire to do it herself. So why did this happen? Did we have a different kind of relationship on another level of consciousness? Did she have subconscious desires she wasn't aware while she was awake?

March 18, 2014

Last night, I woke up in the vibrational state. It was subtle, smooth, and a very high pitched tone rang in my ears. It kept going while I went to the bathroom. Afterward, I went to my practice area, our living room. But, I was too awake. I recited affirmations for a long time, and eventually drifted off to sleep.

I went into a dream in which I was a child, lying in bed, and I (as the child) was experiencing the vibrational state. I wanted to get out of my body, and I screamed (in my mind) an affirmation "Now I'm out of body!" And I rose up and away … then the dream ended.

March 20, 2014

This long dream started out in a classroom inside of an eight or ten story building. It was in the shape of a cylinder. I was with about six people, and I was teaching them how to have an OBE.

I was leading them in a practice in which they visualized sinking deep into the earth, and I ended up leaving my body in the process. [To be extra clear, this was a dream, and in it, I was having a dream-OBE.] I went through a wall, then beneath an air duct, and felt trapped inside, like I was under a pile of pillows. I got scared and felt like I couldn't breathe although I was completely cognizant of the fact that I didn't need to breathe in the OBE state.

I began to whimper out of fear. When the session was over, my students asked me about it, and I described my experience to them just as I have in this writing. We took a lunch break and my next task was to teach the stage after relaxation, the techniques for preparing for "lift off."

I decided to teach the rope technique, and they were excited about that. I wanted to first take them outside of the building to look around it so they could use what they saw in their visualization.

But, a student who reminded me of [another friend from Steve's group] said she needed to see the nurse before continuing, because she had car pain. I was fine with waiting for her to return.

Then the dream shifted to a scene back inside the building, on the ground level. I was with the students, waiting for the one who went to see the nurse, and eating a white, powdery substance out of my hand as a snack.

Someone else came by and said I needed to keep my folks collected or they would go off in different directions. Then I noticed that the students' attention was indeed becoming scattered. So, I tried to move them to a seating area, which looked like the inside of an airport terminal. The dream ended there.

To prepare for this evening's experience, I used three affirmations that I created for myself:
"I love OBEs, now I'm out of body."
"I enjoy OBEs, now I'm out of body."
"My dreams go lucid, then I *go* out of body, now I'm out of body!"

I think the energetic, positive, emotional and specific quality of the affirmations is what led to such a powerful dream. As I drifted to sleep, I could feel subtle energy flowing in my lower legs. Yesterday afternoon during my OBE practice, I had a strong energetic adjustment to my right foot, as if someone were physically touching it.

Commentary: It's not unusual to have sensations of someone touching different parts of your body while practicing these techniques, or relaxing afterward. You will need to determine for yourself whether someone really is touching you, or whether it's your brain's interpretation of whatever is causing the sensation.

Sean McNamara

Remember, the answer doesn't have to be one or the other. Sometimes, it could just be your imagination and other times, it could actually be some type of helper *out there*.

March 26, 2014

Had an upsetting dream this morning. I was driving up a snowy mountain road. I had a sense that this was a car that my father had given me. The windshield was covered in snow and ice. I was too scared to drive that way, so I jumped out while it was on a slow roll, to try and scrape the windshield while it was moving.

But the car rolled to the side, then into a rock wall, then it bounced off the wall, and went off the road on the other side, rolling down the mountain. I was cold and my jacket was inside the car, and I was concerned that my dad would be pissed. No cars would stop for me. Then it got worse.

I walked down the road far enough to see a lower road. I saw that my car had crashed into another vehicle down below, and the people inside of it were probably hurt.

Analysis: this dream reflects my desire to be able to see what's ahead clearly - to a fault. This wish forced me to step out of the car while it was moving, which led to a loss of control, and further loss after that. This shows me that I need to "drive" my life, keeping my hands on the steering wheel, even if I can't see where it's headed or what lies ahead.

This is at a time when I'm nervous about real estate being slow, knowing it's not my true calling, and really wanting to teach more, or find work that suits me better. I am working on my book, also hesitant because success isn't guaranteed. Overall, I'm frozen, and it's the most damaging state for me to stay in.

156

March 26, continued

Yesterday (March 25), I went to Mayu Sanctuary to practice the orb technique while taking a footbath. I realized that I always kept the visualization of my orb sort of dim, or gray, instead of bright white. So, I focused on making it much brighter, as if there was a big bulb inside of it.

Suddenly, a very bright flash came down from the orb, and my whole body felt the impact. This was an *almost physical* event. It didn't hurt, but there was a moment of feeling stunned, and not knowing how to react.

This (the very bright flash) couldn't have come from me, I hadn't intended for this kind of impact. I think it came from "other," from something, or someone, else. I think it was something *real* as opposed to my imaginary visualization.

March 27, 2014 - Bardo of Tantrikas[8]

I dreamt that I was in a hotel or dorm room gathering up my practice implements [bell, drum, etc.] for my puja table. A group was getting ready to practice the sadhana[9] together downstairs.

On my way down, I saw Charlie walking up the steps. He was full of energy, and very happy. He stopped to say "hi," and it seemed like this was the first time he saw me in the building. He asked if we could have a drink together soon. I got the sense there was a bar or restaurant somewhere in this place.

---

[8] A "tantrikas" is a practitioner of one of the many Tibetan Buddhist lineages in the Vajrayana tradition.
[9] "Sadhana" here means the tantric liturgy, rituals, visualizations and meditations associated with a specific practice.

I wasn't lucid, so it didn't strike me in the moment that this was the first time since our shared death experience that I've seen him. I agreed to meet him at a later time, because right now I had to meet the other meditators downstairs.

I entered the meditation room and saw row after row of tantric meditators sitting at their low tables, chanting out loud and playing their bells and drums in unison.

I woke up from this dream feeling extremely upset. It didn't last long, and it wasn't very complex, but I was left with a profound understanding. Seeing Charlie there tells me that this building was a place in the "afterlife," and the people there had crossed over (died) yet, they were still practicing the same sadhanas they'd been doing while alive on physical Earth.

What this tells me is that while they were alive, their spiritual efforts had become rote. They were nothing but ineffective, repetitive rituals. And instead of experiencing a true spiritual transformation or any kind of liberation, they passed into the next life only to continue what had become a simple habit. They just kept doing the same old practices, still believing that it would eventually lead to enlightenment.

The message to me was that this practice led nowhere, at least for me personally. This was the same practice I'd been initiated into all those years ago in Vermont with Rinpoche. It was also the same practice Steve initiated us into after he left his old organization and started his own lineage. It was a practice I'd coached many new tantrikas on myself, showing them how to ring their bells and beat their hand drums at the same time, how to do the various hand mudras, and how to visualize the deity.

Perhaps this ritualized practice *actually worked* for the many generations of yogis practicing in India and Tibet. Maybe it even had some benefit for some of the westerners who adopted it after Tibetan Buddhism came to the west in the

20th century. However, this vision made me wonder if any of my peers were actually reaching enlightenment, or gaining any kind of insight at all by doing this practice. Or was it all just a show, a way to *feel special*, to feel spiritual *without actually having a truly transformative experience?*

In all fairness, it's not my place to judge whether anyone other than myself was getting anywhere with this practice. But to be honest, and at risk of sounding arrogant, the dream allowed me to take a look around and consider everyone I knew, including Steve, and ask myself if they seemed to be getting anywhere with it. My answer? No, they weren't. No one had really changed.

And I hadn't either.

Looking back on my time as a Buddhist practitioner, the meditations that had the most impact on me were the simple ones, in which I'd sit quietly and watch my mind, and watch the awareness behind it all. The complicated, exotic sadhanas hadn't added anything to my development, even with all the colorful empowerment ceremonies.

But, over all those years, none of it had done anything to quench my thirst for real, experiential answers about death and what happens afterward. The *only thing* that had provided real answers to my most important question was having an out of body experience.

Although the message from the dream was clear to me, I still wasn't ready to walk away from my tantric practice, my community, or Steve. In fact, there was another fire puja retreat around the corner, and I was preparing to go and assist Steve with running it.

April 18, 2014

The last couple of weeks, I've been too busy to write. I've been covering for Emily at work while her mom Carol has

Sean McNamara

been in the process of dying from cancer. I've also been preparing for the fire puja, which is where I am now as I write this (at the retreat center).

Last night, I dreamt that I was sitting on a dais next to Dilgo Khyentse Rinpoche, and we were on our way to take care of a dying person. I asked Khyentse Rinpoche if we were going to heal that person's body, and he replied "Of course *not*, why would we? The body is *supposed* to fall apart." Our whole conversation happened without spoken language. We used mental communication instead, but the meaning was clear.

Commentary: Dilgo Khyentse Rinpoche is a well-known and beloved figure in Tibetan Buddhism, not only in Tibet, but across the world. Even the current Dalai Lama considers him one of his teachers. I've never met him, and he died in 1991, even before I'd started on my path. It's unusual that he should appear in my dreams.

April 20, 2014

I had another dream which resembled some type of "night school" training session. I was in a large room, trying to guide a stream of fiery sparks to draw several discrete shapes on the wall. Somehow, I figured out that the sparks would follow *the direction of my intention*. Instead of focusing on the sparks directly and trying to force them to move a certain way, I had to focus on the place on the wall where I wanted the sparks to land. I'd place my focus on a specific point on the wall, then *move my focus* in a line or a curve, and the sparks would follow.

Commentary: This idea not only had to do with learning how to use my mind during OBE training. As you'll read later on, it was crucial to learning how to do psychokinesis, also known as mind-over-matter.

160

April 22, 2014 - Pre-cognition during "tonglen"[10]

This morning during the tonglen portion of the sadhana, I decided to focus on sending compassionate feelings toward Carol who, as far as I knew, was in a hospital back in Denver struggling with her cancer. As I sat there quietly visualizing her, I heard her voice in my head. She sounded strong yet tender, telling me "I know this is a hard time for Emily, but I'm alright, and I'll see her again someday."

After the meditation period ended, I broke the rules about maintaining silence so I could sneak away to my room and check my phone for any voicemail messages or emails. Opening my inbox, I read Emily's announcement for Carol's upcoming memorial service. Carol had died four days previously, toward the beginning of this retreat, and without my knowing.

Commentary: It seems the act of sending Carol loving energy served as some kind of bridge or signal which she, now departed, could use to communicate with me. I prefer to be cautious about statements like these, since there's no way to prove she was actually communicating with me. Therefore, I should say that sending loving energy to her served as a way for my mind to open up, and to be able to receive information (from where?) indicating what had happened to her.

April 24, 2014 - An attack

I woke up at 2:00 am, having set my alarm so that I could attempt the interrupted sleep method while on retreat. I

---

[10] Tonglen is a Mahayana Buddhist practice for generating compassion. In it, one visualizes sending positive qualities (love, understanding, healing energy, and other resources) to someone who is suffering (physically, emotionally, etc.), and then receiving that person's suffering in exchange.

went out to the lobby to lay down on the couch. Everyone else was asleep, and all the lights were off. I listened to some soothing massage music while doing the target technique. A long time passed, and I remained awake. Then, I listened to some hemi-sync for a while before taking out my earbuds and dozing off.

The vibrational state began, and then something strange happened. Someone, or something tackled me, and shoved me *out of my body* in the process. We started wrestling immediately, even though I didn't have any visual perception. I was blind.

This felt like a different "zone" of experience, a place or locale that I've never been in before.

At first, I was in shock, but the feeling quickly took on a fun and playful quality. This creature felt like a friend, not an enemy. This wasn't an attack, after all, but I was still very surprised. After a few seconds, I was back in my body. I could feel the vibrations inside of me. I was too alert to do anything else though, and couldn't exit my body again.

April [date unrecorded]

Our retreat center is near a town where a Tibetan teacher, a bona fide Rinpoche from another lineage, happens to live. I've never met him in person, but I know what he looks like from photographs, and many Tibetan Buddhists in the United States and Asia speak highly of him.

In the dream, I entered what looked like an old Irish castle. It was a single tower, several stories tall, constructed of large blocks of stone. Once inside, I saw this Rinpoche sitting down at a table, waiting for me to join him. I sat down.

Before I had a chance to say anything, he began to slowly turn his head left and right, while looking directly into my eyes. The motion of his head indicated a "No," in response to a question I didn't even need to ask out loud. He had read my mind.

His face expressed an emotion anyone would feel when sharing bad news with a friend. In fact, he felt like a very old friend to me. The unspoken question he was silently responding to was "Does this path, Steve's path, *actually* lead anywhere?"

Suddenly, an earthquake struck, shaking the walls of the castle. A powerful wind blew the doors open, sending debris flying around the room. The walls trembled more and more until blocks of stone began to fall from above, pounding the earth and landing dangerously close to where we still sat.

The dream ended abruptly. Clearly, it had become too intense for me. I lay in bed feeling a mixture of sadness, shame and confusion. This Rinpoche seemed to be looking out for my best interests, but in doing so, he'd criticized my teacher. Although I'd already had my own troubling thoughts about him, it didn't feel good to think that there were people outside of our situation who thought badly of Steve, and of everything he was teaching us.

On a deeper level, I knew that this wasn't merely about what this man thought about my teacher. It was about admitting *to myself* that I had doubts about him. On top of that, the fact that my dream included another person meant I needed to share my feelings *with others*, and this was far more uncomfortable.

Commentary: This dream happened during the retreat, but I didn't write it down at the time because of how much it disturbed me. It's embarrassing to say, but there are only two reasons I fail to record a dream or OBE as soon as it happens. The usual one is sheer laziness. The other reason is either the experience is so positively transformative that I'll always remember it, or it's so troubling to me that *I'd rather not*.

In fact, the only reason I'm recording this dream now, as I'm writing this book, is because of something that will happen several years later. As you'll eventually see, it's something I could never have predicted.

May 1, 2014 - Another attack

I drifted off to sleep after listening to hemi-sync music and doing some affirmations. I'm not sure if what happened afterward was a dream or an OBE.

I found myself inside some kind of workshop. The room had a table with various devices on it. There was a man there, who asked me to hold up one of the devices to my chest. It was square, and reminded me of an old 1800's camera, the kind that stood on a wooden tripod while the photographer ducked behind a black cloth to look through the viewfinder.

This man was trying to do something to my heart. He activated the device, which released a surge of energy. The impact threw me off my feet. I was sent sliding back across the floor, still pressing the box against my chest. I looked up to see him looking down at me, smiling.

At that moment, I started to wonder if I was dying or passing out, and the whole experience began to fade away.

I opened my physical eyes, and realized that I felt completely fine, including my chest and heart, thankfully.

Commentary: Ok, I'll be the first to say it. This sounds like a scene from the movie *Ghostbusters*. Was I the ghost in someone else's reality? Was I a willing participant in an experiment, or was I tricked? I can't tell. The idea bothers me, even if this was "just a dream."

May 23, 2014

Last night, I went to the massage table and did the target technique. After a while, I turned on my side, got really comfy, and fell asleep. Then I became conscious of the vibrations. I kept calm and gave up all control. Then, I felt myself automatically separate, then float out of my body.

I could see out the window, and as I moved toward it, I set the intention that it would *not* behave as a portal, and that I'd really get to the actual street outside. It worked. I flew over the street, slowly heading north. The environment was bright, like daytime.

I decided I wanted to go down to walking-level, but instead of landing on the street, I kept sinking down, beneath the asphalt, going underground. I kept flying in a forward direction, but I couldn't see anything. It was all blackness. I returned to my body soon after, probably out of exasperation.

Our old apartment on S. Pearl St., where I had my first out of body experience. We lived in the upstairs unit on the left.

CHAPTER 18 THE PROCESS OF SEPARATION

The final journal entry from the previous chapter is the first to give a simple and clear description of the separation process during an OBE. I think many people have the idea that a person simply lies down, does a visualization, and finds themselves floating away without any break in consciousness. That makes sense, and I also thought that's how it was before I'd had several OBEs of my own.

In my experience, the most common way I've had OBEs is like this. First, I lay down and do a technique (visualization, affirmations, energy work, whatever...). This is either in bed at my usual bedtime, or in the middle of the night as part of the *interrupted sleep* method.

Whether or not I experienced any strange sensations, it didn't matter. After finishing the technique, I'd allow myself to fall asleep, gradually letting go of paying attention to the process.

Sometime after falling asleep (this could be seconds, minutes, or longer), I'd become mentally conscious and aware - while my body was still asleep. The thing that would activate my awareness was one of the *separation signals*, the vibrational state. Sometimes I'd realize my whole body felt like it was vibrating. Other times, there would be a strange "whooshing" sound, *pulsing* inside the base of my skull. Or, I'd hear a gunshot inside or next to my ears, or a roaring sound like being beneath the crashing ocean waves. As you've already read, it might be the sensation of someone touching you or of a presence in the room.

It's at this point, after realizing that I was aware, yet asleep, when I'd follow Buhlman's instruction to point my mind to another part of the room, or to another location. For instance, I've directed my attention to my door, or to the hallway, while intending to go there. As long as I stayed calm, and acted patiently, it's at that moment when I'd feel myself floating or moving out of my place inside my physical body. At this stage, I typically didn't have the ability to "see," but as soon as I'd stop moving and "land" somewhere, vision would come on its own, or I'd use the "Clarity now!" command to make it happen.

Over time, though, it became more common to suddenly find myself in another location, without feeling the vibrations or other signals. I've spoken to other travelers who have similar experiences. But you should be prepared to have a unique experience of your own. If it happens differently for you, don't worry, you haven't done it "the wrong way." Instead, you've done it *your way*, which is the best way.

An OBE feels as real as, if not *more real* than, this physical experience. It's as if you've walked through a doorway into another room, and you turn back to see your body still lying in the first room. But you are not there, you are not that body. *You* are here instead, in a new place.

The information above pertains to voluntary, initiated OBEs. Yet, there are stories about marathon runners, women giving birth, and people in life-threatening situations who spontaneously left their bodies. Near-death experiences (NDE's) fit that last category. I personally know someone who spontaneously left their body while meditating during a retreat I led recently.

So, there's definitely more than one way to leave your body. Doing it safely, calmly, willingly, and with clear intention, has its obvious advantages.

CHAPTER 19 EVEN MORE OUT OF BODY EXPERIENCES

July 9, 2014 - An after-life healing environment

Note: This experience marks the end of a two-month "dry spell"

3:00 am - Woke up to use the bathroom, almost went back to bed but for some reason, I decided to try for an OBE instead. I went to my new "chair," an antique wooden reclining chair we just bought at the farmer's market. The salesperson said it was an *opium chair* from the 19th century.

I spent some time relaxing in it while doing the target technique and the 100-count[11]. After a while, I decided to lie down on the couch and just keep my awareness open as I fell asleep. I remembered the important lesson from the most recent book I read, by Robert Peterson, "Out of Body Experiences: How to Have Them and What to Expect." He wrote that this is a process of *allowing*, not trying. Luis Minero's book, "Demystifying the Out of Body Experience" talks about two types of anxiety - fear and anticipation (or expectation). These are reminders for me to *allow* - which I haven't been doing for months now.

As I started to relax, I heard a new sound, the tinkling of bells. I knew they were separation signals as soon as I heard them, and got excited. I reminded myself to relax and calm

---

[11] The "100-count" will be described in detail later.

down, and just keep my attention on the technique itself rather than on my body and whatever I felt or heard in the process.

I relaxed while doing the target technique and imagining myself inside Mayu Sanctuary, and the sound of tinkling bells returned. This time, I did a good job of ignoring them. I let myself drift off, and then the vibrations came. With the thought "Up, up…" I separated out while feeling a brief sensation of movement.

I opened my eyes (for lack of a better word) and found myself standing near what looked like a couple of swimming pools. These weren't lap pools, but more like lounge pools with curved edges. Several young women in dress clothes stood in the water. Then, I noticed there were children in the pools with them. They weren't swimming, but gently immersing themselves.

The pools were on my left. To the right, there was a building like an outdoor cafeteria, with a gently sloping lawn in front of it. Kids of all ages were sitting on the grass, looking dazed, mostly. There were more young people in the cafeteria area. Most of them also looked lost, or bewildered.

I decided to fly away from there and reached out my arms "Superman" style, and then remembered that I didn't need to do that anymore. With that thought, my body dissolved and my awareness moved through some trees, into the sky, eventually landing in a new area.

This new place reminded me of the "quad" at my old college campus, a big, flat grassy area with buildings nearby. I took on a body form again and sat down in the grass. I realized that, so far, this was the longest OBE I'd ever had. I started fading out so, to stay there longer, I moved my hands through the blades of grass to *feel* the environment, which helped to keep me *connected* longer. The grass felt as real as it does here, "here" being *this* physical Earth.

It worked, and I was able to stabilize myself there. I also realized that I'd made a friend, a boy had followed me there from the pools. He was about ten years old, with sandy brown hair, and an endearing face. I felt an instant kinship with him. He seemed clear-minded, unlike the other children. The boy and I walked to one of the buildings nearby and I encountered someone who looked very familiar to me. It felt like I'd known him a long time ago. We started talking as if it was just yesterday.

"You're dead?" I asked him. "Yeah," he replied, simply. He motioned with his hands near his throat to indicate a blockage of some type. He told me that "they couldn't figure out how I died," but somehow he knew he probably just choked. He seemed surprised to see me there.

Then I took the boy to another building, but instead of walking, we just went there instantly, as if we were teleporting in a sci-fi film.

We entered a special room, and saw a two-way mirror, the kind you see in police shows. We watched what was happening inside. There were two elephants wearing suits in the room. They were trying to find a way out, but for some reason, they only concentrated on one wall, as if there was an exit hidden inside of it. They also seemed to be arguing with each other.

I turned to the boy and said "Look! They don't see that if they tried the door (instead of a wall), they'd be free. I swung the door open, and they came out - but as people, not elephants! Something about the room or the window had made them appear as elephants to me.

We went outside, and the two guys from the room were sitting down on the steps, eating sandwiches. They were either a father-son duo or older-and-younger brother. I had the sense this special room was a place where people went to resolve lingering issues between them. These two were trying to work something out.

I wanted to introduce myself to them, and started with "I'm not actually dead, I'm having an out of body experience, my body is down in Denver." And with that sentence, I faded out of the place. I realized that I'd made the mistake of thinking about my physical body. An instant later, I opened my eyes. I was back.

I checked the clock, it was 3:30 am. This was surprising because on the other side, it felt like I was gone for around forty minutes. On *this* side, after going through all the techniques and relaxation, I'd probably been gone for just five minutes.

I woke Cierra up to tell her about where I'd gone. She suggested I send a "thank you" to my guide in case there was someone out there who had helped me, and to thank the boy as well. I sent off a prayer of gratitude to my mystery guide and to the boy, then drifted off to sleep. Even this afternoon as I write this out, I miss him deeply, but I don't understand why.

I can tell part of me is working hard to adjust to this experience, which I think is my first real visit to a *consensus reality*.[12] Also, the fact that I had direct, meaningful contact with multiple people in one OBE is also taking some adjustment.

Commentary: If you, the reader, feel odd or confused after reading this entry, that's perfectly alright. It's a mind bender, and I still don't

---

[12] A "consensus reality" is an environment where people (or other inhabitants) with similar beliefs, mental states, karmic patterns or stages of development naturally gather together. Their shared beliefs have a great deal to do with shaping the environment itself. An example in your own neighborhood would be a local church, mosque, synagogue or temple. In the non-physical realms, or the *afterlife*, there exist countless consensus realities.

fully understand it. One thing I've realized is the mind works differently, it *understands reality* differently, during an OBE, or even a lucid dream for that matter. I think it's because the process of knowing and perceiving isn't limited by the physical brain, which we know filters out a great deal of information while we're awake, simply to help us navigate physical existence efficiently.

Many of the insights I've had during an OBE have been subdued or forgotten upon returning to my body. Other authors have talked a lot about a "veil" between this world and the next. It's a kind of amnesia, and some people believe we agree to this kind of existential "forgetfulness" when we choose to be born here. I don't think the veil is any kind of mystery. I believe the veil is nothing other than *our very own brain*.

The 100-count technique is something I developed based on Thomas Edison's technique for entering the hypnagogic state during his afternoon catnaps. He'd fall asleep while sitting up, holding some steel balls in one hand. As he'd approach sleep, his hand would relax, releasing the balls. The sound of the fallen balls would wake him up, and he'd start all over again. For him, it was a new opportunity to dwell in the hypnagogic state, which is a rich source of inspiration, creative thinking, and problem solving.

In the 100-count, you lie down while keeping your forearm raised in the air, and your upper arm resting on the mattress, bending your elbow 90 degrees. Then you relax while slowly counting backwards from 100 to 1, as if receiving anesthesia before surgery. Relax your body and mind as you continue counting, and if you fall asleep too soon, your arm will drop, stirring you up and bringing you back. With this technique, you can learn to hang out on the edge of sleep and wakefulness, which is a productive state to be in when trying to stimulate an OBE.

August 19, 2014

I had a series of nightmares throughout the night. They were pretty simple, the appearance of scary figures. I don't remember them clearly, but I do know one was the classic "scary clown." These figures would just appear in the dream scene, and I'd retreat from them in fear - not wanting to see them, and turning away.

This is the type of response I'm very familiar with. Instead of facing situations and making necessary changes, I tend to just look away and pretend I don't see them at all.

After the final nightmare, I became aware of my habitual response to these fears, and even had a feeling of being fed up with them, both the fears and how I usually responded to them.

Sometime after going back to sleep, I dreamed I was lying down on a cushion or on the floor, on my right side. Behind me, also lying down, was a feminine presence, perhaps a woman. I didn't have a visual experience of her, but I knew she was there.

Communicating without words, she gave me specific instructions for how to lie down. I remember her guiding me to lay my arm against my side and thigh, just like I've read about in books about Tibetan dream yoga. Then, the dream ended.

Was this my guide from other dreams and OBEs? Why did she show up now? Did I need to face some fears before my mind was open enough to have this experience with her?

August 22, 2014 - Accidental lucidity

I dreamt that I was on a road somewhere at night, in some other city. I encountered a guy who asked me where we were. Even though I had ordinary, limited dream awareness, I began to tell him that *we were in a dream*! I began to shake him gently by the shoulders to help him become lucid. At that very moment, I became lucid! I was so happy, ecstatic even.

173

It must not have been a very strong lucidity though, or perhaps I was tired, because it didn't last long and I soon returned to a deep and dreamless sleep.

September 8, 2014 - Using a lucid dream to have an OBE

I woke up at 4:00 am to pee. I took some galantamine, then did the orb technique in my practice area for about 45 minutes. Then I went back to bed, as Cierra would soon be waking up to use the practice area herself to do her morning meditation. I drifted off while doing the target technique. First, I had a dream of [a friend from Steve's group] playing ultimate Frisbee, which is something she actually did in real life many years ago.

Then I dreamed I was sitting at a table in a cafeteria eating rice and beans. There was a guy sitting across from me with a spaced out, dumbfounded look on his face. I finished the dish, then looked down and watched as small clumps of food began to appear on my plate. I ate the new food, then looked at my empty plate and saw even more food appear.

I decided to see if I could change the appearance of the food just by looking away from the plate and then looking back down at it. It worked. Then I looked at the guy sitting across from me and *instantly realized that I was dreaming*.

Interestingly, I was behaving *as if* I was lucid, but only became lucid afterward. This time, I didn't feel especially blissful, just very aware. I looked around the cafeteria briefly to see what else I could do within the lucid dream, but realized that I'd rather have an out of body experience instead.

With that very thought, the dream ended, and I became aware and conscious of my body. I could feel the vibrations beginning. After setting my intention to go out, I let go and relaxed.

I travelled upward through layers of bright light, and then it seemed dark. I "opened" my eyes, and discovered I was in outer space. There were countless stars all around me. So many more, and so much brighter, than I have ever seen from Earth in the waking state. It was just beautiful.

I "moved" around to see where the sun and the Earth were, in order to get a sense of location. But, they were nowhere to be seen. I felt disoriented by the movement and lack of reference points, which is probably what caused the OBE to end.

I opened my eyes, then tried to go to sleep to see if anything else might happen. But I was too excited, too happy, and too satisfied. Getting out of bed, I had that feeling of wholeness and reconnection to myself that only OBEs can bring.

Commentary: Galantamine is a medication used to treat dementia in Alzheimer's patients. It's sold over the counter in low dosages, and is becoming increasingly popular as a lucid dreaming supplement. It helps by increasing a dreamer's "memory function," which is also why it helps with dementia. Somehow, the increased memory also makes it easier, for *some* people, to become lucid during a dream.

Even though I have journal entries here which mention galantamine, I stopped using it after only a few times because first, it hurt my stomach to take it in the middle of the night. Second, there was a qualitative difference in my dream and OBE states, one which I didn't like. I also didn't like relying on anything other than my own intention paired with a helpful technique.

September 22, 2014 - Looking for a witness

Last night after exiting via the vibrational state, I found myself gliding just about 50 feet above the sidewalk in a city I've never been to before. I landed and began to walk among the bystanders there. It was obvious they couldn't see me. I made a mental demand to find a person from the physical plane who I knew would be an excellent witness, if I could get her to perceive.

At that moment, I felt a strong desire for some kind of proof this was really happening. That feeling may have been a hangover from the other day when, in the waking state, I told a friend about my OBEs, and realized he didn't believe me at all.

Suddenly, I was whisked away and found myself inside a bar/restaurant that was built into the side of a theater. I figured that this is where my requested witness would appear. I walked around, still invisible to the people around me.

But, as I was walking past a man-woman couple, the woman whispered at me, "Hey!" I was surprised, and asked, "You can see me?" She told me that she could, but was talking under her breath because she knew that no one else in the room could. Except for her husband, that is, who asked me if I remembered him.

I've never seen these two people in my current life, yet while in this state, I *did* know him, I remembered him, and I also felt immense love for him. I couldn't recall the details of how or when I knew him, but it was as if my heart had never forgotten his. I can't say for sure if this was a brotherly, fatherly, friendly or other type of love, but it was ancient.

He seemed to really appreciate hearing me say that I hadn't forgotten him and still cared for him. During most of my time out, and at this location, I'd been repeating "Clarity now! Awareness now!" in order to maintain my awareness and prolong the trip.

But then, a few people in the bar started getting rowdy for some reason, and the manager came out of his office, yelling at them to cut it out. This distracted me too much and I faded out, instantly returning to my body.

My gut feeling is this wasn't the physical Earth I know, but perhaps some other Earth-like realm. In the end, I suppose I got my needs met, to be witnessed, although it wasn't the way I thought it would happen. The woman wasn't the friend I'd intended to find at the beginning, but maybe she was the better option for me to learn from.

September 25, 2014

Last night, as I drifted to sleep and into what I think was ordinary dreaming, something strange happened.

The best description I can come up with is that a burst of energy in the form of sprinkles or flecks of light came over my inner perception, as if someone had thrown sand in my eyes.

I couldn't tell if this energy came from within me, or from outside of me. I also couldn't tell if it was meant to cover over (hide) what I was about to see in the dream, or to simply bring me back to the present waking state, which it did.

I moved to the couch at 4:00 am, read books about OBEs for a few minutes, then drifted off. I dreamt about remote viewing, and the dreams had a dramatic tone to them. This isn't surprising because yesterday, I listened to the audio book "Psychic Warrior" by David Morehouse, and his personal accounts are filled with dramatic events. And today, I began working with Morehouse's "The Remote Viewing Online Training Course."

I've been learning more about remote viewing lately, and am very interested in experiencing it as another avenue for learning about consciousness.

Sean McNamara

September 30, 2014 - Directions to a portal

Three nights ago, I was in the practice room early in the morning. I dreamed there was a small figurine on a stone table. It resembled one of those Japanese "good luck" cats. It began talking to me, and I became frightened. I started walking out of the room, but decided not to let the fear control me, and to stay and hear what the statue was saying to me.

It was telling me to "look up," and that something was happening that I needed to pay attention to. I lay back down on the couch (still in the dream), and looked up at the ceiling. There above me, was a purple triangle about 2 feet long on each side, acting like a window or some kind of portal. Images and blocks of information were coming through like a television signal. I don't remember the details of what I received, though.

Then, I had some early morning dreams. In one, I was walking down a wide hallway with a woman. We were inside someplace like an airport or train terminal.

On a very large wall in front of us, a purple circle appeared, about 8 or 10 feet in diameter. The edges were bright, but it got much darker toward the center. I needed to concentrate to be able to see it at all. As I looked, it looked like a dark tunnel, as if I could've entered it myself, or something could come out of it. Then the dream faded out.

October 6, 2014 - Precognitive OBE

Awoke at 2:00 am, my body felt very energized, as if in a pre-vibrational state. I simply *felt* confident that an OBE could happen very soon. I went to the couch and did the target technique. I heard a strange sound, the single chime of some kind of digital or electronic bell. I took it as a vibrational state phenomenon, a separation signal. Then I drifted off to sleep.

178

I became conscious of the vibrations, but in a way, I was *too* conscious of them. I felt too solid. I drifted back to sleep again, confident that I still had enough energy to make a second attempt.

Again, I became conscious, and rolled myself off the couch, landing on the floor. I stood up, but as I reached for the armrest for support, my hand went right through it. At that point, I realized that I was out of my body. I must've been at a very low vibrational rate because I felt sluggish and dense, almost physical. I decided to walk to the bedroom.

Cierra was lying in bed, and I saw a faint glow around her head. Her cat Jack was lying on her pillow, and he had a little glow around him too.

I backed out of the room and went further down the hall and into the kitchen, through the back door, and down the stairs which lead down past the first-floor apartment and into the basement. Half-way down the stairs, I decided to try something new. I commanded "Sukhavati now!"[13]
My trying to go to Sukhavati with the command "Sukhavati now!" was as an experiment in purposely traveling to a consensus reality. As I uttered the command, I jumped up, as if I'd fly away or be taken away to someplace new. But, no such luck.

Instead, I stumbled, and my hand smashed against the wall of the staircase, which felt quite physical in the moment. It felt like I'd shattered some glass, though there wasn't any glass around.

---

[13] Sukhavati is a Buddhist "Pure Land," known as a place that people can be born into after they die. The tradition says it's a place filled with wise and compassionate beings, and that being born there assures one of a life of advanced spiritual development, leading all the way to enlightenment. As I write this paragraph, I realize the irony that Vajrayana Buddhism makes an analogous claim for *this* life, as do other religions.

179

I looked down at my hand and saw that it had a small scratch on it. I was bleeding!

Still cognizant of the fact that I was in the middle of an OBE, I realized this was some kind of illusion. There was no pain, so I shook it off, looked at my hand again, and saw the scratch had disappeared.

I went back up the stairs, through the kitchen door, across the hallway, and down the front stairs. But then, a new idea came over me. I decided to look at my physical body lying on the couch. Instead of walking up the stairs again, I floated up, gliding over them, passing right through the railing and the wall, finally arriving in my living room.

Hovering near the ceiling, I saw my sleeping body below. It faced the back of the couch, and looked like I was wearing a white shirt, and cradling a red-hot water bottle.
I knew the risk of looking at myself, that I might be drawn back into the physical, and that's exactly what happened. After a couple moments, I was in my body, opening my eyes.

Doubt overcame me right away as I looked at my shirt. I was wearing a dark tee shirt instead of a white one, and I was facing away from the back of the couch, opposite of what I'd seen when I was looking at myself from above. And there was no red water bottle to be seen.

I told Cierra about my doubt the next morning, and she reminded me that my visual experience didn't prove that I wasn't out of the body. She said that it was possible that what I was looking at while I was out of the body *also* wasn't physical.

But if I was out, what was I seeing on the couch? Was it an energetic projection from my physical body? Or was it just a mental projection? My doubt lingered through the rest of the day, until something unusual happened.

Cierra needed to do some laundry, and carried a basket of clothes down the back stairwell to the washing machine in the basement. Along the way, she got startled by something (she doesn't remember what) and scraped her hand on something on the wall. She wasn't bleeding, but it did hurt. She showed me the part of her hand she'd scraped. I was surprised to see it was the same part of my hand I'd "hurt" during my previous night's OBE.

Commentary: Could it be that during my OBE, I'd somehow moved forward in time? Not only that, had I also entered into Cierra's personal experience? If so, then the blood I saw on my "astral hand" was a symbolic manifestation of her future injury. If so, then this was a precognitive mental projection. I'd seen, and felt, someone else's future experience.

One might think, "It was just a little scratch, shouldn't it be something more significant to make this kind of point?" I wonder the same thing. It just seems so...insignificant. But, I also wonder if it was just this level of harmlessness which made it possible for this to happen. Wishing something more significant had happened might be like wishing I'd "broken" my astral leg during an OBE, then Cierra breaking her physical leg the next day. I wouldn't want that at all, *even if* it served as a lesson about precognition. The scratch then, was *just enough* to get the point across.

November 19, 2014

Fell asleep last night after taking some galantamine and listening to "Astral Aerobics" by Magic of Dreaming. A lengthy event followed.

I floated out and walked down the hall to find a different version of the apartment. Looking out the kitchen windows, I saw lions and other large, dangerous animals outside. I was completely aware of what I was experiencing, including the fact that this scene was a subjective projection from my mind, as happens in lucid dreams. So, with the blink of an eye, I turned them into harmless birds like cranes and peacocks.

Then, I flew down to the ground outside, taking in the new environment, which was a garden with small trees around. I wanted to make the most of being out, so I decided to do something I've never tried before. I attempted to invoke my Buddhist deity, the one whose sadhana I'd been empowered to practice.

I commanded "Vajrayogini now!" I thought since I'd been doing her meditation for several years now, certainly she should show up as some kind of objective figure, right?

Wrong. After several attempts, nothing happened.

Then I tried something different, "Spiritual guide now!"

After a couple of determined requests, William Buhlman appeared! I was very pleasantly surprised. He was a few yards away. Looking around, he asked "Did somebody call me here?"

He didn't have his usual beard (I've never met him; I'd only seen photos and videos online). He also looked thinner than usual. But his appearance began to shift, and continued shifting for the duration of my OBE. For this reason, I think it wasn't the *real* William Buhlman, but only a visual projection. Whether the projection came from my own mind or someone else's, I don't know.

The scene shifted, and we entered a room with concrete walls. It had an underground feeling to it. Other "OBE students" were there, and Buhlman led us in an exercise about looking at our reflection in a mirror. I picked up a piece from a broken mirror which had been laying on the ground, and saw my face reflected in it. I appeared a little younger than I am now, especially my hair. It was entirely black, even though in actuality I have a fair amount of gray hair, surrounding a balding crown.

Then, a woman showed up, who needed all of Buhlman's attention about some personal issue. She had a "needy" feeling about her. I watched as he took her over to some kind of exercise machine and helped her onto it. I got bored right away, feeling finished with the experience, and then the whole thing faded out. I instantly opened my physical eyes, and I was back in my living room, lying on my couch.

November 22, 2014 - The void, a question of manifestation

Woke up around 4:00 am and took some galantamine, then listened to some Astral Aerobics until I fell asleep. I woke up to pull the earbuds out, and turned over on the couch. I felt the surges in my head and, eventually, subtle vibrations up and down my back. I resisted the urge to open my non-physical eyes too soon, recognizing that an immediate feeling of departure doesn't always indicate separation has occurred yet.

Finally, after becoming sure that I'd lifted out completely, I "looked" and saw that I was drifting toward the wall and ceiling above the doorway. Instead of trying to force myself downward so that I'd pass through properly, I decided to let go of control and move through in the direction I was heading, where the wall and ceiling met, above the doorway.

I moved through it easily enough, then found myself in a place of darkness, or rather, blackness. This place had no dimensions whatsoever, no reference points. I think this is "the void" I've read about in OBE books.

I willed myself forward, further into the darkness, looking around and hoping for something to appear. Some faint glimmers of light began to appear, but I knew this was my mind trying to produce something in that space. I knew if I held my attention in that way, wanting something to appear, that something would. But, it would only be my own mental projection. That wasn't going to satisfy me, so I decided to try something else instead.

Sean McNamara

I decided to meditate.

I crossed my non-physical legs and put my hands together in front of my heart. I formed an aspiration, inspired by my Buddhist training, "I meditate so that I may be of service to others." Making the aspiration had a second purpose to it, which was to stabilize my awareness the same way uttering "Awareness now!" did.

Then, I remained in a state of open awareness, without doing anything, simply remaining present. After a few moments, a golden light began to fill the darkness.

An instant later, I was back in my body, opening my eyes.

Commentary: Reflecting on my brief time in the void, I realized something which has stuck with me ever since. *There's no such thing as objective reality.* The void seemed like a fundamental aspect of reality, or the basic field, from which, or in which, various experiences occur. It's like a blank slate, and everything that appears on it is only a temporary manifestation.

During this OBE, I came to understand this by noticing my act of looking for something in the emptiness was enough to start manifesting an object of my searching. The "faint glimmers" were the beginnings of something, stirred out of the nothingness by my simple act of looking. I wonder if this is how things really are, ultimately. And how far does it go? Is this non-objectivity limited to non-physical ideas and mental projections, or is this what produces physical reality as well? Is this what makes psychic abilities, miracles and manifestation possible?

Note on location change - in January of 2015, Cierra and I moved out of our apartment in Platte Park and into a high-rise condominium on the southern side of Denver.

January 2, 2015 - Using dream momentum to cause an OBE

Sometime in the middle of the night, I moved to my meditation space in the living room and practiced sitting meditation for about an hour. Then a *knowing* told me to just lay down on the couch, which I did, while maintaining the state of meditation. This meant that I was simply staying present, not drifting into memories or thinking about the future, and using the sensation of breathing to help me relax and pay attention.

Energetic sensations flowed through me, but these were even more subtle than the usual vibrational state. After a while, they became muted and I realized that I was in the "mind awake, body asleep" state. I wanted to let go further, so I drifted to sleep, immediately entering the dream state. I was lucid, completely aware that I was in a dream.

In it, I was lying down in the back of a car while a friend was driving. As the car turned a corner, I felt the force of the momentum acting upon my dream body. Instinctively, I decided to use this feeling to stimulate an OBE.

The driver took a particularly sharp turn around a corner, and I focused on the sensation of the centrifugal force. I felt as if I was being thrust from the car. With that feeling, the dream faded. My awareness was in the room, inside my physical body, though my body was still asleep. I felt my non-physical legs floating up and out of their physical counterparts.

My excitement almost ended the experience, but I caught myself and allowed my emotions to mellow out. Once I was fully settled, I continued. I decided to rise up to a standing position next to the couch.

This felt *so* physical, including the feeling of gravity, that I wondered whether or not I had truly separated, or if the OBE had already ended and I was simply standing up in my physical body. I didn't dare to look at the couch, because if I was still having an OBE, looking at my body would almost certainly end it.

I decided to walk through the sliding glass door to the balcony, and to do it slowly enough so that if I was in my physical body, I'd merely bump against the glass without breaking it. The embarrassment would've been worse than the cuts and bruises.

But after only a millisecond of feeling resistance, my body continued moving through the glass, and then I was outside, standing on the balcony. We'd moved to a condo on the 10th floor, so I was still a bit nervous, and overly cautious. I walked right through the railing, thinking if I was awake, it would prevent me from going further. But it didn't, and I began to fall. The descent was slow enough to reassure me this wasn't a physical experience, so I decided to stop worrying and start enjoying it.

After a soft landing, I walked around the empty parking lot. I mentally repeated "Clarity now!" to keep myself present and prolong the OBE as much as possible.

Across the street, I saw some teenage boys playing catch. I asked myself, "Are they part of my mind, or do they have their own existence? Are we 'all one'?"

With that question, I phased out and was back on the couch, opening my eyes. As with many of my other OBEs, I felt that wonderful, fulfilling sense of wholeness. I felt like I'd reconnected to a part of myself that I frequently disconnect from in the course of living this physical, stress-filled existence.

For me, this *wholeness* is one of, if not *the most precious* gifts of the out of body experience. It heals me deeply.

January 16, 2015

Woke up at 3:30 am, moved to the couch, and read about OBEs for a while. Then I repeated "Now, I'm out of body" for a long time, imagining my awareness moving away from my body with every exhale. I did this until I fell asleep. Then, I woke up to full vibrations, though they were different than I remember, these seemed to have some *heat* to them.

I pointed my attention across the room, and after a few moments, I floated out, feeling pulled toward the window. I didn't want to go yet, so I fought it. I turned around to see if I could see my body on the couch, but this time, I couldn't. The couch was empty, and my body was nowhere to be seen.

I wanted to see Cierra lying in bed, so I floated down the hallway to find her. But, the OBE ended before I made it all the way to the bedroom.

I waited to see if I could exit again, but my heart rate was up. I was just too excited. I was very happy since it had been sometime since my last OBE, and I really wanted to have another one.

Interesting to note that this OBE ended another "dry spell," and occurred the day after I emailed Steve telling him I wasn't going to continue with the new meditation technique he was offering his advanced students. I think the thought of letting it go released an invisible weight in my mind.

Commentary: Several weeks before this OBE, Steve offered another meditation technique to his senior students. The practice was related to the tummo (inner heat) practice from the Six Yogas of Naropa, mentioned early in this book.

If I hadn't yet had lucid dreams and out of body experiences, I would've been very excited to learn the Six Yogas. Steve was going to teach them to us step-by-step, a process which could last several years. Yet, now I knew that this complicated process, with the teacher offering breadcrumbs slowly over time, wasn't necessary.

The non-religious techniques I'd learned from books provided all the information I needed, in plain and simple language, in order to have the experiences I was looking for. Also, OBE authors and instructors weren't setting themselves up as gurus, as far as I could tell. And no special blessing or permission was required in order to have these experiences.

Given that, the most important aspect of this journal entry is this is the first time I'd ever said "no thanks" to receiving a new practice from Steve. I had initially accepted his offer, and began the training. But, after a few weeks, it felt like I was banging my head against a wall and wasting my time.

Emailing him to say I wouldn't be continuing that particular practice was a way of releasing myself from the weight of an unspoken commitment I'd made to him and to the practice. That I ended up having an OBE the following day was a good sign that I'd made the right decision.

> February 10, 2015

> Early this morning, I went to the meditation area of my living room and fell back to sleep lying on the floor. I hadn't been doing much lucid dream training lately, so the following happened unexpectedly.

> This began as an ordinary dream. I was in a house, talking to a woman who looked like a 10-year-old girl. When I asked her if she really was only 10, she seemed offended and said it was only how she *appeared* to my eyes. Then a man appeared, who also resembled a child, and they climbed into two small cars, like go-carts.

> They put helmets on and raced around the house, somehow setting the curtains and furniture on fire. I saw the flames, and while waving my hands in downward strokes, I willed

the fire down lower and lower to the ground, *extinguishing it with my intention.*

Realizing what I was doing, I instantly became lucid. With increased awareness, I decided to prolong the dream by crouching down to touch the floor and touch it in order to feel more physical "input" from the dream, anchoring me there.

After a while, I stood up, and saw others entering the room. I felt sexual urges toward one of the women, which I think caused the experience to end at that point.

February 26, 2015
Dreamed I was with Steve and we were on a boat, manned by other community members. He wanted me to take over as captain for some reason. He also wanted me to treat the passengers the same way he did, which was aggressive and mean. I didn't want to do that, but he made me see that some individuals needed "firm instruction," otherwise they'd cause problems for everyone else.

Commentary: This is the first journal entry in which I criticize Steve's treatment of other people, calling him "aggressive and mean." By this point in time, I'd heard more reports of Steve being unkind to students and staff members. Sometimes, it happened behind closed doors, sometimes via email, and sometimes in front of everyone while the person was standing at the microphone.

I may have also been feeling guilty at this time because recently, Steve had me and another senior teacher talk to one of the junior teachers on his behalf. Steve was unhappy with how she was advertising herself online and representing his organization. Instead of speaking to her directly about it, he had us do it for him instead. It didn't feel good, or appropriate.

Sean McNamara

March 3, 2015

I've spent the last several afternoons doing OBE practice.
Last night, around 3:00, I moved to my training area and did
some reading for half an hour. Then, I lay down on the floor
and did affirmations as well as the target technique.
Eventually, I turned onto my side to fall asleep. At one point,
I became aware of intermittent surges in my skull. I lost
consciousness, but then became aware of the vibrational
state.

I floated up and completely surrendered control, allowing
something else to do the driving. Once I was sure I had been
taken to another place, I "opened my eyes" in order to see.
The vision was incredible.

The easiest way to describe it is to say this was as if God was
giving me a tour of other worlds. I was passing through outer
space and seeing planets I've never heard of before. There
were all of different sizes and strange, beautiful colors.
Oddly, they weren't in heliocentric formation, so there was
no way for me to possibly identify what I was looking at.

Then I decided to look at myself, so I stretched out my arms
in front of me. At first, they looked like dark silhouettes.
Then, sparkles of green light appeared all over them, and
through them. I turned my palms over to look at them,
wondering where the acupuncture point for healing energy
was located. As if to answer my question, the center of each
palm lit up with the same green light that was speckled
throughout my arms. But these particular lights, in the center
of each palm, were about the size of a quarter.

March 11, 2015

This morning, I went to my training area to practice sitting
meditation from 5:00 to 6:00, and then went back to sleep. I
dreamed I was standing next to a massive block of ice, about

190

the same size as a car. A group of people were sitting at a long table nearby, chatting with each other.

I spontaneously decided to "karate chop" the ice, and felt the physical impact on my hand. The onlookers began clapping and congratulating me, but I had doubts about whether I'd actually broken the ice or not. I took a close look and realized that my self-doubt was unfounded - I'd successfully broken the ice.

Commentary: This dream occurred around the time that Steve had contacted his most senior students, asking who among them would like to be considered for another level of training and empowerment. He wanted to know who was interested in becoming a lineage holder, which was a really big deal.

I would've jumped at this opportunity a year or two before, but now I wasn't so sure. Being a lineage holder meant becoming familiar with the full "menu" of practices Steve taught, then teaching them to others the same way he had. I wondered if this was how I wanted to spend all my available free time?

If I did, there certainly wouldn't be any time left to continue my other path, with OBEs, lucid dreams, and the other experiences I'd yet to have. I figured that it also meant a tight leash. He'd want us to do it a certain way, *his way*, and the margin for error would be miniscule.

Later that morning after the dream, I emailed Steve telling him that I did not want to become a lineage holder. The act of telling him that left me feeling free and at ease. I believe the dream of breaking the ice block either told me what I needed to hear in order to send the email, or simply reflected a decision I'd already made deep down inside.

Little did I know several months from now, I'd make an even more significant decision about Steve, his organization and community. Until then, though, there would be several more dreams and OBEs.

Sean McNamara

March 19, 2015

Got up around 2:45 am, then meditated for a while. Then, I lay down to do the 100-count technique. Unable to settle down all the way, I shifted into doing the target technique instead. Eventually, I rolled onto my side and drifted off.

Then, I felt the surges inside my skull, then the whole vibrational state, and I let the separation from the physical happen automatically, at its own speed. I "opened my eyes" to find myself standing outside a large, square-shaped house, with very tall walls.

I knew I was having an out of body experience, so I floated right through the door. The inside of the house looked very spacious, and the walls were lined with marble. Walking around, I found a man lying on the floor of the bathroom. He looked as if he was passed out, but I sensed dark emotions inside of him. Somehow, I was told he was "bad" and needed to be left alone. I faded out and came back to my body, opening my eyes.

Then, I drifted off to sleep, eventually reaching a dream state. In the dream, I was back in the same house I'd gone to during my OBE. I was lucid and very aware this was only a dream and that I hadn't left my body again.

This time though, Steve and several community members were inside. I approached him and told him that I'd just been in the house while in the out of body state. He responded with "She...has given you this gift." I knew he was referring to Vajrayogini, because he often spoke about how this tantric deity had the ability to create circumstances in our lives in order to help our spiritual growth.

Silently, I disagreed with him. I was confident that everything I'd experienced so far was a natural, intrinsic aspect of existence, available to any person, regardless of their spiritual or religious background. To me, it sounded like he was trying to color over my experience and take ownership of it, so that it would fit into *his* paradigm, *his* version of spirituality.

Commentary: In waking, physical reality, I still hadn't told Steve about my interest in, or success with, having out of body experiences. That was still to come.

June 4, 2015

Last night, I set an intention for that night's dreams. I wanted to know what my *true role in life* was. I've been more and more unhappy as a real estate agent; the work isn't a good fit for me on many levels. My inner connection to Steve and this lineage is weakening. Have I been wasting years of my life?

"Dear dreams, please tell me what my role is."

This is what I dreamed afterward. I was at a meditation retreat, and we were given a long liturgy to recite. The letters were in a language I've never seen before in waking life.

There were many people inside the shrine room, but I could hear a woman crying in another room, one of the offices. I found her, and asked her why she was crying.

She said she didn't want to do this practice or chant the liturgy. It felt too foreign, too complicated, and too much about something that had nothing to do with her actual life and spiritual path.

One of the staff members came into the office and asked her to return to her meditation cushion in the other room. I watched as she stood up and walked away obediently, with a sad look on her face.

Something came over me, and I stood up to go find her. I found her as she was sitting down on her cushion, and I leaned down to tell her that *she was right*, that all of this was wrong for her, and that she should leave. I repeated the fact that she was right, reiterating only she knew what was best for herself, not them.

A look of relief came over her face, and she was happy that someone else understood her, agreed with her, and supported her. And then she left.

Is this my role?

Commentary: Asking yourself, or your guides, or anything/anyone else, or your dreams directly to bring you information in the dream state is a technique called "dream incubation." In my opinion, it works best when you have a real need, an emotional desire for the answer, guidance, or whatever ideas you're seeking. The answers might come from your subconscious mind, or they might come from somewhere, or someone else. Finding out for yourself is part of the learning process. As I wrote before, there's no dogma here.

June 18, 2015

Dreamt that I was at a retreat center in a city I've never been before in waking reality. Steve was there with a handful of students.

I approached him, then began to tell him that I was leaving, and would no longer be one of his students. Before I could finish the sentence, the dream got interrupted and I woke up.

Commentary: The day after I recorded this dream, I emailed Steve's assistant to make an appointment to see him in person. I was finally going to do what I've been putting off for months now. Unfortunately, the assistant said he was traveling overseas at that time, so I wouldn't be able to see him for a while, after he returned.

CHAPTER 20 LEAVING MY TEACHER

Later that summer, I finally got my appointment with Steve. I'd been thinking about leaving for months, and I could've done it sooner with a simple phone call or by emailing him, since he was traveling so much. But it was important for me to do it in person. I had many dreams over the years, mostly unrecorded, in which I ran away from a frightening dream character. Sometimes, though, I stood my ground. I would only have one chance in life to say goodbye face-to-face with Steve, and to be completely honest about why I was leaving. I needed to face my fear this time, instead of turning my back.

And I owed it to him. He'd been my teacher for many years, and many good things had come out of it. He introduced me to the joy of teaching, and that led to many wonderful experiences leading programs at the retreat center and guiding my students in Denver. It hadn't all been bad.

I drove to his home, and we sat down at his dining room table. I remember the sunlight coming in through the large, panoramic windows. He didn't know why I'd asked for a meeting, and he seemed happy to see me. He probably thought I wanted to talk about meditation, or an idea for leading another group retreat.

I'd heard enough stories about him blowing up at students when he felt challenged or contradicted, so I felt nervous and scared, not knowing exactly how to begin. On the fly, I decided to offer him some backstory first. I talked about my life-long fear of death, and how it eventually led me to study Buddhism, leading up to becoming

Sean McNamara

his student. I also talked about how, even though I'd learned a lot about Buddhism, I still hadn't found substantial answers to my particular questions about life, death, and reality.

"So I decided to try something different. I had this idea that if I could have an out of body experience, then I'd know for sure that I wouldn't completely disappear when I died. And about a year and a half ago, it finally happened." I smiled weakly, waiting for his response.

"Was it drugs?"

His first response told me enough to feel confident that I'd made the right decision to leave. It was clear that he didn't know what I was talking about. I assumed he would though, because of certain "advanced" Tibetan practices I'd believed he was familiar with. Maybe I was wrong.

I was also wary of his use of the word "drugs." I remembered an old friend who either got kicked out of the community or left on his own (perhaps there'd been an ultimatum) after telling Steve about his interest in using ayahuasca[14] as a spiritual modality. Steve was strongly against his students using entheogenic plants, even if it was something shamans and aboriginal people across the world had done for thousands of years. I think he didn't like the competition.

"No, I figured it out on my own, and I'm not afraid of death anymore."

Note: Before I continue describing what happened next, I must be honest and say I didn't record the conversation in writing afterward. I'm piecing sentences together from memory. The exact words are gone, but I still remember what was said.

---

[14] Ayahuasca is a South American brew made from several plants, and whose active ingredient is Dimethyltryptamine (DMT). It causes one to enter an altered state of awareness, with the potential for spiritual revelation, healing, and other kinds of experiences.

"I'm not sure about this path anymore, and I don't think it's helping me. But more than that, things have changed. I remember when you left [the other organization], we were this little group and we were all so connected to each other. You really cared about us individually."

As I think back, I can't even remember the expression on his face as I continued. But clearly, this wasn't the kind of meeting he'd been expecting.

"I think you're more concerned with the organization these days than with the actual students."

So far, so good. He hadn't stopped me yet, but his eyebrows were lifting in concern. I wondered if I was hurting his feelings. But I had to keep going, without holding anything back.

"And you're *hurting* people. I don't think what happened with me and Trish was fair. And I've heard from other students and the staff, you're acting more and more aggressive."

Now his eyebrows revered course, and they pointed downward toward the bridge of his nose. He was getting angry. It was time for me to finish up.

"I don't think what you're doing is right, and I don't know what to do about it, but I know that I'm done. I've received so much from you over the years. Thank you. But I can't be your student anymore, I can't support this organization anymore."

I paused, hoping for the best. I wanted to stand up, but my legs felt like jelly, and he still had his turn to respond.

"Sean! How can you say this? Don't you understand that we need an organization to make this work?" I thought I'd made the point that my issue was about students being deprioritized, and it seemed he was coming back from a different angle

And then came the sentence that confirmed my decision to leave, "How can you say that I'm hurting anyone? I'm not hurting anybody! Don't you see? *You're believing your own thoughts*, you're being judgmental."

Over the years, he'd given teachings about how the conceptual mind is a poor model for reality, and as such, led to much of people's internal suffering. When someone judged someone else, or a situation, they were apparently doing it from their "ego's" point of view, and so the judgement was never to be trusted. Believing one's own conceptual thoughts was antithetical to seeing "reality."

There was never much talk about common sense or using one's discernment wisely. It was usually an open ended "Never judge....." kind of message. And now, he was telling me that I was judging him, and that my viewpoint was flawed.

"Why can't you see that? You need to see things *my way*." His voice was stern, concerned, but he wasn't yelling.

And that was it, now I was really done. He was asking me to set aside everything I'd seen and heard, and realize that I was wrong and he was right, that he was treating people appropriately and nothing wrong was happening. If he was a regular guy off the street, his response would have far less weight than it actually did.

But he wasn't just a guy off the street. He was the head of the lineage, the guru. The implication, taught across many, if not all, Tibetan Buddhist traditions, is that *the guru is always right,* and the teacher's view is aligned with ultimate reality. Everyone beneath him is just confused, egotistical, and judgmental, albeit trying to improve themselves on the path of dharma.

There was a time when I thought the same thing. I'd been a true believer, a committed student, a serious disciple. I'd bought into the age-old propaganda, if you join the lineage, ask for the guru's blessing, and do the "advanced" practices, you'll reach enlightenment in one lifetime.

But I didn't believe it anymore, at least where he was concerned. He was an excellent meditation teacher, no one could argue that. But he was also a terrible administrator, had control issues, and responded poorly to criticism. The community had become an organization. It had become his business, his sole source of income, and his legacy. And it seemed to me like that was his ultimate priority.

But he isn't an enlightened being. He is just a man who enjoys power.

"I'm not going to ignore what I've seen, Steve. I'm not going to pretend nothing's wrong. I have to go."

In a flash, I remembered everything I'd heard over the years from students, senior teachers, and even the executive members of his staff. He had a way, a power, to convince people to see things from his point of view, and it was almost beginning to work on me now. I summoned the memories to be sure I wasn't making anything up, and to help me stand my ground.

We both stood up. I can't remember if we bowed to each other or not, though it would've been a natural thing for us to do, even in this awkward and painful moment.

I took a couple of steps toward the door, and then heard Steve's voice behind me.

"Wait!"

I stepped back, walking closer to hear what he had to say.

"Can we agree to leave the door open?"

I could tell that saying goodbye was really hard for him. He had sounded angry and frustrated less than a minute ago. But now, his voice was soft, and tender.

"Sure," I replied, saying something that could never be true. I simply felt bad for him at that moment. He seemed happy to hear me agree to leave the door open, that this might not really be "goodbye." We gave each other a hug, and then I left.

I drove back to Denver, mostly in shock. I was done, free, and on my own. No more guru, no one to tell me where I could find enlightenment, or any kind of spiritual fulfillment for that matter. I no longer represented him, his teachings, or his organization.

I felt sad, though. I knew that I'd hurt his feelings. He really believed that he hadn't hurt anyone, and my words must've felt like an unfair accusation. I knew what a terrible feeling that was. How it truly felt for him, I'll never know.

But, even though he appeared soft and sad at the very end, I knew he was likely to continue hurting other people. This form of hurt wasn't something illegal. His actions were emotional, psychological, and difficult to pin down. It was the kind of stuff you can't arrest the perpetrator for, but which still produces victims.

I knew that no one would be able to change him, or stop him from trampling over another person. But that person, a student, staff member, or teacher who realized they were being treated badly could still get out of the way, and leave. As I had. I realized that I probably wasn't the first to do this. I remembered others who'd quietly left in the middle of a retreat, or who simply stopped showing up. No, I wasn't the first.

Unfortunately, even though I was out of the way, I soon realized I wasn't out of his reach. A couple weeks later, people began contacting me asking about a strange email Steve had sent out. Some were my current students in the Denver group, and others were people I hadn't talked to in years. It seemed like Steve must've asked a staffer to go through old registration lists to make sure this letter reached anyone in Colorado I'd ever met.

It was a smear campaign, and a cover-up. The first paragraph reads, "[Sean] expressed that he feels our lineage and community are no longer helpful to him in his own journey." That was a lie.

If this was an honest letter, it would've said "He expressed concerns about Steve's personal treatment of some of his students and staff members. He is also concerned that Steve has placed the organization's priorities over those of his students, which is incongruous with an authentic student-teacher relationship."

The letter went on to say they'd be sending someone down to Denver soon to replace me as the leader of my group, and those who wanted more support from the organization could contact them directly, that my students would be welcomed to continue on underneath Steve's.

I was shocked to read it, and angry. Most of my students had never been to one of the organization's retreats or even met Steve in person. Their relationship had always been solely with me. And our group met regularly inside of Mayu Sanctuary, *my wife's meditation center*. Did he really think they could just send someone over to take my place?

The arrogant, aggressive and territorial nature of the letter left me upset, and worried. I remembered the times when Steve would address a room full of meditators to explain why someone had left, or why someone was "taking some time away." I realized that his version of the facts was probably untrue. Now that I was the most recent escapee, what stories would he tell them in my absence?

Fortunately, my students could tell something was iffy here, and they didn't ask me to explain it. But, I needed to tell them something. I knew I had to be careful. I didn't know how far this man was willing to go once he felt threatened or abandoned. Would he lash out again? What else would he do?

Initially, all I allowed myself to tell them was that I'd observed things within the organization which concerned me, and which I couldn't support any longer. Eventually, I told them a bit more, including the

Sean McNamara

fact that I'd realized, through teaching myself how to leave my body, that the guru-disciple model was a power-and-control mechanism more than anything else, at least with Steve, and I couldn't allow it into my life anymore.

I told them I would continue teaching, but would no longer use a shrine, the liturgies, or anything else that was connected to his organization or the tradition. But if they felt they wanted to stay connected with Steve's group and leave mine, I would respect their decision.

The idea of controlling people had never been on my radar until now, and I was extremely cautious about doing anything to influence people's decisions. I felt free, and I wanted them to feel free too, even if it meant no longer meditating with me.

Some left, still wanting to pursue the path structure that Steve had created over the years. Most stayed, usually with the same remark, "I'm here because of *us*, because of our group, *not* because of him!"

CHAPTER 21 DISSOLVING CONTROL SYSTEMS

While I continued teaching meditation with my Denver group, I had to strip a lot of things away. The chanting, incense, making offerings to statues, and even bowing to each other...I discarded all of it. I still loved meditation because ultimately, a good meditation technique offers a way for someone to look directly at their mind, which is both the projector and receptor of his or her life experience.

Over time, I'd read enough books on psychology, behavioral economics and environmental influence to learn how symbols and rituals had a direct impact on people's beliefs, values, and behaviors.

When a student and teacher bow their heads to each other, is it truly on equal footing, a sign of mutual respect? What if the teacher is sitting *just a little bit higher*, on some type of pedestal, chair, or throne? Could there be a subconscious affect upon the students, causing them to unknowingly surrender their ability to think independently, behave freely, and retain their own authority?

The rituals and chants, did they really do anything to help people meditate? Or did these activities create the facade of spiritual transformation? I realized the framed portraits of teachers hanging on the walls of the various retreat centers I'd seen over the years had a subconscious effect on people. Many of the daily chants and sadhanas included "supplications" to these figures, praying for their blessings. Combined, these symbols and activities trained people to think the teacher on the pedestal *has what you need*, and they are of a higher position than you in life.

For me, the meditation practices of simply looking at one's mind could set one free by de-conditioning the mind, reducing its emotional reactivity, and finding peace. But the extraneous rituals, gestures and images did the opposite. They conditioned, or *programmed* a person's mind by imprinting a spiritual self-image, such as "I'm a yogi," "I'm a tantric practitioner," "I'm part of a special lineage," or "I'm a student of so-and-so."

Of course, this isn't limited to Tibetan Buddhism. It's in every religion, because religions are not necessarily genuinely, spiritually transformative structures. Their main scope is usually about social organization and political oversight.

It was a difficult adjustment for the Denver group, and I wondered sometimes if I was being extreme. Maybe I shouldn't have taken the rituals away from them. Maybe that's why some of them left. But I still had to do it. The plain fact was that for some reason, every time I looked at something that reminded me of Steve, a jolt of adrenaline would shoot through my veins, and anxiety would fill my mind.

Months later, I dissolved the group. Even though I'd done away with Steve's rituals, getting together every Sunday night to meditate still reminded me of the man. But, just as importantly, I found out by talking to some of the group members that most of them weren't even meditating at home. Our Sunday night meditations had become what Sunday mass is for many Catholics. It was their one hour of concentrated spiritual practice for the week.

I just didn't have enough in me anymore to keep the group going. I wanted to work with people who meditate consistently, in a serious way, so that real transformation could occur, instead of just paying it lip service. There were only a handful of people like that in the group, and I knew that they had the inner-compass and self-motivation to find their own way even after I stopped leading the group.

Today, I can look back and admit that more than anything, I was frustrated, confused and sad. By leaving Steve, I'd also lost most of my closest friends, the ones who were part of his community from its earliest days. Losing all my friends at the same time was something I was familiar with while growing up, but it didn't feel any easier.

Aside from losing a path, a teacher, and my oldest friends, I was also surrendering my titles, like "senior teacher" and "meditation instructor." I didn't mind the loss though. In fact, it was an immense relief. I had no idea how much influence these titles had over my identity. I realized *giving a spiritual seeker a special title is probably the most damaging thing you can do to them*, because it makes them think they've finally gotten somewhere.

I don't want to carry Steve or Rinpoche along with me for the rest of this book. I have other things to share with you, the reader, and it's time for me to let this go. I'll cut those cords now by bringing this part of my story to a close.

Sometime before writing this book, multiple accusations of sexual assault and abuse were brought against Rinpoche. The incident with Andrea was relatively mild compared to what he'd done with many other women over the years, and now they were going public. Eventually, he sold some of his properties and fled to India.

Today, his organization still operates in centers around the world, of course. The many complicit teachers, administrators and instructors left behind still have their own identities and titles to defend. I think it's likely he'll return one day, since people tend to have short attention spans these days, and forget things easily.

As for Steve, reports of a different kind of harm, psychological and emotional in nature, were made public by a small, courageous group of ex-students. Their letter was intended as a warning to anyone thinking about joining the group. Soon after, and emboldened by the initial report, more and more ex-students and ex-staffers shared similar accounts of mistreatment online and in private correspondence. My case was very mild compared to theirs. I was glad to know *I wasn't making things up* that day when I told him I was leaving.

CHAPTER 22 MIND OVER MATTER

Leaving Steve, then dissolving my own group in Denver had the wonderful effect of giving me back a lot of that invaluable resource, time. It gave me the mental space to look backward and reflect on my dreams, out of body experiences, and things I'd never experienced before, like hearing Carol's voice inside my head after she'd died.

I thought, perhaps naively, that eliminating my fear of death through consciously leaving my body would be the end of my journey, mission accomplished. But it was only the beginning.

I began to read a lot more, and spent time browsing in bookstores and libraries every week, especially the sections labeled "Metaphysics," "Ancient Mysteries," and "Spirituality." Too many years had passed since I'd ventured into these genres. Since I'd read just about every book on OBEs I could get my hands on, I decided to widen my scope and learn about other kinds of experiences.

I started with some of the classics. Raymond Moody's "Life After Life," of course, was required reading, especially since he's the one who coined the phrase "near death experience." Bill and Judy Guggenheim's "Hello from Heaven" came next, since it covered "after-death communication." I often thought about that afternoon when I heard Carol, who I didn't know had already died, talking to me inside my head. From reading about "ADCs" I realized this kind of thing happens all the time. I also read "The Dead Are Alive," by Harold Sherman, which seemed like a natural pairing to "Hello from Heaven."

Claudia, from one of the online OBE forums, recommended "Testimony of Light" by Helen Greaves. It's a record of telepathic communications between the author and her dear friend, Frances Banks, after Greaves had died.

I also began to watch YouTube videos featuring subject matter experts in the field of the afterlife. One day, I watched a presentation by a woman named Cherylee Black at the 2014 conference for the International Association for Near Death Studies, also known as "IANDS". Her presentation was entitled "My NDEs, After Effects, and What I'm Doing About Them Now."[15]

In it, she described three different near death experiences she'd had at different stages of her life. She was also able to see lights around people, have out of body experiences, and produce RSPK, or "recurrent, spontaneous psychokinesis." These were poltergeist-like effects during which objects would move, sometimes violently across a room. As part of her process to understand these phenomena, she began to explore "non-spontaneous psychokinesis", meaning that she learned how to move objects with her mind *on purpose*.

As she described her research, a video played on the screen behind her. In it, a pin-wheel constructed of tin foil and balanced atop a needle was rotating. Her hand was nearby, apparently producing the effect. To show that this wasn't simply the effect of heat or wind, she placed a glass jar over the pin-wheel and was still able to produce the movement.

I was captivated. I hadn't had an NDE, but I'd certainly left my body many times by having OBEs. I wondered if I could do psychokinesis like Cherylee.

One thing I loved about my OBEs was *they were mine*, and had nothing to do with the two teachers I'd left behind. I learned the techniques, practiced as much as I could, and worked through all the kinks and obstacles I encountered along the way. Eventually, I succeeded, and no one could ever take them away from me.

---

[15] Find the link to this video at www.RenegadeMysticBook.com/links

I told my Denver group just a little bit about my OBEs, but I knew it would be hard for some of them to believe me. To be honest, I worried that they might think I was beginning to lose my mind. And, it wasn't the kind of thing I could just *show* them. But telekinesis was different. It was objective in that, unlike OBEs, other people in the room would be able to see the effect of my intention by watching a physical object move.

Cherylee's video was only the first of many I'd find online, of people exhibiting telekinesis. For example, I also watched black and white footage of the Russian psychic Nina Kulagina taken during the Cold War. Most recently, a man named Trebor Seven had a whole YouTube channel dedicated to the topic, in which he demonstrated his abilities.[16]

Telekinesis *is a real thing*, I realized. And it was the kind of thing I could show to other people standing in a room with me. If I could demonstrate telekinesis, then I could inspire and educate all kinds of people, and encourage them to see that they are more than just blood and bone. They could know they are a non-physical consciousness, and they're as essential to this universe as anybody else.

I set up a little telekinesis practice area in our living room, the same place where I'd learned to leave my body. But now, I'd stay *in* my body, wide awake, while some non-physical part of me, perhaps my mind, reached across space to move a physical object in front of me.

It was a simple setup. I found an old pink eraser in a desk drawer, and stuck a sewing needle into it, with the sharp end pointing up. Then, I folded a piece of tinfoil, leaving a rounded crease to keep it from getting pinched on the needle. Finally, I put a large, glass flower vase over it to prevent any air movement.

I wasn't interested in fooling myself, and I knew that I needed to be careful. Most of the alleged telekinesis videos I'd found on YouTube

---

[16] Find the link to videos of Nina Kulagina and Trebor Seven at www.RenegadeMysticBook.com/links

were, in my opinion, made by people who were either fooling themselves or worse, trying to fool the public. If they were fooling themselves, how were they doing it? Was it really that difficult to distinguish wind currents from whatever psychic force was involved?

That wouldn't be a significant question until much later on. For now, my only goal was to make that little piece of tinfoil move. Somehow, something had to happen between me and *it*, something with enough energy to push it, perhaps. I really had no idea how to do this yet.

At first, I'd sit down in front of the flower vase a couple times a week and just stare at the tinfoil. Sometimes I'd try to "push" it with my mind, which is something difficult to describe. It's easier if I suggest to you, the reader, to stare at that cup or pen or whatever else is in front of you and *will* it to move. Demand it. Push it, shove it, or silently yell at it, even. See if anything happens that way. That approach didn't work for me, and fortunately, I didn't spend too much time on it.

I found a video by Trebor Seven, in which he described how, whenever he wanted to do a "pull," meaning to make a standing piece of tinfoil fall toward him, he would inhale a certain way then hold his breath to make it fall.

Hearing him describe his process made something click inside my mind, and I realized that he was essentially describing a rudimentary form of what I recognized as "pranayama," from my meditation training.

Various meditation traditions across the world seem to agree on a particular concept regarding the breath. Everyone is aware of the physical breath, exchanging oxygen for carbon dioxide as we inhale and exhale. Then, there is the "prana," also referred to as "chi" in Chinese, or more generally as "life force" in English. Just as oxygen flows through every blood vessel, subtle energy flows through every subtle channel, or meridian, in the body.

Sean McNamara

By paying attention to one's physical breath, a person can tune in to his or her subtle breath. The simple act of paying attention can affect it in certain ways, such as to intensify its sensation, or to send it to specific parts of the body, which is often done for healing purposes by energy workers.

Related to that, the quality of this energy, how it moves, feels, and whether it's clear or stale, has a direct effect on a person's mind. If one's energy is lethargic, it can make a person sleepy or distracted while trying to meditate, or even when performing at work or driving a car.

Much of my prior meditation training had to do with meditating by focusing on various parts of the physical body, as well as on the chakras, the subtle energy centers inside the body. Anyone who focuses on a specific part of his or her body while "breathing into it" will soon notice an increase of energy flow to that location.

Briefly put, *energy flows to wherever a person places their attention for a sustained period of time.*

And that's what clicked for me. I asked myself, "Why not treat that little piece of tinfoil *out there* the same way I would treat a chakra *in here*, inside my body, and see if that does anything?" I decided to make this my new meditation.

For nearly two and a half months, I'd spend anywhere from 20 minutes to an hour, almost every day of the week, experimenting with different breathing styles while staring at the piece of tinfoil, which I referred to as "the object." And all that time, it just sat there, refusing to move.

Then one night, I went to bed, and something strange happened while trying to fall asleep. The room was dark and my eyes were closed, but an image of the object arose inside my mind. It was turning on the needle, the way I imagined it eventually would during my daily training sessions.

210

This image was spontaneous. I didn't plan on it, and much as I tried, I couldn't stop it. It was like a movie being projected to the area inside my forehead. Minutes later, the moving image disappeared on its own.

The following day, I sat down to give it another go. After taking some time to relax my body and center my mind, I set my intention and settled in for another staring contest. But a few minutes later, the object finally began to turn.

I felt like a little boy as I went to the kitchen to find Cierra, blurting out, "I did it!" Ever the supportive partner, she responded with, "I knew you would!" How often had she woken up in the middle of the night, alone in bed, realizing that I was in another room, struggling to achieve an OBE? She never complained, knowing how important it was to me.

Now, I'd been spending many hours over many days, weeks and months, seated alone in another room, trying to project my energy, mind, or whatever else may be involved across a distance in order to nudge a tiny piece of aluminum. Other people might have suspected insanity, or that this was some form of unhealthy obsession, like Richard Dreyfuss' character Roy in the movie "Close Encounters of the Third Kind." But not Cierra. She was open, patient, curious, and always respectful. She was kinder to me than I was to myself.

The next few months, I focused on two goals. First, I wanted to improve my ability. Second, I needed to make sure this was the *real thing*, a truly psychic effect. I was vigilant about static, making sure the table and glass were always free of dust, and that I never wore clothing, such as long sleeved sweaters, which could produce a static field that would attract the object.

I'd seen enough videos of other people waving their hands near their object as it danced and wobbled in response. They were sure it was telekinesis, but I think anyone else could plainly see this was just static electricity.

Sean McNamara

Over time, I realized that if I used the same piece of tin foil over and over again, I could get it to move sooner at the start of each session, and with less effort. It would also react more specifically to my breathing pattern. For example, after getting it to turn, I could hold my breath and shift my mental state, and the object would come to a halt. Then, exhaling slowly, it would begin moving again, but in the opposite direction. Or, if I changed the speed of my breathing, the object's speed changed with it.

I was as if the object had its own memory, or as if *we'd formed a relationship.*

As time passed, I became more proficient at affecting the object. I'd started off by having my hands an inch or two away from the glass, thinking that some kind of energy was emanating from my palms to push on the object. But eventually, I could leave my hands in my lap and still move it with my mind.

I reached a point where I could scooch back in my seat a foot or two and still get it to move. Eventually, I tried standing up and taking a few steps further back. If I moved away too far, too quickly, it was as if an invisible link had been broken, and it would stop. But if I stayed present, moving away slowly and only when it really felt like we were connected, the effect would continue.

One evening, I had the intention of going to my training area to spend some time with the piece of tinfoil, whom I'd named "Tinny." This little thing had become a friend of sorts. I entered the room and saw Tinny there, across the way, under the glass, waiting for me as usual. Then, as I took another step toward it, it moved, so that one end of it pointed right at me. I seemed as if it was looking at me, like it *knew* I was in the room.

There were other anomalies too. For example, sometimes I'd spend a half-hour seated in front of Tinny, who refused to move no matter what I tried. Frustrated and exhausted, I'd turn my head in resignation, intending to stand up and go do something else for a while. Then, in that moment, *when I'd just given up,* Tinny would begin a nice full turn on the needle. This happened often enough for me

212

to realize that by giving up my effort, by surrendering, something got out of the way. For lack of a better word, it was my ego. I'd prevented anything from happening by trying too hard.

Sometimes, after sitting there for 30 or 40 minutes without success, I'd begin to daydream, or drift toward sleep. By now I'd been meditating for nearly half of my life, so I was familiar with the mental drift that can happen when concentrating for too long. I began to notice that oftentimes, it was at this very moment of slipping into daydreaming when Tinny would begin to respond. I realized the key to affecting Tinny was found through relaxation, not exertion.

Eventually, I was able to refine my technique until I could move Tinny with confidence, on demand, and repeatedly. I created a formula for myself, which I called "TRIAM," meaning that the combination of time, relaxation (mental and physical), intention, and how one paid attention to Tinny would result in movement.

The first four variables, time, relaxation, intention and attention, were common elements in meditation. But telekinesis was different because of the resulting movement of an external, physical object. In a sense, Tinny served as a simple biofeedback device. If I was patient and relaxed enough, and paid attention properly, Tinny would move. But, if any one of those qualities were missing, or there was too much tension, Tinny would stop.

After teaching ordinary meditation to a variety of people over the years, I knew the number one reason why people quit meditation is because of the boredom, and the inability to tell whether they're doing it right or not. I realized that telekinesis could offer a solution.

Telekinesis was a form of meditation, but its value lay in that a person could easily tell if they were doing it right or not, by how the object moved. And, it was intriguing enough to keep the meditator from becoming bored, as often happens while focusing on one's breath for a long period of time in common forms of mindfulness training.

I realized that I was thinking like a meditation teacher again. I loved teaching. I felt an urge to introduce telekinesis to people who didn't already know about it (it turns out that most people still don't know about it). One day, I went to an electronics store and bought a cheap little digital camera. That night, I hung up a wide piece of black cloth in the hallway, set the video camera on a tripod, and started talking.

Once the video was finished[17], I created a YouTube channel to host it, along with a website. I chose the domain "MindPossible.com," inspired by leaving the well-worn paths I'd adopted earlier in life, and eventually doing things which most people thought were impossible. The entire universe is experienced within one's mind. All possibilities are there, within it, waiting for us. Yet, as long as we keep your attention where other people tell us to look, we'll never see them.

Going public about my telekinesis experiences added a whole new dimension to my journey, specifically, that of dealing with other people's opinions. Naively, or stupidly, I thought I'd hear from people happy to see my work, and interested in learning how to do this themselves. And there was some of that.

For a long time, though, most of the emails and video comments I read came from trolls, pseudo-skeptics, and frightened religious people. I can't count the number of times I had to endure accusations of fraud or that I was summoning demons and doing the devil's work.

By then, I'd read enough books on parapsychology and quantum physics to understand that telekinesis was simply the "observer effect" in action. Scientists had already done experiments determining that subatomic particles like photons and electrons behaved differently when a human was paying attention to them. It was clear to many of them that consciousness had an impact on how these tiny particles moved, and they could measure and record these effects.

---

[17] Find this video at www.RenegadeMysticBook.com/videos

Telekinesis isn't a religious matter, and has nothing to do with "good versus evil." And, it isn't fraud. But it didn't take me long to realize that it was impossible to convert, convince, or argue with anybody on the internet. Eventually, I learned about the "backfire effect" from a variety of psychology books, and realized the reason these online debates were usually fruitless.

Simply put, the *backfire effect* means that when people are presented with evidence which contradicts one of their beliefs, they tend to double-down on their belief instead of correct their thinking in light of the new information. It's one of those stupid things that humans do, probably some kind of survival mechanism embedded into our very thick skulls.

I made it a policy to stop arguing with people and ignore them instead. It worked. Without anything to push against, the online attackers got bored and went away to find other people to bother.

I also made it a policy to prevent bullying on my YouTube channel. Bullying me was one thing, but it was especially upsetting to see an adult viewer skewering a child who'd posted a supportive, positive and optimistic comment about telekinesis. It was also difficult to see children being cruel to other children. I figured since I wasn't the government, and none of them were my children, I was under no obligation to allow their hurtful behavior on my channel.

But sometimes, comments came across as a healthy challenge or an innocent question, like "Is that all you can do?" and "Can you move anything else?"

I asked myself the same questions, and began to train myself further to expand my ability. Over time, I succeeded at moving two or three objects at the same time, either all inside the same container, or separately, and even from across the room.

A piece of paper the same size as tinfoil weighed about three times as much, but I eventually succeeded in moving that too. To challenge myself further, I glued two toothpicks to a piece of heavy

seansokok

paper so I could balance them on the needle. After many attempts and a lot of frustration, I succeeded at moving them too.[18]

But I wanted to look ahead, and see if anything really big was possible. I remembered Nina Kulagina and the black and white footage of her moving toothpicks, salt shakers and heavier objects across the surface of a table.

I wanted to learn more about her, and obtained a copy of "Psychic Discoveries Behind the Iron Curtain," an important reference about paranormal abilities, published in 1970. In it, I learned her feats would occur over an eight-hour period, exhausting her completely and causing detrimental effects to her body. Her heart would race, and after weighing her at the end of the day, the scientists saw that she'd somehow lost several pounds of body weight. Eventually, she died of a heart attack.

On YouTube, I found videos of a young Turkish man named Fade Mir who also displayed powerful abilities, such as knocking over a pack of cigarettes from across the room. One day late in 2017, I read the sad announcement on his Facebook page he'd suddenly died of a heart attack or some kind of aneurysm, or both. I had to translate the comments posted beneath his most recent videos from Turkish to English to understand what had happened.

Remembering their deaths was enough to caution me against pushing myself during my telekinesis training. Kulagina and Mir's videos clearly show them *physically straining* to move their objects. My technique went in the opposite direction. I relied on a deep state of relaxation in order to aid consciousness and the transmission of energy, or information, or whatever was really happening, to produce the effect.

Still, there were many times when I ran out of patience while filling up with frustration, and I'd I suddenly find myself straining, just like Kulagina and Mir, in complete contradiction of my own TRIAM

---

[18] For this and a selection of other of my telekinesis videos, visit
www.RenegadeMysticBook.com/videos
216

instructions. At a certain point, I would feel an uncomfortable pressure in the center of my chest, whether inside or around my heart, I'm not sure.

Whether the discomfort was physical, energetic, or psychological didn't matter to me. Given my medical history, especially the fact that I'd already undergone a heart procedure, I wasn't willing to risk having another one, or worse, dying. Eventually, I had to ask myself, "When does it end? When is it enough?"

Since I decided to stop going heavier, I wondered if I could go in a different direction. I looked for new books, hoping to find one written by a telekinetic psychic willing to share his or her techniques. Many authors have written excellent instruction manuals for having an out of body experience. So, I thought surely there must be an author who was equally clear, specific, and effective at teaching someone how to have other types of experiences, especially on the topic of mind-over-matter. If there was, I wouldn't have to reinvent the wheel.

Most of the books I found were concerned with psychic perception, such as clairvoyance, or mediumship, and I wasn't interested in those topics at the time. That would change later on, of course. At this point, I was only interested in good instructions for how to do psychokinesis.

One book had a back cover with a description which included words like "invaluable advice," "secrets," "lessons," and "exercises." I bought it right away, hoping it contained the elusive instructions I'd been looking for.

I took it home and read it in a single sitting. I turned each page hoping to read something along the lines of "first you do this, then you do that ..." But there was no such page. There were no instructions, no practical advice. Only stories. The book was an opportunity for the author to brag about his experiences on and off the stage. He was a performer. I realized that he was more than likely a magician, and that everything he did was some form of an illusion, a trick. In my opinion, the book was nothing more than advertising to help his career. I became angry for being deceived, and because the book I was looking for didn't seem to exist.

So, I decided to write the book myself, to write the very book that I'd been looking for. Of course, I couldn't write about how to do things I hadn't done myself, but I knew that there were people out there in the world who were starting from nothing, and wanted to do what I was able to do by that point in time.

That's when I wrote "Defy Your Limits: The Telekinesis Training Method," which took the reader step-by-step through the TRIAM method.[19] Each chapter included links to videos I'd created so that people could actually watch what I was describing in my writing. I wanted my book to be everything that the stage performer's book wasn't. I wanted to inspire and inform people without holding anything back. No secrets, no prerequisites, and unlike so many spiritual traditions, no special permissions or blessings were required.

As I improved my telekinetic ability, I realized I needed to write a second book to share the new experiments. I wrote "Meditation X: Telekinesis," in which I propose telekinesis is a valid and productive form of meditation and worthy of consideration by a wider audience. It also teaches the reader how to move multiple objects in multiple containers, how to move an object from another room while using video conferencing applications like Skype and Zoom, and more.

My videos and books attracted more attention from the public, and I would eventually receive invitations to give interviews and conference presentations, and to be included in a TV show and a movie project, "Super Human: The Invisible Made Visible," by Caroline Cory.

I was happy to share my experiences through these formats, and optimistic that more people out there could discover and explore

---

[19] Find the link to this book at www.RenegadeMysticBook.com/links or at www.MindPossible.com

their inherent abilities. Maybe others were looking for a new way to empower themselves.

At the same time, something entirely different was going on *in here*, inside of me. My perspective was slowly and gently becoming altered, and I don't know if I was doing this myself, or if other forces were involved. In fact, I wasn't fully aware of what was happening to me until I reviewed my old journals in the process of writing this book. I believe that some of the changes are reflected in a few of the dreams and out of body experiences I had in the years surrounding this time in my life.

CHAPTER 23 FURTHER EVOLUTION

September 9, 2015

Dreamt that I was part of a special event, helping or watching people go into what I initially interpreted to be a spaceship. But then I came to understand the scene differently. These people were climbing a structure resembling a staircase, one that was physically part of this world.

But, after reaching a certain point on the stairs, the people disappeared completely. This staircase was some kind of junction point to, or with, a different dimension. This junction point was a place where this world and another occupied the same place. Within this point, the two worlds became transparent to each other.

Somehow I knew this was a planned event. Two gateways had been brought into coincidence so people could pass through it. I didn't see any aliens, which makes me think I was incorrect to interpret the structure to be a spaceship.

Interestingly, the concept of coinciding a specific point here in this physical world with a point in another world for the purpose of creating a passage is not an idea I've ever conceived on my own. And there was never a reason why I would purposely think of such a thing. But now, I'm reminded of the movie "Otherworld" by Freddy Silva, where he explores stone doorways around the world, doorways that lead to nothing.

The scenes from the movie don't match my dream in any way at all, but I wonder if there's a link. Have there ever, or will there ever be a way to join two worlds at a specific location, creating a passageway across space and, perhaps, time?

October 7, 2015

Two dreams. In the first, I was in a room containing an aquarium. I opened the cover, and two exotic fish, angelfish to be exact, floated out of the tank and up into the air. I had to hold on to their long belly fins as if they were balloon strings. After a while, I pulled them down, close to the water, and they went back inside.

In the second dream, I was visiting Grampa. I couldn't tell if Granny was there. This wasn't their house, though, it was a house I'd never been in before. Jen, and Ma, and maybe Dad were there too. Grampa was acting grumpy and mean.

December 9

Playing catch-up. For the last few months, I've stopped reading about OBEs or training for them. Instead, I've been working on telekinesis, with very real success. One side effect from the TK work is an increase in an energized state during naps and during the hypnopompic state (waking up). It's not quite the vibrational state, at least as I've experienced it in the past.

It could be a new aspect of that state, or something totally new, I don't know. Needless to say, what happened last night was completely unexpected. Just to note it in case it makes a difference, Cierra and I split a full bottle of saké with dinner last night, so I was very tired.

At some point, time unknown, I emerged from a dream state and became aware that I was in the vibrational state. I was so tired; it was easy for me to remain calm and passive while

221

it happened. Slowly, gently, I coaxed my awareness out by repeating "Up, up ..." and then felt the familiar sensation of drifting out beyond the physical boundaries of my body.

I came into an environment I can only describe as being completely filled with a beautifully rich blue color, in the form of rays resembling countless laser beams. I had no sense of bodily form or shape. Still, I felt a profound sense of wellbeing. It was sublime. It only lasted several moments. Upon the instant of thinking about my body, I was back, opening my physical eyes.

I suspect the non-effort, non-intention, the new energetic side-effects from TK practice created the ripe circumstances for this to happen.

January 19, 2016

I had two significant dreams last night. The first was brief. An invisible figure gifted me with a special pen, perhaps the most beautiful pen I've ever seen. In waking life, I don't have any kind of affinity for pens, so this was a little bit odd. There was a silent understanding that somehow, I had earned this pen on behalf of my entire clan, my family. Receiving this pen symbolized our newly elevated stature. I felt profoundly joyful, a sense of celebration and accomplishment.

The pen looked like a large, old-fashioned calligraphy pen. The main body was a deep, cobalt blue. The middle portion was shaped into ripples, or a set of rounded sections with diamond like jewels embedded in them.

The wonderful feeling faded as I entered the second dream. I was on a large, wooden ship, and other people were there, including John H., the property inspector I used for my real estate transactions.

I noticed some oddities in the construction of the ship. Some sections were designed to be raised and lowered like moving cages, or elevators. An outer wall was open to provide direct access to the ocean, or perhaps to a beach.

I can't remember if John said something or if I just knew it - we were passengers on an ark. The purpose was the same as Noah's ark. "The End" had already occurred, and the planet was flooded. All the knowledge, history, and capability of humanity was utterly gone, and only a few people like us were left to attempt survival.

Even after waking up, I felt a profound sadness, as if the great loss had actually occurred. If I'd allowed myself, I could have wept.

Yet, I'm not pessimistic about the dream. I still remember other catastrophic dreams of planetary destruction from years ago. Even though these dreams tend to accompany some kind of loss or failure in my life, their deeper meaning is of an important shift in the direction of my life. Those shifts have brought me here, to this moment. So, I can only be grateful for everything that has happened, even if I didn't feel that way at the time.

April 3, 2016

Catching up on journaling. It's been a stressful time since I haven't had a real estate deal in months. But in the last few weeks, I've placed two homes under contract for my clients, so the stress is markedly less now.

Five nights ago, I had my first OBE in months. I woke up in the middle of the night, feeling a nice energy flow in my body. I moved to the couch, holding on to the energetic feeling as I settled in. As the energy grew stronger, I simply set my intention to leave my body, then allowed myself to drift off to sleep. Moments later, I floated out of my body and moved through the hallway of our new condo. I felt less than 100% clear-headed, but remained present enough to know what I was doing. The floor plan was a little different than the physical version. After noticing the difference, the experience ended and I was back in my body.

Two nights ago, I awoke in bed like before, and transferred to the couch again. This time, something brand new happened. My consciousness condensed near my solar plexus, and I exited out through the middle of my back, behind the solar plexus. It felt like what I imagined going down a drain might feel like. It was even slightly pleasurable.

Next, I was surrounded by total darkness. I think I was in the void again. I'd recently read something about the void in Frederick Aardema's "Explorations in Consciousness." Did I reach the void again simply by reading about it?

The darkness felt wonderful, freeing. I made swimming motions in order to stretch out my "limbs," and this felt expansive and relieving.

I moved back "up" through my body, into the living room, then continued out through the front door, across the hall, into our neighbor's unit. I perceived yellow, red, and brass decorations, reminding me of one of the meditation centers I used to visit.

Moving through their farthest wall, I found myself floating over a coastline. In the physical world, there's a large reservoir in that direction, a few miles away. But this didn't look like that. This was more like the coastline of an ocean.

Feeling lost, and with my awareness fading, I returned to waking consciousness back on the couch.

August 13, 2016

Dreamed that I was visiting a place here on Earth where angels hang out together. These angels looked like what I'd grown up envisioning in church, with the robes, sandals, and even wings. This place reminds me of Wyoming.

Apparently, I'm an angel too, but they can't be sure until I show them the palm of my hand, where there's something hidden, like an invisible barcode.

Then, I dreamed I was helping a man in an electric wheelchair use the toilet. He's making a mess, peeing on the floor and I see feces everywhere, but it's like the little turds that mice make. The toilet is flooding over onto the floor. He's embarrassed because of a pretty woman who's also helping out. She has some issues with her wrist, and she appears to suffer a little bit from cerebral palsy, but seems to be healthy overall.

Then another dream. In this one, I'm showing photographs of shamans and their drums to an Asian man. I think he's Mongolian. He misses his home.

September 27, 2016

I dreamed that I was floating in the sky, and saw a large silver disk nearby. Then, the disk expanded into a large sphere, but it wasn't a perfect sphere. It looked fluid, its surface was moving, contorting, as if it was a giant drop of water or quicksilver moving through the air.

October 4, 2016 - A shared dream, perhaps

Last night, I drank some Guayusa tea before bed. I woke up at 3:20 am and moved to the living room for a long meditation session followed by a few rounds of microcosmic orbit (a Chi Kung technique), then falling asleep on the couch.

I became conscious of "energy sounds" inside my head, and then I lifted out of my body. I floated out to the balcony. I looked down to see a city far below, which made me suspect I was having a lucid dream, not an OBE. I floated down to the city. I saw a giant sculpture, a glass of iced tea about five stories tall.

Then, I entered a shopping mall and saw dozens of people walking around. I was fully aware of what I was experiencing, and realized that I should try to do something constructive, some kind of experiment.

I decided to will everyone inside the mall to stop moving. I yelled out "Everybody freeze!" and they did. It was just like hitting the "pause" button while watching a movie.

But, there was one guy who didn't freeze. He had shoulder length, dirty blond hair, a short beard, and was in his 30's. He wore large headphones over his ears. Was it possible he didn't "freeze" because he couldn't hear me?

I mentally "released" everyone, turned around, and began to walk away. Suddenly, I heard someone behind me yell out "Is there another dreamer in here? Is someone sharing my dream?

I turned around to see the person yelling was the guy who'd been wearing the headphones. I replied "Yes!" and approached him. All we could do was smile at each other, we were both shocked.

Was this guy more than just a dream figure? Was I having a real shared dream, but with a stranger? The excitement forced me to wake up before we could say anything else to each other.

November 2, 2016 A strange beacon

Swooshing sound in my head, then lift-off. I could tell I was still in our condo. I walked toward the door. I was blind, my visual perception wasn't working quite yet. An alien face appeared, and I followed it to the front door as if it was leading me like some kind of beacon. I passed through the door and could see the hallway, but it looked like a fancy hotel's hallway instead of the physical version.

Different people showed up, some looked like Kung-Fu fighters, and Julianna, a marketing specialist on our real estate team, showed up too, in a white dress (she doesn't usually wear dresses).

I remembered that I'd previously set a goal for whenever my next OBE occurred. It was to try to see Cierra lying in bed. I walked back through the door of our condo and into the bedroom. I saw her in bed. But, next to the bed was our loveseat, and I saw Cierra's astral form lying down in it, asleep just like her body.

Her eyes opened as I approached. Her hair looked blond (she had darkened her hair by this time), and curlier than usual. Her cheeks appeared more full, like those of a child. I began to talk to her, asking if she could see me and knew who I was. Then the experience faded and I opened my eyes, back on the couch.

This one felt like a combination of a dream with an OBE.

Commentary: I'm a bit surprised as I transcribe this journal entry for the book. I'd completely forgotten about this experience. Strangely, I don't even remember the part about seeing an alien face, or what it looked like. Judging from the especially poor handwriting, it seems I wrote this down immediately upon my return to my body.

November 8, 2016

I dreamed I was somewhere in Africa, and groups of people were fighting each other. I headed to the ocean and swam with the dolphins. The water was crystal clear. I dove down deep underwater to touch the sand on the ocean floor, and saw that all the sand was gone. A strange sort of print pattern covered the floor, and it looked artificial, man-made.

I returned to the beach and saw dead bodies, trash, and other things that had been dredged out of the ocean. I intuited that industrial forces had taken all of the sand, but why, I don't know. As I continued walking, I passed through a village and saw people everywhere protesting.

November 11, 2016

I dreamed I was with a teacher-figure and other students. We were in a forest or nature setting, and the ambience had a pagan or shamanistic feel to it. We were in a circle, and one at a time, the students took turns turning themselves into all kinds of animals including rabbits, squirrels, birds and more. We were being taught how to shapeshift. It seemed like I was just there to watch, and I don't recall turning into an animal myself.

November 30, 2016

Last night I had a terrible nightmare. It's been a very long time since I've had one this bad. I awoke, still filled with absolute terror. But the terror had a gift for me.

As I went back to sleep, I made an affirmation unlike any I'd used before. *I asked for help.* I asked for any guides *out there* to help me, to keep me safe, and to dispel my fear. The nightmare which had woken me up involved a dark, formless personality which threatened me greatly somehow, and I didn't know how to deal with it.

After asking for help, I let myself drift back into the darkness of sleep. Just before I was all the way gone, I received a message, an intuition perhaps, and I think it came from whoever *out there* had received my call.

The wordless instruction was to imagine myself in a place where I felt protected. Without hesitation, I thought of the large, enclosed tropical plant exhibit at the Denver Botanic Gardens. This is a place I'd visited from time to time, especially when I wanted to replenish my energy by spending time among its vibrant and beautiful plants.

Suddenly, the exhibit's appearance changed in my mind's eye, in a way I'd never envisioned before. It was brimming with light. A white energy filled the entire space of the building, and streamed out through the glass domed ceiling, shining out into the night sky.

Following the silent guidance, I imagined myself sitting inside the exhibit and surrounded by plants. I was also surrounded by the intense white light, and I felt safe. In fact, I was then able to send feelings of love and compassion from my imagined location inside the exhibit, out to the dark being who'd been pursuing me in the earlier nightmare. My fear completely dissolved, and my heart felt tender as I drifted off into the blackness again.

I woke up this morning feeling happy and invigorated.

Sean McNamara

Outside and inside the tropical display at the Botanic Gardens
(see Nov. 30, 2016 journal entry)

CHAPTER 24 PSYCHIC PERCEPTION

Although I didn't mention this in my journal entries from that time period, I felt confused and unsure about the fact that sometimes, a guide or teacher would appear in my dreams and OBEs.

After feeling deeply hurt and disappointed by "real life" spiritual teachers, I'd sworn off asking anybody for guidance. Unfortunately, but understandably, I'd developed serious trust issues, and I was on guard against anyone who identified him or herself as an authority figure.

Also, teaching myself how to have an OBE and do telekinesis, albeit with guidance I'd found in books and online, had given me a powerful sense of independence and self-empowerment. I had absolutely no interest in giving up my own authority by placing myself under anyone else's wing whether in "real life," dreams, or non-physical realms.

I have to consider the possibility that my nighttime interactions with guides and teachers at this point in my life was a form of preparation, because even though I didn't know it at the time, I was about to become someone's student again.

In April of 2016, Cierra surprised me with a most unusual birthday gift. She knew I'd been watching programs about spiritual mediums like James Van Praagh, John Edward, Gordon Smith, and John Holland. Watching these mediums, along with movies like "Astral

City" (Nosso Lar)[20] was a natural next-step after reading books about near-death experiences and after-death communication.

A metaphysical bookstore close to Mayu Sanctuary named "Goddess Isis Books and Gifts" had advertised a *gallery reading* by a local spiritual medium named Jude Starks. Cierra thought it would interest me, so she reserved our seats. I was delighted, since I'd never been to anything like this before.

When the night finally arrived, we entered the bookstore's classroom, which hosted a wide variety of metaphysical events almost every day of the week. On this night, a couple rows of chairs were set up as a semi-circle. There, sitting in front of the room, was Jude.

I was almost disappointed to see that she appeared...normal. I suppose that even though most of the mediums I'd watched online wore normal clothes and spoke like regular people, I must've made some unfair assumptions about the kind of people who taught classes inside metaphysical bookstores.

But Jude wasn't really "normal." She greeted us and the other sitters warmly, making us feel comfortable as soon as we came in. She'd been a medium for many years, so she probably knew exactly what the shy, guarded or confused looks on her visitor's faces meant whenever they attended one of her programs for the first time. We were all there to see if this person could actually talk to dead people, particularly people we used to know while they were alive. She was in her comfort zone, and we were not.

That didn't last long, though. Her warm sense of humor, and the way she exhibited playfulness by clapping her hands to get our attention, put us at ease right away. She had a warm personality and was 100% professional. What became abundantly clear that night was that she wasn't really working for us, the people sitting in the room. The people she was really working for didn't have physical bodies anymore.

---

[20] See the *Movies* section in "Recommended Resources" later in this book.

Before getting started, Jude let us know that she was trained as an "evidential" medium. This was a style of mediumship favored in Great Britain. Being evidential meant that she wasn't just going to stand up there doing cold readings on people while making broad statements like "Aunt Edna's here and she just wanted to let you know she loves you and is waiting for you on the other side." These kinds of readings had probably done a lot more damage than good for the field of mediumship, leaving the door wide open for accusations of fraud.

Evidential mediumship raised the bar by requiring the medium to acquire specific, verifiable facts about the spirit, the sitters (the people sitting in the room), or both during the séance. Typical examples of evidence include what the spirit looked like while he or she was alive, personal names, locations where they lived and worked, their relationship to the sitter, and their cause of death.

I'd had my OBEs and performed telekinesis, but have to admit that some part of me was eager to see what Jude could do. Incredibly, I had my doubts. It seemed that some part of me was never satisfied by what I'd already experienced, and always looked for a way to disprove everything. This was a part of my personality which never changed, even after everything I'd experienced. Whether it was caused by religious programming, or if it was just how my brain was wired, or both, I'm not completely sure.

After introducing herself, and answering any preliminary questions from the dozen people in the room, she clapped her hand gently, then rubbed them together as a way of settling in. She bowed her head as if to quiet herself for a couple moments. Then, she looked up and away, as if she was peering out into a distant horizon somewhere. I could tell she wasn't really looking with her eyes, though. She appeared to be listening, feeling, and yes, looking. Not outside, though, but *within*.

"Ok, I have a man here, someone's father or grandfather."

Sean McNamara

I was sure that half the room had a dad or grandpa on the other side. Jude had asked us to reply "Yes" if, and *only if,* the description matched someone we might know. Several of us replied, "yes."

"This man died a while back, a few years ago. But he knew someone in this room while he was alive. Can anyone take this?"

"Yes," I replied, hoping for more. This wasn't enough to convince me.

"I'm feeling something like a swelling or an enlargement, or some kind of issue on his abdomen." One of her hands glided up and down above her own belly, indicating where she thought the abdominal problem was.

I can't remember if I said "Yes," or not, but I should have. Grampa had suffered a hernia at some point in his life, before I was born. As long as I'd known him, Grampa had a very noticeable bulge that always protruded from his belly. How many times had I sat on his lap, snuggling into him as he draped his arm around me to keep me close?

"But that's not why he died…" She was right. Sitting on the edge of my seat, I waited anxiously for her to say more. Could Grampa be talking to this woman right now? Does he know I'm here?

"He had a lot of heart problems, I think he had surgery too…."

"Yes," I replied. She was close, but the heart attacks and valve replacements aren't what killed him.

"There was something with his mind, like he was really foggy. Something was making it difficult for him to think in the end."

"Yes!" She was right. He'd suffered from dementia, which eventually took the ultimate toll on his life, killing his brain, and taking his body with it.

I was amazed, excited, and in awe. I had offered no clues whatsoever, only replying "Yes" and nothing more. I'm sure some people might've reacted by saying that the idea of someone's grandfather having abdominal, cardiac and mental issues at the same time was not extremely uncommon, especially for his generation. They could be right.

As if to put the kibosh on any remaining doubt, Jude spoke again.

"This is your grandfather, I'm sure of that now. He says I need to tell you something. There's this thing that all the men in your family do. You do it, and so does your father. When you guys get angry, you stop talking. You don't communicate."

I was aghast. There was absolutely no way Jude could've correctly guessed this most unfortunate truth about the men on my dad's side of the family. There was more than a little bit of German-Irish in all of us, and we all did the same thing when someone close to us wanted to argue or discuss a difficult topic. We clammed up. "End of discussion!"

Thinking back, I can remember Granny becoming a lot louder while Grampa remained angrily stoic during disagreements. My dad does it too. For him, it's definitely useful since my mom's Latin, passionate reactivity can assault him with the energy of a hurricane.

And I was that way too. How many times had I refused to answer the phone for a worried girlfriend who was trying to make amends after hurting my feelings? How many times had someone pleaded for me to "just say something," when I felt more in control by keeping my mouth shut and turning my back?

Somehow, three generations of men had learned the art of stuffing one's emotions down inside as deeply as possible. God help anyone in the room when we got too full and had to finally let it out. It wasn't pretty.

"He says to tell you 'it doesn't work.' He regrets having been that way, and he just wants you to know it doesn't work."

235

She was really hearing from Grampa. What was that like? Did she hear his voice? Did she see his face?

And, what was it like from his perspective? Was he actually in that room? If so, was it anything like having an out of body experience and visiting another place? Was he visiting from some other realm, or was he always close by? Or was he doing some type of long-distance communication, tapping into Jude's mind using some kind of trans-dimensional telepathy?

These questions burned in my head while I absorbed the emotional impact of that evening. She had me convinced that evidence-based mediumship was legitimate, and served an important purpose in helping people understand the cycle of existence on a deeper level. My OBEs had already removed my fear of death, and Jude's mediumship served as a helpful confirmation. I was immensely grateful. And increasingly curious.

A few months later, I saw something else I couldn't stop thinking about. It was an email announcing the upcoming year-long training program to become a certified medium taught by, who else, but Jude.

The deadline to sign up grew closer, and most of the thoughts filling my mind anytime I thought about signing up were along the lines of "Who do you think you are?" and "You're not psychic, there's no way you can do this!"

Looking back, it seems funny to me that even though I'd learned telekinesis and had experienced many out of body experiences, I hadn't thought of myself as a psychic. I'd already begun teaching telekinesis to other people, and saw how easy it was for anybody to learn, as long as they were willing to follow the instructions carefully. I also believed anyone who wanted to, could learn how to have an OBE.

But, for some reason, I thought of telepathy, clairvoyance and talking to dead people as things only special people could do.

Yet, if that were really true, what would be the point of offering a class on these topics? This was a certification program, which meant Jude expected her students to actually become successful at receiving communications from the other side.

So, on a cold winter night in 2017, I walked into a classroom full of students who, in an oddly comforting way, seemed as nervous and awkward as I was. I think we all thought the same thing, "I better not tell my friends I'm doing this."

Jude was every bit as warm and funny as she'd been during the séance eight months earlier, which quickly put us at ease. She explained that we'd spend the first six months of the program developing our ability to psychically see, feel, hear, and even taste and smell things in different places, and from different *times*. After developing our ability to receive this kind of information without using our physical senses, we'd spend the final six months using it to communicate with those who'd crossed over.

It soon became apparent the key to developing our extra sensory perception was simply to use it as if we already had it. Because, it turns out, we did. I like to compare Jude's teaching style to that of a swimming instructor who simply throws the child into the deep end, trusting that she or he will quickly figure it out, because it's the most natural thing in the world.

Week after week, we'd engage in simple yet highly effective exercises, such as sitting across from someone, and after giving the appropriate instructions to our own minds, describing what kind of home he or she lived in.

In another exercise, students would write a personal query on a slip of paper, fold it, and hand it to their partners. After holding the folded paper in their hands and using their minds in a particular way, their partners began to feel, see, or simply know information pertaining to what had been written down.

Jude would also put us through many exercises related to "remote viewing." For example, she would hold up a large manila envelope and ask us to write down whatever came into our minds pertaining to the enclosed photograph. Then, she'd reveal what was inside after we'd written down our impressions.

Without fail, we'd begin each new exercise with reluctant, incredulous expressions on our faces, and comments like, "Oh no, I don't think I can do that," and "There's no way I'm going to be able to get anything this time." This went on, week after week, even though we'd all had some level of success the week before.

Jude Starks[21]

Perverse as it was, there was something oddly comforting about the fact that everyone else expressed the same self-doubt I did. But Jude would have none of it, and this is where her professionalism shone. As soon as we began to moan and groan about how we'd surely fail this time, she stopped us in our tracks. She'd remind us to stop doubting ourselves and *just do it*. We were to take a chance, and write down whatever came into our minds. She wouldn't allow us to

---

[21] www.JudeStarks.com

diminish ourselves with negative self-talk. And if we lacked confidence, she made sure we knew that she was confident in us.

Fifteen minutes later, Jude would pull the photo out of the envelope, and our jaws would fall open in astonishment, as we compared it to whatever we'd written down.

We learned how normal it was to perceive flickers of imagery, or hear snippets of things, or feel emotions which didn't make any sense whatsoever. We simply wrote down whatever came through, without trying to filter it. We never seemed to lose the sense of wonderment when we realized that the jagged line, color, name, or feeling we'd recorded was a clear match for a significant aspect of the target image.

Week after week, Jude put us through her exercises. I could call each one a "test," but they were simply meant to remind us of an ability we already possessed. She knew it, and her job was to remind us of it. Time and time again, we'd moan and groan with doubt. And, time and time again, our jaws hit the floor when we realized that the thoughts and images flitting through our heads was real information, and it connected to the target we'd set our minds upon.

Every night after class, I'd come home excited to show Cierra my notebook filled with drawings and words accurately describing the evening's targets. She was as amazed as I was, but never surprised. Ever the patient watcher, I think she always knew it was just a matter of time until I'd succeed, no matter how much I doubted myself along the way.

Eventually, I asked Cierra to help me with some "extracurricular" training at home. I'd begun researching ESP, looking for reliable sources of information, especially anything with a "how to" quality to it.

One book, now a classic of the ESP genre called "Mental Radio," was especially interesting to me because it included photographs of drawings produced during experiments between the author Upton Sinclair and his wife Mary Craig Kimbrough.

"Craig," as she was known, had a history of psychic experiences throughout her life, and Mr. Sinclair became interested in doing a systematic evaluation of her ability. They designed an experiment in which either Mr. Sinclair or his secretary would make a drawing and seal it inside an envelope. Then, Craig would lie down on her couch while placing the envelope on top of her solar plexus with one of her hands over it.

After a while, she'd reach for a nearby pen and paper, and sketch whatever came into her mind. The incredible results are printed inside "Mental Radio." I was also delighted to see Mr. Sinclair had included Craig's specific instructions for how she did it, in chapter 21 of the book.

Craig's instructions weren't very different from Jude's. They both taught three keys to using one's psychic ability. First, to relax. Second, to set one's intention to perceive the desired information. And finally, to simply wait for the impressions to come into one's awareness, then record them just as they were.

Craig's style of relaxation was quite similar to some of the meditation techniques I'd used over the years. These involved relaxing both the body and the mind, the principle being that these two aspects of a person are interrelated. To relax the mind, one begins by seeking out any tension within the body. Then, one releases that tension through breath work and visualization. As the body softens, releases and relaxes, so does one's mind.

This will sound familiar to anyone who's ever tried the popular technique called "progressive muscle relaxation," in which one focuses on various parts of the body, head-to-toe, relaxing each one-by-one until wholly relaxed and calm.

After reading "Mental Radio" and other books, it seemed I was at no risk of "recreating the wheel." There was no wheel to be found. All my sources, including David Morehouse's remote viewing book I'd read a couple years before, echoed the same instructions. Relax, quiet the mind, set one's intention to perceive, then patiently wait for the impressions to arrive.

Could it be that simple? I'd already answered that question for myself in Jude's classroom. The answer, in big, bright letters, was "Yes! It really is that simple!" But in the spirit of adventure, and with a little help from Cierra, I decided to repeat Craig's experiments.

Cierra would make simple drawings using a marker, then place them inside a folder. Following Craig's example, I'd lie down and spend a good deal of time relaxing my body and mind. Once I felt ready, I'd place the folder over my solar plexus and intend for my mind to retrieve the image. For a few seconds, I'd generate a *strong desire* to know what was inside the envelope. Then, I'd just let go of that desire, return to a calm, neutral state, and wait to see what arose in my mind afterward.

Here are some experiments done over a few days that May (next pages). In each set, the first image is the "target" drawn by Cierra, and the second is the drawing of what I perceived. These were done over a few days that May.

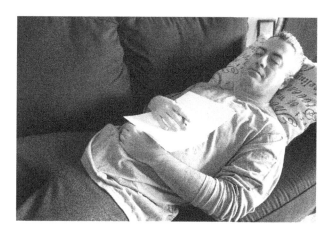

Lying on the couch with the folder on my solar plexus
containing the "target image" drawn by Cierra

Sean McNamara

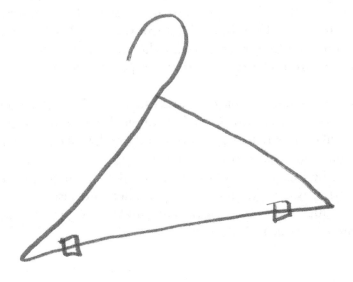

Target image (above)   Perceived images (below)

242

Target image (above)   Perceived images (below)

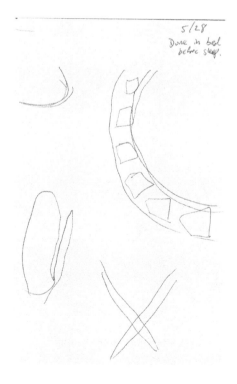

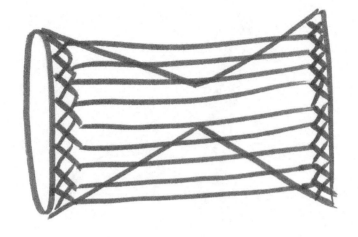

Target image (above)   Perceived image (below)

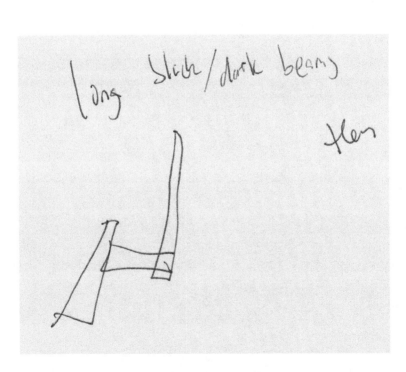

"long black/dark beams"

Target image (above)   Perceived Images (below)

"yellow"

Sean McNamara

Target image (above)   Perceived images (below)

"Done sitting up at dining table after dinner."

Target image (above)   Perceived images (below)

"in bed" (meaning I did the session lying in bed)

Sean McNamara

Target image (above)   Perceived images (below)

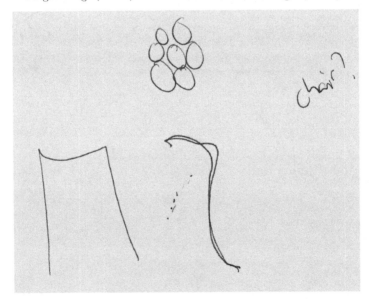

"chair?" (my conscious mind attempting to make sense
of the perception)

Notice the dots in the center of the transcript.
Was I connecting with the dots on the strawberry?

248

As we can see from this small set of experiments, receiving psychic impressions about a simple line drawing comes with significant challenges. Inaccuracy is most obvious, as none of my drawings were exact matches for their targets, not even close. At best, my drawings show that I had picked up on particular, but disorganized features of each image, like scattered puzzle pieces.

However, in each experiment, Cierra could have drawn *anything in the universe* within her artistic limits, as my target. That my perceptions contained salient aspects of her drawings, is significant. We can call these "hits." Of course, there were also plenty of "misses," experiments where my sketches had no connection whatsoever to the target.

The inaccuracy, lack of clarity, and fractured quality of my perceptions were a far cry from the way Jude received information during the séance with Grampa. His hernia, heart issues, dementia, and his comment about our communication issues were quite on target.

What Jude saw, felt, and heard were whole pictures, and a far cry from what came through for me when trying to perceive one of Cierra's line drawings. After six months of training, the focus of our training changed from clairvoyance to mediumship. Not surprisingly, my first thought was "I don't think I'll be able to do this."

It seemed everyone in the class felt the same way. We hemmed and hawed like we'd done so many times before. As always, Jude encouraged us to dive in and take a chance.

One aspect of mediumship, as Jude teaches it, involves developing a working relationship with one of our spiritual guides. She told us these beings on the other side helped us to form a communication link between our deeper selves and the deceased. The first step, then, was to meet our guides for the first time in order to establish that relationship.

Sean McNamara

This was difficult for me to hear. By spending time with Jude, I realized that it was alright to trust other teachers again, and that most people weren't at all like the two teachers I'd had previously. But trying to connect with a spiritual guide, someone I'd never met before was a difficult concept for me.

Helpers of one kind or another had appeared in some of my dreams and OBEs, but those were spontaneous, and I couldn't help that. I didn't like asking for help. I didn't like the idea that I couldn't do this on my own, and I didn't like the idea of meeting someone else who might let me down.

Still, I trusted Jude. And, I had enough self-awareness to know the psychological roots of this particular discomfort. I knew this was my issue and my responsibility, not hers, nor anyone else's. I swallowed my pride in preparation to meet my guide.

That evening, Jude dimmed the lights to help us relax and open our minds. Then, she used a special induction to take us even deeper, so that we were in the proper state of consciousness to perceive and communicate with our spiritual helpers.

At a certain point, I felt like I was in a beautiful outdoor area, like a park, sitting on a bench. I was instructed to wait and see who would enter the scene and approach me. My body was sitting in a plastic chair inside the bookstore's classroom, but *my mind* was somewhere else. Was I simply absorbed in my own imagination, or was I really tuning in to a different reality? I wasn't sure.

Eventually, a figure appeared at the edge of the park, and began to walk toward me. The image in my mind's eye was blurry, but cleared up a bit as the being came closer. I couldn't tell right away if this was a masculine or feminine presence, but it felt like a spiritual presence, like this wasn't an ordinary person. This being had a special presence, an energy unlike anything I'd felt before.

As it drew closer, I could see it was a male presence. Then I saw something which confirmed this was not simply my imagination. He had wings. That's right, like an angel. He was clothed in a very

250

bright robe, and I even noticed sandals on his feet. The figure standing before me was such a cliché, I was sure this wasn't my imagination. I would never have created this experience on purpose, it just wasn't my style, especially after practicing Buddhism all those years.

I could hear Jude's voice in the background, guiding us in our introductions. "When you are ready, ask your guide what his or her name is."

I did, and the name I heard inside my mind sounded as cliché as the wings and sandals he was wearing.

"Ezekiel."

I couldn't believe it. I was disappointed and became unsure about the whole exercise. I had no idea who Ezekiel was, but I was fairly sure his name showed up somewhere in the Bible, and I just wasn't interested in heading that direction.

Everyone in the classroom met their own guides, and the exercise concluded. Several people shared some of what happened during their introductions. I don't recall anyone else having met someone with that "classic angel" look.

I drove home feeling confused and unsure about what happened. But, I also felt curious. I decided to do an online search when I got home. After typing the search phrase "angel Ezekiel" into my browser, several metaphysical websites appeared. Many of them were owned by channelers who claimed to be able to let angels speak through them.

Several of these channelers' messages agreed on one point, that Ezekiel had to do with personal transformation, which usually involved a loss or change in personal identity, or a change in the way a person decided to live their life. Cierra was nearby, so I read the descriptions out loud to her. She could see how I was feeling by the way I rolled my eyes.

Sean McNamara

"Don't you see?" she laughed. "This is absolutely perfect for you right now; it makes complete sense!"

She was right. I'd been changing a great deal since my first out of body experience, leaving my previous teacher, and learning telekinesis. Attending the mediumship course was also expanding my horizons, particularly through the clairvoyance exercises in Jude's class and at home with Cierra.

Cierra also knew that I'd been extremely unhappy with my job as a real estate agent. I'd chosen that career with the intention of helping people, since buying or selling a home can be emotionally difficult. But over and over again, my clients reminded me they weren't interested in emotional support. Most of them just wanted to beat out their competition, get the house, or sell for as much money as possible.

I was in the wrong field, and by now, even my own body was telling me to get out.

Every Monday morning, the whole team would gather to review what each agent was working on. And every time we met, without fail, it felt like an elephant was sitting on my chest. My heart physically ached from the minute the meeting began, to shortly after it ended. I was beginning to wonder if I was going to have a heart attack, even though I knew this pain came from emotional stress.

The worst part was that I didn't know what I would do if I were to quit. The anxiety-producing thought of starting over, yet again, acted as a counterweight to the stress I endured by staying in that job. I felt stuck, and scared.

Cierra was right, it made perfect sense that Ezekiel, as a New Age representation of change and representation, should appear in my life at this time.

Next, I wanted to learn who Ezekiel was in the Bible. A quick search showed that he was a prophet who lived nearly 600 years before Christ, and that one of the books in the Old Testament is named after him. More interestingly, the book contains specific details of the visions he experienced.

The first chapter of the Book of Ezekiel is particularly strange. Verse 4 reads "I looked, and I saw a windstorm coming out of the north—an immense cloud with flashing lightning and surrounded by brilliant light. The center of the fire looked like glowing metal." It goes on to describe strange, winged animals gathered together inside the fire.

Verse 12 describes how they moved in the air, "Each one went straight ahead. Wherever the spirit would go, they would go, without turning as they went.

Then in Verse 16, describes strange wheels located next to each creature, "They sparkled like topaz, and all four looked alike. Each appeared to be made like a wheel intersecting a wheel."

The description gets even more strange. Verse 22, "Spread out above the heads of the living creatures was what looked something like a vault, sparkling like crystal, and awesome." Verse 24 then goes into more detail about how they moved, "When the creatures

Engraving of Ezekiel's "chariot vision" by
Matthaeus Merian (1593-1650)[22]

[22] https://commons.wikimedia.org/wiki/File:Ezekiel-Vision-Merkaba.jpg (public domain)

Sean McNamara

moved, I heard the sound of their wings, like the roar of rushing waters, like the voice of the Almighty, like the tumult of an army. When they stood still, they lowered their wings."

To me, this passage seemed to describe some kind of futuristic aircraft, or even an extraterrestrial ship. Given that the Wright Brothers invented powered flight in 1903, that doesn't leave many options for one's imagination.

I didn't have a strong sense of what I should do with Ezekiel. We'd been introduced, and the implication was that he'd be working with me on the other side to help me connect with people there during my mediumship training. I decided to leave it an open question, and avoid overthinking it.

One evening, I decided to try something I hadn't done for a very long time. My work stress was worse than ever, and I didn't know what to do about it. I felt stuck, and scared at the thought of leaving my real estate job. I turned out the bedroom light and settled into bed.

And for several minutes, *I prayed.*

Cierra was sleeping next to me, so this was a silent prayer, from my heart, and my mind. I called out not only to Ezekiel, but to "any and all" of my guides out there who might be willing and able to give me guidance. I didn't know for sure if anyone was listening, and after a while, I dozed off.

Then I had two dreams. I don't know exactly what time they came, but it was still dark outside when I awoke with a clear recollection of them.

The first one contained a single image. It was a "quetzal," a bird from my mother's country, Guatemala. We'd lived there when I was in kindergarten, and visited often in the years after we moved away, since my grandmother on my mom's side was there. I remember hearing somewhere, these beautiful jungle birds tended to die quickly after being caught and held in a cage.

254

The dream was simple, and highly symbolic. I stared at the quetzal, and he looked right back at me. His tail and feathers looked damaged, as if it had just endured a tremendous struggle. I was given the understanding this bird had just escaped its cage, and was now free. He was happy, and everything was going to be alright. With that vision, I was filled with simultaneous joy, and relief.

The dream faded, and the second one followed on its heels.

> I found myself sitting in the office. It was a Monday morning, and our team meeting was concluding. As everyone stood up to leave, I approached the two team leaders and asked if I could speak with them. They were happy to chat, so I followed them back to their shared office. As the dream continued, I told them everything I'd been feeling lately, and resigned. They understood, and responded by telling me their utmost wish was for me to be happy, no matter where I went next.

Quetzal[23]

---

[23] Photo credit: Victoria Bahena Lanzagorta,
https://commons.wikimedia.org/wiki/File:Quetzal_en_el_zool%C3%B3gico_de
_Tuxtla_Guti%C3%A9rrez.jpg

I'd fallen asleep asking for guidance, and the dreams couldn't make it any clearer that not only did I need to leave my job, but I'd be deeply happy after doing so. Yet, I felt more unsure about the dreams with every minute that passed after waking up. Did I really have to quit? The fear and hesitation I now felt had been curiously absent during the night.

It just so happened that I'd rented a vendor table at a metaphysical fair in a town named Loveland, that same weekend to promote my telekinesis books. Once in a while, I'd leave my table and visit the other vendors. One booth stood out among the rest. It displayed immense pieces of artwork depicting various spiritual scenes, and many of them had a particular feeling to them. They reminded me of some of my out of body experiences.

I approached the artist, a woman named Sonya Shannon, who appeared to be waiting for a customer to return so that she could give her a psychic reading. Sonya was an oracle-card reader, and had created her own deck using her artwork. I suddenly felt an impulse to request a reading from her. Her customer was nowhere to be found, so she was able to do it for me right on the spot.

As she shuffled the deck, she asked me to set my intention for the reading by holding my particular question in mind. I repeated the request I'd made the night before, to receive guidance about what to do with my life. Then I selected the cards for her to turn over and read.

I can clearly remember the final card, because shivers went up my back as she turned it over. In big letters at the bottom of the card was the word "Liberation." The image above it was of a man on his knees, seemingly restrained by a ball and chain. On closer inspection, though, I saw the chain was broken, and he was free.

I was out of excuses. So, the following Monday morning after our team meeting was over, I approached my team leaders just as I had in my dream. They agreed to talk with me, and we went to their office. And just like in the dream, I told them how I'd been feeling, and let them know that I would be leaving. They responded with full support, expressing their desire for me to be happy even if it meant saying goodbye. Just like the man on the card, I was free.

It would take some time until I figured out what to do for work. Meanwhile, I continued my training with Jude. By the end of the course, we tested our skills by inviting the public to come to the bookstore and allow us to try our mediumship abilities with them.

Many books have been written about mediumship, so I won't attempt to go into detail about my experiences here. One important point is that during a mediumship session, I was able to receive far more information than the fractured images which came through when trying to perceive Cierra's line drawings.

Sometimes, I got what a person looked like. Other times, there was a feeling or message included with the image. Or, the visual image would be missing, but I'd still receive some kind of guidance which seemed specific to the sitter.

If there was a single indication telling me that I was indeed communicating with a deceased person, it was a particular wave of love-energy that would fill my whole being during the session. I knew this feeling hadn't come from within me. Rather, it was as if I'd tapped into a different plane, or a different state of existence, and the love-energy was coming through from there.

I came to understand this was possible because the people on the other side are still alive and filled with energy. Psychic communication with them was a two-way street. By comparison, a few lines of black ink drawn on white paper is, for all intents and purposes, dead, and it's left to the clairvoyant to retrieve the information on their own.

After 12 months, I received my certificate, and that was enough for me. I'd learned so much, but felt this wasn't my calling. However, if there had been another purpose to my time with Jude, it would become obvious later on.

The "Liberation" card
from Sonya Shannon's Transformation Oracle[24]

---

[24] Many thanks to Sonya Shannon (www.Sonya-Shannon.com) for allowing me to include her Liberation card here.

CHAPTER 25 CONTACT

From my dream journal:

September 1, 2017

Had an interesting experience while lying semi-awake in bed this morning. This felt like a type of spontaneous clairvoyance, as if a window had unexpectedly opened inside my mind. I perceived a small humanoid figure, surrounded by golden light. It was so bright; I couldn't make out any details like its face or gender. This being seemed to be inside some kind of doorway. The being was holding it open so that it could keep looking at me. Or was this happening so that I would see it? Did it want to be seen? I couldn't tell. I tried to mentally say "hello," but apparently, I was too slow. The experience ended a moment later.

September 18, 2017

Something happened last night, I don't know what time it was. While I was sleeping, I suddenly became aware of a white light turning on inside my head. It turned off, then back on a few times. Sometimes it was small, the size of a pearl, and other times it seemed to fill the entire space of my head.

I opened my eyes to see if there was any moonlight entering the room, unsure of the light source. But, our curtains were drawn, and it was pitch black. I closed my eyes again, and the light returned.

Sean McNamara

This time, I saw a face in front of me, in my mind's eye, looking right at me. It wasn't human. It was bald, with a broad forehead and cheek bones tapering down to a slender chin, which framed a small, closed mouth. Its eyes were dark, almond shaped, and larger than human eyes.

Eventually, the light faded and the face disappeared, and I fell back asleep.

Commentary:

I felt strange and uncomfortable not only that day, but for several days afterward. I hadn't asked for this kind of experience, and felt like I had no choice in the matter. If I had to guess, I think this being wanted to make it clear that it could see me whether I wanted it to or not. It wasn't particularly aggressive, but this was so different from anything I'd experienced before, that I was left feeling nervous and unsure about the experience.

The discomfort faded with time, and the next few months were filled with more of the normal dreams and OBEs I was accustomed to.

Then, something else happened.

May 10, 2018

I'm writing this almost two weeks after this event occurred. It's still clear inside my memory, almost as if it happened last night.

This experience was semi-lucid. It involved a being that I don't think was human. It wore some type of skin-suit which entirely covered its body. It fit loosely enough that I could tell this was a costume, or a disguise, and the being inside it could have looked very different underneath. The skin-suit was of a greenish-brown color, and had a rough, mottled texture. This being looked humanoid, with two arms and two legs.

260

The being approached me and, even though I couldn't visually perceive its gender, the energy coming from it felt feminine. And sexual. She straddled me as I lay down on my back. I noticed an opening in the crotch of her suit and felt inside with my hand. The flesh inside was soft, warm, and moist.

I entered her and ejaculated, or so I thought. I suddenly became conscious of the bedroom and opened my eyes. My visual field was filled with yellow paisleys, bright blue squares, and other shapes. After a few moments, I could see the bedroom normally again.

Feeling myself beneath the sheets, I couldn't find any evidence of having ejaculated. Had I had some kind of "dry orgasm"?

Commentary:

This wasn't an ordinary orgasm. Although I didn't journal the details, I still recall the burst of pleasurable energy that moved up my spine, into my skull, then spread out through the rest of my body. It was sublime. Was this a gift? Was it something other than just a really good orgasm? What was its purpose? I don't know the answers.

Taken from my journal entry May 10, 2018

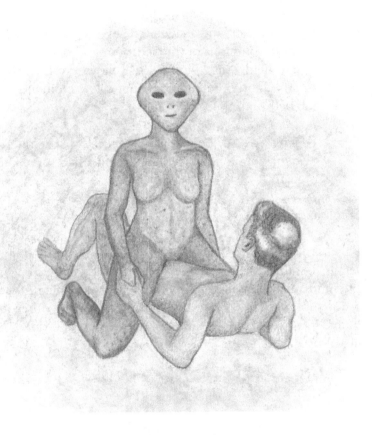

Depiction of my experience the night of May 10, 2018[25]

---

[25] Thank you to artist Paige Losen (instagram.com/paigerefresh & www.PaigeLosen.com) for her faithful representation of my experience. Color image at www.RenegadeMysticBook.com/pictures

Not having answers was something I needed to get used to. Leaving my real estate job felt like the right thing to do, particularly after receiving the guidance I'd requested. But there was no clear path forward in terms of the practicalities of making a living and paying the bills. I began doing massage therapy again, but I knew it was just a temporary solution.

One day that summer, I felt particularly worn down by my anxieties about not knowing what to do with my life. I had the whole day off, so I decided to visit the Botanic Gardens. I knew it was a place I could relax, soak in the ambient energy, and reconnect with myself and the earth.

I felt drawn to lie down on a gently sloping hill next to their iconic science building, which looked like a cross between a stealth airplane and an Egyptian pyramid. I took off my shoes and relaxed, allowing my mind to drift as I inhaled the lush air, infused by various scents of grass, trees and flowers.

Hours passed, and I could feel my anxiety melting away. Cierra called, and I invited her to come join me since she was already nearby. Twenty minutes later, she found me on the hill and lay down next to me. We had no agenda, no time restriction, and no other desire than to continue soaking in the sun and feeling the earth on our skin.

After a while, Cierra nudged me with her elbow and broke our peaceful silence by asking, "Do you see that up there?"

"What, where?" I replied, not sure what she was talking about. The sky was blue, and it was the middle of the afternoon. Only a couple of clouds lingered far above us.

"There, between the clouds, toward the very top. There's a dot or something…"

My eyes followed her finger as it pointed to a spot between the two clouds. Then I saw it. This thing up in the sky appeared round, but it was so far away it was difficult to tell for sure. What was more obvious to me was the color, a beautiful shade of teal I'd never seen before, almost opalescent.

We looked at it for a few minutes. It wasn't moving at all. This wasn't an aircraft of any kind, as far as we could tell. Then it disappeared. It just blinked out, leaving nothing behind but the blue sky.

"What do you think it was?" I asked her.

"I don't know."

Depiction of me and Cierra on the hill where we
saw the strange object in the sky.

We fell silent again, and returned to watching the clouds drift by as we soaked in the sun. And then *it* came back. Like the first time, it didn't seem to be moving in any direction.

"How high do you think it is?" Cierra asked me. I told her it seemed to be really far up there, higher than airplanes normally flew. But to her, it seemed much closer than that. The fact that it wasn't moving and that there wasn't anything else in the sky to compare it to made it difficult to be sure. We continued watching this beautiful teal *thing* for several minutes.

"Look, it's gone again!" I remarked. It had blinked out, like the first time. "I think it's a UFO," I said. I was getting excited. I stood up, wanting to find someone nearby to get a second opinion, but there was no one around.

"I don't know, I'm not so sure," she replied. She knew as well as me that I was probably biased to think it was a UFO because of the night time experiences I'd had over the last few months.

The little sky-blob came and went a couple more times, until it disappeared a final time. It was time for us to leave too, and return to our daily routines.

Cierra seemed unaffected by the experience. But I, on the other hand, felt a certain something inside, a "something" which lingered for a few days. The best way for me to describe it is that I felt *a sense of grace.*

This was the polar opposite of the feeling which lingered after the night the strange, non-human face projected itself inside my mind without warning, or my permission. Still, I didn't know whether these were connected or not, or if any of it was even real. My night time experiences could've been mere dreams, or hypnagogic phenomena, those hallucinations which naturally occur on the borderline of sleep. The tiny teal thing in the sky could've been, well … I don't know. But that didn't necessarily mean it was a craft from another world.

However, I remained curious. That November, in 2018, I decided to attend my first "UFO Conference" to see what I could learn. I decided to attend as a vendor, so I could sell some of my books and offset the cost of traveling to Nevada.

This was the Starworks USA conference in Laughlin, founded by UFO researcher Paola Harris. I was excited to meet her because I'd begun watching some of her videos online. She is clearly one of the most informed researchers in the field. Her professional background is in journalism, and she uses her training for all her research, particularly when getting witness testimonies.

Sean McNamara

Remarkably, Paola makes it a point to interview witnesses, contactees, political and military leaders in person, like a reporter. She says she can see it in a person's eyes when they're telling the truth, and when they're not.

When I was teaching myself how to do telekinesis, I had to be discerning when watching and hearing other people talk about their psychic abilities online. Some of them seemed legitimate, most did not. In the field of UFOlogy, a person needed to be just as, if not more, discerning when considering their sources.

On my way out of town, I felt an urge to get some reading material for my trip to Nevada. Trying to decide where to go, a single bookstore came to mind, called "Shining Lotus." It was out of the way, but I had plenty of time, so I went there anyway.

Quickly scanning their "used books" section, I found one called "Entering the Circle" by Olga Kharitidi, M.D. The back cover described it as an account of a Russian's apprenticeship by a shaman in the Altai Mountains of Siberia. The clock was ticking and I had to get back on the road, so I paid for the book and left. I drove to Moab, spent the night there, and arrived in Laughlin late the following day.

I had no idea if I was about to enter a circus filled with lunatics and pushovers, or if the conference participants would be "normal." I was happy to see right away that these were people just like me. Some were curious, others were there because they'd had their own strange experience and were seeking answers of their own. Several were researchers, like Paola.

As a vendor, I needed to stay at my table outside of the conference's ballroom, with the other vendors. Towards the end of the weekend, though, I found myself alone in the vendor area. It seemed everyone else had snuck into the ballroom to listen to a presenter named Ricardo Gonzales. All I knew was that he was a researcher from Peru. He'd traveled around the world over the years, looking for information about historical UFO contact events among the local populations.

266

I decided to join everybody else, and snuck into the ballroom. Ricardo was on stage, well into his presentation. Images were projected onto a screen behind him as he spoke. My heart skipped a beat, and a thrilling sensation spread across my skin as I realized what I was looking at.

Ricardo was describing an archeological discovery from Siberia, in which the tomb of a young woman had been unearthed. The archeologists believed the tomb to be two or three thousand years old. The images on the screen were of the tattoos which were still clearly visible on her well-preserved skin. The archeologists also believed her to be a priestess, or a shaman.

The reason for my reaction to what I saw on the screen was the night before, I'd been lying down in my hotel room, reading the twelfth chapter of "Entering the Circle." In it, the author described learning about the discovery of *this very same woman*, the "Siberian princess" as many others referred to her.

What were the chances? It was a last-minute purchase, and I'd almost randomly pulled the book off the shelf when I bought it in Denver. It wasn't even a recent work, since it was published back in 1996. Now, one of the main presenters at this UFO conference was making direct references to an important figure in a chapter I'd been reading just the night before.

I'd experienced many types of synchronicity over the past few years. The rate of incidents increased drastically after I began my telekinesis training, mostly in the form of calling or texting Cierra at the exact same time she was calling or texting me. But this synchronicity was on a whole other level.

On the final day of the conference, I was able to greet Ricardo briefly while he signed copies of his books at one of the vendor tables. There was no time to chat, so I wasn't able to tell him about the synchronicity. I had no clue what I was supposed to do with it.

I didn't need to wait very long to find out, though. Just a few months later, I saw that Paola was promoting a special event to take place in

Sean McNamara

August of 2019. Ricardo Gonzales was going to lead a weekend program about UFOs in the San Luis Valley of central Colorado, in a little town named Crestone. I had to wonder, was this the purpose for the synchronicity? Was I meant to go to Crestone?

Crestone is known as a very spiritual place. It's filled with retreat centers connected to Hinduism, Buddhism, Christianity, and to a variety of metaphysical groups from all over the world. I think another reason for choosing Crestone for Ricardo's program is the lack of light pollution, which makes night time sky watching near the cities nearly impossible.

Apparently, it was normal for Ricardo's participants to have UFO sightings of their own during his programs. He saw his first UFO as a child in Peru, and has continued to see them into the present, often surrounded by other witnesses.

Crestone is only four hours away from Denver, so there was no excuse for me not to go. I still had questions after my strange night time experiences with non-human beings. Was it all in my head? Was any of it real? Was the little teal thing in the sky that afternoon at the Botanic Gardens something from another world, or just a weather balloon? I hoped spending a weekend with Ricardo might provide some answers.

The weekend arrived, and we spent most of each day inside a conference room at the local branch of the Colorado College, called the Baca Campus. Ricardo devoted several hours to sharing his personal experiences with us. More than that, he shared details about a continuing relationship he'd forged with an extra-terrestrial being named Antarel, who communicated with Ricardo telepathically.

This would sound crazy to anyone, until they found out about the "programmed sightings." Antarel sometimes gives Ricardo a specific time, date, and location for Ricardo and others to witness Antarel's craft. And they always come, right on time, for everyone to see.

268

Ricardo's lectures that weekend were intensely moving and provocative. I remained guarded though, very aware of the risks and limitations of blind faith. Anyone can conjure a good story to draw a crowd. From what I could tell online, there seemed to be indications that UFOlogy was becoming like another religion. The internet is brimming with self-proclaimed authorities, "insiders," and participants of secret government programs. Many of them have attracted massive followings, yet without producing solid evidence for their claims, as far as I could tell.

I trusted Ricardo, though. He knew the risks of being involved in this field, including some of the questionable personalities taking advantage of it. More than once that weekend, Ricardo repeated the dictum to *not take anything he was telling us on faith*.

As it turned out, we didn't have to.

That Friday night, after sunset, we gathered on an empty plot of land outside of town. There were about fifty of us, and we formed a large circle with our camping chairs. After settling in, Ricardo led us through special meditations which helped set our group's intention for that night.

When the time was right, we all leaned back to stare up at the night sky, and wait. The stars twinkled brightly, and it was quite easy to see the Milky Way spanning out overhead. As time passed, I could feel my mind shifting back and forth from a heightened sense of expectation to utter boredom.

And then, among the innumerable points of light above, a new one appeared. Someone spotted it first, and commented aloud while pointing to a specific spot in the sky. Someone else had a powerful laser, and shone it in the direction of this "new arrival" to help the rest of us locate it among the stars.

As if to acknowledge our awareness, the little pinpoint of light suddenly expanded, appearing many times larger than its original size, then quickly returned to its original size.

Sean McNamara

The following night, we did it again. I had no idea what the chances were of repeating the experience, but it turned out I didn't need to worry. Ricardo guided us through a special visualization, then we repeated a special mantra he'd used before. These exercises were a way of connecting us to the earth, raising our energy, and reinforcing our intention to connect with whoever was out there.

Just like the night before, a new light appeared in the sky out of nowhere. This time, it slowly coasted against the backdrop of stars. It only took a few moments for everyone in the circle to locate it. As soon as all our attention was placed on it, it released a pulse.

Ricardo Gonzalez and Paola Harris
during the 2019 event in Crestone, Colorado.[26]

---

[26] Photo credit: Paul Sperry

Ricardo suggested we mentally request a *second pulse* as a type of confirmation. He must've known that some of us would have doubts about what we were witnessing. In his presentations during the day, he'd made it clear that he was still careful not to take anything for granted. He seemed cautious against fooling himself about what he saw in the sky, similarly to how I'd been cautious when learning telekinesis.

Our circle fell silent as each one of us mentally requested a second pulse from the little light, far above us. We gasped in unison as a second pulse burst out from the pinpoint. Then it blinked out, disappearing entirely. We waited patiently, hoping for more.

I was seated on the southern edge of our circle, facing north. I turned my head to the right, to scan along the Sangre de Cristo mountain range. I could only make out its silhouette against the sky. As my eyes turned left, moving back to the northern end of the range, until I was once more looking straight ahead.

Out of nowhere, a bright green stripe of light, like ribbon, shot down from the sky, straight down toward the earth. The green stripe seemed to disappear before hitting the ground.

With only the distant silhouette of the mountains many miles away, it was impossible for me to tell how high this thing was when it began its descent, or how low it got to the ground before disappearing. I couldn't even tell how wide this stripe of light was. It was fast, but much slower than any shooting star I'd ever seen. This was no meteor.

Many of us, but not all, saw it, including Ricardo. He commented that maybe, just maybe, this was something he'd heard about somewhere else. He said it was possible this was a craft changing its vibrational frequency as it passed through the atmosphere in preparation to go under the surface of the Earth. He also made sure to say it was just a possibility, a hypothesis, and that he didn't know for certain.

Setting up our sky watching circle.

It was up to us individually to come to terms with what we'd seen. Nobody was pushing any dogma or belief system on us, which I appreciated a great deal. Ricardo was there to share an experience with us. Whatever each of us believed about it was our choice to make.

He did have a message to pass on to us, however. It was a message from the beings he'd received communications from throughout his life. It's about the direction our society is headed in, and the possible consequences of our actions.

I'll try to share some of that message here to the best of my memory. What I'm writing down here are my words, not his. Any mistake or misrepresentation is purely my fault.[27]

> Beings out there are watching us, but they will not and *cannot* solve our problems for us. We need to figure this out ourselves.
>
> The solution is not an external force, but an internal one. If we can open our hearts, increase our sense of compassion

---

[27] To read his message directly, find his book "Contact from Planet Apu" in the Recommended Resources section.

and interconnectedness, and find peace with each other, then we'll have the solution.

I didn't have any trouble hearing this message. Whether or not it actually came from extra-terrestrial beings didn't matter to me. They weren't saying anything surprising. Our world really is in deep trouble, and it won't improve without drastic behavioral changes from its human inhabitants. Behavior is rooted in how we feel inside, where the most important change needs to happen.

We remained in our circle for a while after hearing Ricardo's comments about the green stripe. Then, for no reason at all, I let my head drift toward the right again, letting my eyes scan the mountain range to the east once more. As my chin moved past my shoulder, I spotted a new speck of light appear just above one of the mountain peaks.

Was this another one? I decided to send a request and see what would happen. Two or three seconds later, the pinpoint of light expanded into a bright halo, just like before, then quickly receded.

I remembered Ricardo's suggestion to seek confirmation. So, I mentally asked them for a second pulse, not completely sure if it even was a "them," or something else entirely. One second passed, then another, and then ...

Another pulse of light, and it was gone.

CHAPTER 26 PREDICTING THE FUTURE

Let us turn back the clock now, and return to the UFO conference in Laughlin where I first met Ricardo. While I was there, I decided to have some extracurricular fun, and try something I'd been learning about related to remote viewing.

I'd been watching a lot of videos by Marty Rosenblatt from the Applied Precognition Project. This is a group of people who specialize in predicting future events, especially sports and stock market performance. They use a protocol called "associative remote viewing," or ARV.

Since I was staying in a hotel-casino which included a "sportsbook," a place to bet money on sporting events, I thought it'd be fun to place a wager on a game using ARV. I needed a partner for the experiment, so I emailed Cierra, who was back home in Denver.

Here's a copy of the message I sent her, which explains the protocol I used:

Email sent on Nov. 2, 2018

Hi sweets,

I know we'll talk later, but I thought I'd save time by writing down the basic steps assuming you have time to help me today. I'd like to place a bet tonight on a hockey game, Hurricanes vs. Coyotes. I know the Avalanche are playing but since we live in Colorado, the emotional connection could affect my work. Here's how you can help:

1. Go online and print out two photos, very different from each other but both have distinct features for remote viewing.

2. Assign one photo to the Coyotes, the other to the Hurricanes. Just write the team name somewhere in the photo.

3. You'll send me a photo of the winning team's image later tonight after the game (or in the morning if you go to bed before the game finishes). You could just snap a photo of it with your phone and text it to me later on at the proper time. You won't show me or tell me anything about *the image assigned to the losing team.*

4. We need to pick a time this afternoon when you can look at my notes and sketches, and let me know which team's image I'm seeing. But you won't show me the *actual* image until after the game, you'll only give me the team name this afternoon, so I can place my bet.

Sound good?
xoxo

She agreed to help me. She went about the task of choosing two distinct images and assigning each to either the Coyotes or the Hurricanes. Around the same time, I went outside the casino to sit on a quiet bench with a pen and some scrap paper I'd taken from my vendor table outside the ballroom room.

I had a specific process in mind. First, I'd take a few minutes to do a "cool down," which for me, meant relaxing my body and mind much the same way I did during a telekinesis session.

Second, I would form the distinct intention for my mind to perceive the image which Cierra was going to text me sometime after the hockey game was over. My singular concern was that image, and I wasted no attention focusing on hockey, or team names, or anything like that. *All I wanted was to see the image she'd send me in the future.*

Third, after setting my time-traveling intention, I'd sit back, relax, and write down whatever spontaneously came to mind.

I was aware the subconscious mind often operated on its own schedule, and might begin retrieving information before the cool down period even began. This possibility was similar to some of my telekinesis experiments when, after using the same object for a few weeks, it would respond to my presence ahead of time, spinning before I consciously began the process to get it moving.

And that's exactly what happened as I sat down on the bench.

Before starting my "formal session," a snippet of something flashed into my mind, and luckily I wrote it down. As you can see in the image below, I labeled the information with the phrase "spontaneous, before official session."

Then, I settled into the process by relaxing, set my intention, then waited for more information to come. I knew it was important to write down *anything* that came, no matter how illogical, confusing or nonsensical it seemed.

What came next was a type of sphere with dark squares like windows or access points of some type all around it. Then, I saw an image which, looking at it now, resembles a birthday cake with tall candles sticking out of it. Or it could've been a building with large antennae on the roof. Or, who knows what else it could've been? I followed the generally recognized remote viewing instructions to *not label* what I saw, because that would involve too much left-brained thinking. I waited for more.

A feeling came over me and I noted it as "Up, rising up." Then a couple others, "animal-feel" and "yellow cubes, like pineapple." None of this made sense.

Then a couple more images came to mind. One was a long, narrow shape with a rounded edge. Then, a different shape, and this one

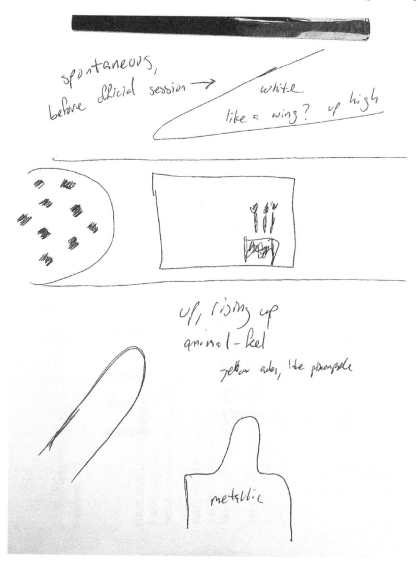

This is the photo of my notes which I texted to Cierra.

Sean McNamara

had a metallic feel to it, so I wrote the word "metallic" right on top of it.

A couple more minutes passed, and I could tell that my mind was now filling up with lots of guesses as I got more and more distracted by the people walking around where I was seated.

I snapped a photo of my notes and texted it to Cierra. Her job was now to compare my notes to the two photos she'd downloaded off of the internet, each labeled either as "Hurricanes" or "Coyotes."

After a while, she texted me saying that my notes seemed to indicate I'd been perceiving the photo assigned to the Coyotes.

She was careful not to send me the actual photo. The team name was all I needed to place a wager. I went to the sports book inside the casino and placed a $30 bet for the Coyotes to win that night.

Then I returned to my vendor table at the conference and tried not to think about that evening's hockey game too much. I was more curious about the *image* Cierra would send me after the game was over. If the Coyotes won, she'd send me the photo she'd assigned to them. If the Hurricanes won, then she'd send me the other one, instead.

Late that night, Cierra texted me the photograph, along with a note of congratulations. We won!

278

Coyotes

The target image which Cierra matched to my notes.

The image of the wing, along with the sense of "up, moving up" were easy to connect to the image. The two shapes at the bottom of my notes reminded me of my earliest experiments with Cierra, when my sketches resembled disconnected puzzle pieces rather than a whole image.

The drawing on the bottom left could've been a wing, or the front fuselage of an airplane. The drawing on the bottom center of the page with the word "metal" written over it could've been the middle part of the fuselage, where the wings connected to the body of the airplane.

As for the sphere and the birthday cake, I didn't see any way these could've connected to the image. Were they just extra "noise" in my head, or something else?

Questions aside, it was nice to win.

Our winning sports wager.

In the e-mail I'd sent Cierra at the start of the experiment, I told her that I wouldn't be shown the alternate image, the one for the losing team. But after winning, I became curious. How different were the two images? How easy was it for her to choose one photo over the other after looking at my chicken scratch?

I waited until the next day to ask Cierra to send me the other photo. I waited because I hypothesized if I saw it too soon, or too closely to when I saw the first image, my mind could've sent me information about that one instead of the other during my viewing session.

So, I thought inserting a half-day's-worth of time in between looking at both photos would be enough to avoid confusion.

When Cierra texted me the second image, I realized I should've waited even longer, or refused to see it at all.

Hurricanes

The alternate target image. This is the one she would have sent me after the game if the Hurricanes had won instead of the Coyotes.

Upon looking at it, my drawings of the sphere and the birthday cake made more sense. There's no way to know for sure, but the associations are too close to ignore. The sphere seems obvious, since the balloon image is filled with spheres.

Was the birthday cake an association with the meaning of colorful balloons? I knew from my mediumship studies with Jude that the subconscious mind often communicated "meaning" through symbols rather than words, since symbols carry far more information than a single noun, adjective or adverb is capable of.

Or, were we simply lucky? It was only because there were a few more images connected to the airplane than to the balloon that Cierra selected the Coyote photo.

We made two more wagers that weekend. We won one, and lost the other. I realized this wasn't a perfect system. Still, I was intrigued, and wanted to do more. A lot more.

Inspired by Jude's teaching style of throwing her students into the deep end, I decided to do the same thing. I already knew who I'd invite to explore remote viewing with me. My meditation students.

I already knew people who meditated were more successful at lucid dreaming than non-meditators. I also thought meditators had an easier time learning my TRIAM method for telekinesis than non-meditators. I was still teaching meditation at Mayu Sanctuary, but by this time I did it without associating myself with any teacher, lineage, or religion. I focused on techniques and direct experience, and avoided dogma and disempowering rituals. This allowed me the freedom to try something new, like teaching them how to see the future.

To make my first class as attractive as possible, I decided we could attempt to predict the Colorado lottery's winning numbers. This was the big lottery, requiring the correct selection of 6 out of 42 numbers, with a jackpot of millions of dollars.

The plan was to spend the morning slowly explaining what remote viewing is, how it related to consciousness exploration, and the specific methods we'd use to predict the 6 winning numbers for that night's drawing. Afterward, we'd do the actual remote viewing, get our predicted numbers, and anyone who wanted to could go out and buy their lotto tickets. Since the lotto drawing was later that night, I'd have to email each viewer their feedback image, the following day.

Each feedback image represented whether a particular number, like 5, or 12, or 41 was either "drawn" or "not drawn." The viewers had no idea which number they'd been assigned to predict. Instead, I gave each of them a 6-digit coordinate, which they were told was associated with the feedback image they'd be emailed the following day. The purpose was to ensure they weren't focused on seeing a lottery number, but instead would keep their mind on the future image they'd be shown.

I was basically treating each number, from 1 to 42, as a hockey game. The viewer who was assigned to the number 1 via a coordinate was singularly concerned with psychically perceiving which image they'd be shown in the future.

If their notes matched the image assigned to the number 1 being "drawn," then 1 would be one of our predicted lotto numbers.

If their notes matched the image assigned to "NOT drawn," then we wouldn't include that number.

In a perfect world, I would have had 42 viewers in class that day, that way they'd only have to do a single viewing session each. I only had 23 viewers, which meant if each person did 2 sessions, we'd produce 44 predictions. Since we only needed 42 predictions, I designed the assignments so that 2 of the targets were "control" targets, not associated with any lotto number.

None of the viewers would know if they were predicting a real target or a control.

The biggest risk was a viewer's subconscious mind confusing their first target image with their second one. Another risk was a viewer accidentally picking up on *another viewer's target* instead of their own.

I knew this was a possibility because of something that happened almost a year and a half earlier, in one of Jude's classes when we were practicing our clairvoyance with each other. During this exercise, we broke up into teams of partners, and our task was to perceive information about our classmate's home life.

Jude sat back, listening while each partner began sharing their perceptions with the other. The room was filled with the noise of

Sean McNamara

simultaneous conversations, but Jude was able to focus on each one, assessing everyone's progress.

I became embarrassed because everything I was telling my partner was wrong. I'd received impressions of the home's design, the furniture, who else lived there, but my partner's response was always the same, "Try again."

Jude picked up on my difficulty and walked over to and asked how we were doing. "Hold on a sec," she replied, after hearing about my difficulty. She walked across the room to another set of partners, and asked one of them to change places with mine. "Ok, now tell her what you were telling your first partner."

I did, and was shocked when my new partner replied that I was doing a great job describing her living situation. It turned out that her previous partner had been struggling just like me. While listening to both sets of partners, Jude realized I and the other "reader" had gotten our lines crossed!

Teaching my "lotto" class, I knew it was possible for the same thing to happen here. Still, it was worth a try. My priority was not actually about winning money, after all. The lottery simply provided a third-party random event generator, of sorts. We could've all worked together to predict a football game, but the benefit of using the lottery was that we'd need a "team style" design to do it. If enough of the viewers' predictions were correct, we'd have a successful experiment.

Being successful in a 42-number prediction required more than 6 targets correctly viewed as "drawn," though. We also needed the remaining 36 targets to correctly indicate "not drawn." Each viewer had to do two sessions that day. If a single viewer's prediction for just one of their numbers was wrong, then our odds of winning shrank considerably.

Everyone took their work seriously, and I did everything I could to keep them relaxed and playful. They turned in their notes and

284

drawings, and Cierra and I went into another room to compare them to each number's two potential images.

The clock was ticking. We had to put together a solid prediction in time for the participants to go out and buy their tickets on their way home that evening.

Not counting the control sessions, we quickly compared 42 transcripts containing each viewer's notes and drawings to 84 paired images. Ideally, the result would have left us with *exactly* 6 "drawn" numbers, and 36 "not drawn" numbers.

Instead, we were left with 12 "drawn" and 30 "not drawn." Statistically, this was already interesting. If no psychic ability was involved, each prediction had a 50/50 chance of going one way or the other, so we would have had closer to 21 "drawn" and 21 "not drawn" predictions. Still, we didn't know the final results, since the lottery hadn't been drawn yet.

I told the viewers which were the 12 "drawn" number predictions, and they each had to decide for themselves which of those numbers they'd select when buying their ticket that evening. I think many of us bought multiple combinations of those numbers hoping that one of them would be a match for the correct 6 winning numbers.

Alas, nobody won. But, out of our 12 potential numbers, 3 of them were *actual* winning numbers. I thought it was noteworthy, given this was everyone's first time, and these were far from ideal conditions.

That was on November 17, 2018.

I taught a similar class that December, and it was a confusing mess. The problem was I thought it would be fun to let the viewers' play my role, and analyze each other's transcripts and potential images.

Looking back, I can imagine the veritable tangle of psychic information in that room as multiple images entered each viewer's mind during each stage of the process. Needless to say, we didn't win.

Sean McNamara

Nearly a year passed by before I decided to try again, in August of 2019.

I call this our *true first attempt* because this time, we did the entire experiment inside our home. And instead of doing this in the context of a paid, public class, this would be a gathering of friends. Everyone in this group was familiar with remote viewing from my other classes, and we all knew and liked each other, which helped us relax.

Still, we lost.

In September, we tried again. They'd had so much fun last time that this event was done by their request, which I deeply appreciated. They saw value in our experiments, and the "wow" factor never seemed to wear off. Even though we didn't pick enough winning numbers, there was astounding evidence in each viewer's transcript to show they'd *actually received information psychically* to one degree or another.

But this time, our objective was to predict the outcome of the local "Pick 3" lottery. This would be easier because we only needed to predict 3 numbers out of 10. Equally important, nobody was here because of the money, especially since the highest jackpot for an "any order" bet was $80 on a $1 ticket. They were here simply to explore the mind together, and to have fun. Again, this helped everyone to stay relaxed during the process.

This time, we won!

With Stacy Linrud and Michelle Cox,
the winning ticket holders from our first group success,
September 15, 2019.

To put it more specifically, 2 of the 8 viewers on our team that day had all 3 winning numbers on their tickets. The problem was, just like when we attempted the 42-number lottery, we ended up with more predicted winning numbers than we needed.

Still, I call this "our win" because it took the whole group to determine the potential winning numbers.

We met in my home again that October, but lost.

But, everyone in the group was still having fun and learning a lot, and still didn't care whether we won or lost. More than anything, this was a chance for us to just hang out as friends and explore the mind together. So, we decided to try it again the following month.

We scheduled our next get-together for Sunday, November 10.

The week before, I became nervous that I might have to reschedule our experiment. For some reason, my whole body felt strangely worn down, and my digestion was giving me a lot of trouble. More worrisome, though, was my mood. I felt deeply anxious throughout the week, but I didn't have any idea why.

I remember trying to keep a sense of humor about it and jokingly telling Cierra, "I'm either going through some kind of spiritual transformation, or I'm about to have a really bad case of diarrhea."

At some point that night, I woke up from a dream.

> I walked into a diner, the kind with vinyl-covered booths and a breakfast bar where people could sit by themselves, on stools. I sat down at an empty booth, and realized that Steve was sitting at another booth nearby. I quickly changed my position in the booth, hoping to find an angle where he couldn't see me. Suddenly, and by some mysterious force, I found myself sitting right in front of him.

> He didn't say a word. As I looked at him, I noticed his eyes were red and moist. He looked sad, and soft. Without using words, he let me know how badly he felt about the way he treated me at the end of our time together. He seemed genuinely apologetic and regretful. I couldn't help feeling bad for him, and wanted to accept his apology. But, the dream ended before anything else could happen.

I wasn't sure what to think about the dream. I wondered if it was connected to the strange feelings I'd had all week, including my abdominal pains. I quickly forgot about it, focusing instead on preparing to host my friends for remote viewing together later that day.

Like we'd done the last couple times together, we experimented with unique ways to boost our psychic abilities in preparation for the remote viewing sessions. For example, we did psychic spoon-bending as a sort of "warm up" for the rest of the day. It turns out that, just like all the other psychic abilities I'd explored, anyone could soften metal enough to bend it when given the right instructions.

And for the second time, we won.

With friends winning the Pick 3 lottery again, November 10, 2019.[28]

This time, about half the group purchased the right combination of numbers for their ticket, since in actuality we'd come up with 4 potential "drawn" numbers instead of 3. Like before, I considered it a "group win." Every person there was essential to the process.

That night after everyone went home, I had the dreaded diarrhea I'd joked about with Cierra. It was bad. I had no way of knowing whether or not it was connected to the mysterious emotions I'd been feeling the week before, though.

About two weeks later, an old friend forwarded me an internal memo written by several board members in Steve's organization, addressed to his "advanced" students. It announced plans to close the organization down. The letter was vague about why this was happening, citing financial difficulties and "other reasons." I couldn't believe it; the whole thing was falling apart.

---

[28] Learn the specific details of how we did it in my other book "Signal and Noise: Advanced Psychic Development for Remote Viewing, Clairvoyance, and ESP."

Was this why I felt the way I did a few weeks earlier? Is this why I had my dream of meeting Steve in the diner? The timing surely was interesting.

As far as I know, Steve never did follow through on appointing anyone to carry on his teachings. I wondered how his students felt after getting the letter. Did he leave them any path at all? Or will they have to find their own way? Will they reclaim their personal authority, or give it away to somebody else?

I can only hope each one of them finds what they're looking for.

For me, reading the letter was like breaking a dark, magical spell. It was a spell which had kept me bound up ever since I'd left him. Now, somewhere deep, I became unfrozen.

I noticed that my body no longer exhibited a stress-response the way it had, anytime someone asked me to tell them about what happened with Steve, or how he'd treated other people. The fear was gone.

If I'd ever had any doubt about my decision to leave, it was now gone for good. There hadn't been anything wrong with me "believing everything I thought," as he'd put it during our final conversation together. I'd been right to trust myself.

That's when I began to write this book. I ignored the drafts I'd begun years ago, when my life was headed in a different direction, before I knew what I know now.

I'd had dreams of Steve ever since I said goodbye, all the way up to the night before we won the lottery for the second time. In some of them, he appeared dark and bitter. In others, soft and gentle, or even needy sometimes. I've chosen not to include those dreams in this book. Sometimes, I wonder if he ever dreamt of me. I'll never know, and I think I'd prefer not to.

It doesn't matter though. After everything I've experienced, most of which I've shared here with you, I know we're all connected to each other in ways we can't possibly understand. At least at this point in our development as a species. Our souls might hold the answers, but the physical brain can only allow so much.

I wouldn't be surprised to meet Steve again someday, perhaps in a different lifetime. The same goes for my other teachers, my family, friends, and traveling companions.

Dear reader, I don't know if you and I will ever meet. But, maybe we don't need to, now that you've read this book.

I hope you find what you're looking for.

EPILOGUE

Thank you for reading this book. Writing it was a deeply emotional process, and there were many times when I thought I couldn't go forward with it, because to reveal some of my experiences to you, I had to relive them again. But there were also blessings waiting for me. Transcribing my out of body experiences caused me to have one spontaneously, which I regard as a kind of confirmation.

Also, there was one night when I found myself on the couch, unable to sleep after writing a particularly emotional chapter. Searching my mind, I realized that I hadn't allowed myself to express everything I'd been feeling deep down inside. Alone in the darkness, I began to weep. But I *wasn't* alone. I was struck by the unseen presence of people I'd known during different phases of my life, before they'd left their physical bodies and crossed over.

As I cried, I could feel them holding, supporting, and witnessing me. I didn't write this book alone, and I want to take this opportunity to thank them for being a part of my journey, in their own way. I also reflect on the many students and friends I've spent time with over the years, some of whom are very dear to me. Without them, none of this would have been possible.

Having finished this book, I feel tired, and complete. Not for the writing of it, but for the experiences I went through in the course of growing up. I've spent the last few years sharing my experiences with people, and teaching them how to have them for themselves. If it's appropriate to you, I hope this book helps you set yourself free from anything or anyone who might be keeping you from your ultimate journey.

As I write above, I'm tired. I don't know if I want, or need, to continue teaching this way anymore. It might be time for me to go *within* again, to be still and quiet, and get some rest. When the time is right, I'll be ready to experience something new, and I'll probably share it too, if I can.

I wish to include two more dreams before we say goodbye, and then I'll explain why.

June 10, 2018

I'm on the porch of an old farmhouse with Dad and Ma. We're in a valley, with houses in the distance and only a few people around. I need to take a walk, or go get something, so I tell them I'll be right back.

After walking away, I notice the mountains in the distance are dark. There's a giant, strange silhouette of the sun on one of them, with a sliver of red light shining out from it. I look up, and see the sky is a deep red, with swirls of black and gray, as if the clouds were burning. The whole atmosphere is on fire, red, and black.

I rush back to the house, but Dad and Ma aren't there. I look across the valley. Heat and fire are rushing from one side to another, burning the grass, brush, and earth along the way. The whole world is on fire. It's the end of everything.

June 13, 2018

I woke up with an idea embedded inside my head, that "It's not about choosing the right location, or putting the right pieces together, but about moving over to a completely different timeline of events." It seems like this knowledge was

Sean McNamara

given to me. But how exactly does one *move into a different timeline?*

People ask me why I've written this memoir now, in my middle age, instead of later, when I'm closer to the end. I have several reasons. First, I felt there was so much information here, that to retain it for several more decades would be impossible. Second, I believe there are readers who could use this information to benefit their lives right now. To wait and give it to them sometime in the future would be far too late to do them any good.

Finally, our world is in trouble. When I began the first draft of this book, Australia was burning. Now, the whole world is gripped by the relentless spread of the COVID-19 virus. There's no way to know for sure what will happen next.

But there is hope. I think there's still time for us to change, still time for us to find solutions. Unique individuals throughout history have impacted humanity with new ideas and inventions. Specifically, there have been scientists, mathematicians, artists, musicians, politicians, biologists and others whose ideas have come to them *while in an altered state of consciousness.* Stories abound of dreams, visions, and encounters with non-ordinary beings giving people crucial information for the benefit of others.

Our planet faces challenges none of us have ever seen before. More than ever, we need to find novel solutions. I believe meditation and psychic development are powerful methods for opening one's mind to receive them. Whether these solutions come from one's subconscious mind or from an external source, doesn't really matter in the end. What matters most are the actions we'll take.

If we truly intend to change our destiny, the ideas I've shared with you here can help. Though, not because of the abilities or experiences themselves, exactly.

I think they can help because to pursue them can change you, even empower you. This type of training has the effect of increasing your creativity, your ability to innovate, your depth of understanding, and

294

your courage to challenge the status quo, whether it's at home, in school, at work, or elsewhere in your life. If the changes we need don't occur during our generation, hopefully they will with the next.

There's no time to waste.

ESSAY: Being with Fear During OBE's and in Daily Life

The two most significant limitations a person faces when training to have their first **OBE** are a **LACK OF KNOWLEDGE** of techniques and second, **FEAR**. I'm writing this essay on fear because truly helpful advice on how to deal with it is difficult to find.

To achieve an **OBE** in the ways I've experienced and taught myself requires that one remains emotionally calm during the following periods:

1. The visualization or meditation process (the application of a technique)
2. While strange sensations or other things occur during #1
3. While you allow yourself to drift toward sleep
4. When you become conscious of the separation signals (vibrational state)
5. As you begin the process of separation (floating or being transported away)
6. While you are completely disassociated and having a full out of body experience

Becoming anxious, nervous, afraid, or tense during any one of these periods may instantly terminate the experience. Of course, it's only *natural* for you to experience fear during your training principally because you're attempting to have an experience which you have *no idea what it will actually feel like when it finally happens.* You are stepping into the unknown. So, let's all agree it's perfectly normal to be afraid when trying something new and strange.

If you recall, I would transfer to my massage table from time to time in the middle of the night to help me slowly relax my body during my visualization process, and to delay the onset of sleep. But there were times when I felt overly exposed. I felt like a child who has heard something go "bump" in the night, then draws their monster-proof blanket over themselves for protection.

In the same spirit, whenever I became afraid during an OBE attempt, I'd not only pull a blanket over myself, but I'd also fold the massage table's legs so the padding was lowered onto the floor. This helped me feel less exposed. I didn't really, or logically believe that anything would come to hurt me, but this confidence came from my logical and sensible "left" brain, and not my emotional, irrational "right" brain. That's the part that matters in the dark.

All that is to say, when you feel afraid, treat yourself with the same level of care and understanding that you would a small child, and do what you need to do to comfort yourself. If you're afraid of the dark, it's perfectly alright to use a nightlight to help you relax as you go through the stages of the training, even if you're an adult. Get yourself a monster-proof blanket. Say a prayer.

I realized something important after examining several instances of fear during my OBE attempts. Whenever I became afraid, I noticed a particular feeling in my stomach, the back of my neck, or sometimes in my legs and body. I realized there have been other times in my life when I've felt the exact same physical sensations. These were times when *something I was looking forward* to was about to happen, such as asking someone on a date for the first time, walking on stage during a graduation ceremony, or applying for a new job.

I realized that on a deeper level, the fear I experienced during OBE training felt exactly the same as when I was having these other kinds of experiences. What do these sensations mean, then? They signify I am about to undergo a change in my identity. More simply, they signal that I'm about to have a novel experience. And nothing is more novel than an OBE, since nothing else in everyday life comes close to mimicking the experience. A person can try to describe what an OBE feels like to you, but when you have one yourself, you'll realize that words just don't do it justice.

Having this understanding of the *sensations* of fear actually helps reduce its emotional potency. Over time, you might still feel physical heaviness or the "nervousness" in your chest or belly during the OBE process. But, you'll be able to stay calm as you remind yourself these sensations are simply signaling that "I'm about to change, I'm getting close to finally having an OBE. This is something *I really want,* and I can't wait any longer!"

There's no way around fear. But you can learn to accept and include it in your journey, and use it to measure your progress.

This is how fear works: You'll start your visualization, and at a certain point, you'll become nervous for some reason. Let's call that "hitting your first wall." You'll basically repeat your training day after day, hitting the same "wall of fear" until you get bored and realize there's nothing to be afraid of.

When that happens, you'll naturally go further along the process until you become scared at a later stage. For example, you might start drifting off after doing your visualization, then perceive a separation signal, like the unexplained sound of footsteps or tinkling bells, or feeling like someone's touching your legs.

You'll have to train day after day, hitting that new wall over and over until once again, you get bored. At that point, you'll go even further. It's the same thing all the way up to and including when you find yourself in some mysterious realm after traveling away from your body and having a successful OBE.

When you finally have one, your relationship to fear will be vastly more evolved and mature than it was when you first began. You'll also be able to apply your new understanding of fear to other types of psychic development.

Most importantly, you'll be able to apply it to material aspects of life, like starting, maintaining, or even terminating a career, relationship, or anything else which is within your power to decide.

ESSAY: Artificial Intelligence (AI), Consciousness and the Voight-Kampff Test

Anyone who's watched the 1982 sci-fi film "Blade Runner" will remember the Voight-Kampff test. In this fictional movie, people have figured out a way to bioengineer what is referred to a "replicant," a custom-designed, enhanced humanoid. The problem is, the design is so good, it's nearly impossible to tell the difference between a replicant and a real person. This is usually the point of conversation when people wax philosophical about whether replicants are truly conscious beings or not. Do they have souls? Do they have an inherent right to exist, to live, work and love as we do? And as far as love goes, can they even have that experience in a way we'd call "real?"

In the movie, the ability to test whether a suspect is real or replicated is important because certain independent-minded replicants are on the run, hiding after causing serious problems for the real people. Luckily, investigators like Harrison Ford's "Deckard" can apply the "Voight-Kampff" test.

During such an examination, the investigator asks the suspect a series of questions while looking for the presence or absence of some automatic physiological response from their subject. Do the suspect's pupils dilate, does their skin conductance increase, or does their heart rate shift when a particularly arousing scene is described? If the suspect isn't a real human, he or she may not be able to fake the appropriate bodily response, and get caught in the act.

We'll never need a Voight-Kampff test in the real world, though. Or will we? As of the year 2020, customers call product or service helplines to complain, get information, or place an order. They believe they're speaking to a real person, but this isn't always the case. Often, they're chatting with a computer program empowered with the benefit of "AI," artificial intelligence. Other people are successfully finding emotional support or relief by speaking to an artificially intelligent persona, even though they fully know they're talking to a computer. I don't think I need to go further after acknowledging the rapidly expanding, AI-equipped robot sex doll industry. It's happening.

If the day ever comes when we'll actually need something like a Voight-Kampff test, I propose another method to answer the question, "Does this being actually have a consciousness like us?" The VK exam might not do the trick. If the quality of replication is sufficiently advanced, Pinocchio's pulse may actually quicken after hearing a deliciously dirty joke.

The alternate method is nothing more than a simple psychic demonstration. If a replicant lacks the aspect of non-physical consciousness I believe makes us "us," then it's fair to think they might not be able to demonstrate abilities like psychokinesis or remote viewing (clairvoyance). Why? Because if they're nothing more than a well programmed sack of blood and bones, then they'll lack that mysterious stuff which connects us to everything else in this universe on some invisible level.

A replicant won't have *whatever that is* which allows a real person to physically alter an object without touching it. A replicant would also be unable to gain visual, auditory, or other data about another person, in some other place, because psychic perception is, at least partially, based on non-physical consciousness.

After training hundreds of people in producing psychic effects, I can say with confidence that each one of them has exhibited some level of natural ability (as long as they were willing to follow the instructions).

The Voight-Kampff-inspired test would simply be to put the suspected replicant through a psychic training course, along with a

Sean McNamara

classroom full of real people, and see whether or not they show the slightest bit of success. The real people will, of course, because it's part of being truly alive. Anyone can show a little bit of ability if you teach them how.

But what if I'm wrong? What if it turns out these future replicants possess even these types of abilities? Does it mean that somehow, a non-physical consciousness has found a new home inside the replicant, like a soul entering a body? Or does it mean psychic functioning doesn't actually require a non-physical component, and rather, it's a physical, albeit hidden function?

Or worse, what if it means we've been wrong the whole time, and none of us are actually conscious beyond the experiences produced by our physical brains? No need to worry too much about it, I think. After all, it was only a movie, and this essay is just a bit of a thought experiment.

ESSAY: Caution When Choosing a Spiritual Teacher or Group

There are several things to consider when you are either getting started with a teacher and/or group, or are wondering if it's time to end that relationship. The section below will help you preserve your autonomy and the integrity of your journey. This is intended as a starting point. Meeting with a counselor or therapist (one who is not a member of that group) could be very helpful in your decision-making.

Before joining a group[29]

Are you clear on what your particular spiritual goals are, or what questions you're seeking answers to? Have you researched this teacher/group well enough to know whether or not they're focused on the same things? Or does their "path" take you in a different direction? Keep in mind if you don't know what direction you want to go in life, other people will be more than happy to make that decision for you, and it could be the wrong one.

Do you feel drawn to the teacher's personality? Take some time to reflect on yourself and see if they remind you of someone you've already met, like a family member you admire, or someone you've lost. You should also reflect on whether or not this teacher might subconsciously fill a role for you, such as replacing your father or mother figure, or an absent lover.

---

[29] Also, see the entry for "Avoiding or Healing from High-Demand Groups/Cults" in the Recommended Resources section at the end.

Is the teacher described as possessing some kind of transcendent quality, such as being enlightened, or having direct communication with a spiritual or otherworldly authority? If so, do you feel like you're able, and allowed to, ask them face-to-face if this is truly the case, and to tell you more about what that's like? If you feel nervous about it, or like it's something which "just isn't done," this could be a sign of trouble. The unspoken suppression of open inquiry could be one way a person or group maintains control over its members.

If the teacher claims their followers achieve certain results or goals, take the time to interview the group members who've spent a great deal of time with the teacher. Ask them if they've indeed experienced those results, or ask how their time with the teacher has helped them.

Then ask yourself if these students demonstrate characteristics which you would like to acquire. Are these characteristics only available here, or have you found them in other groups as well?

Analyze the business aspect of the organization. It's completely fair for a teacher or group to earn money. School teachers, doctors, and personal trainers make money for their work, since in our society, this is how we take care of ourselves. People who believe a teacher should work for free might never have had to make a living themselves (children), are still being supported by their parents (dependent adults), or can't accept that the days of bartering service or items of value in exchange for teachings are long past.

Spiritual teachers need to pay the rent like everybody else. But there are two questions. Are you getting what you're paying for? In other words, who's getting the benefit here? You, or the teacher? Is it an equal exchange, or does it feel imbalanced?

The second question is, is the teacher's income appropriate to their role? For instance, when the CEO of a non-profit dedicated to helping the homeless and underserved earns a multi-million-dollar salary, society raises its eyebrows, as it should. If your spiritual teacher's income is similarly inflated, it's worth taking a closer look. There's no objective answer. In other words, you have to decide if the situation feels appropriate to *you*, personally.

Is this person a full-time teacher, meaning, do they earn all their income from this, or do they have a regular job, and teach on the side? If they make most of their income elsewhere, this increases the chance they can act with integrity and not be concerned with attracting more followers to give themselves a bonus or raise their standard of living.

If they have a "day job," there's a greater likelihood their feet are firmly on the ground, and they can relate to life's ordinary challenges rather than descending from their pedestal to "save you."

Do an online search about potential issues attributed to the group or teacher by using terms like "abuse," "harm," "cult," "fraud," "sexual assault," and "high demand." Online watchdog groups might have already identified the teacher as problematic. However, in the end, you'll need to decide for yourself.

I make this final entry in this section since there seem to be more and more groups forming around people with "special" or "secret," information concerning UFO/UAP, or extraterrestrial phenomena. In some cases, they resemble spiritual ministers who go from town to town, attracting followers and donations as they share their revelations to people hungry for meaning. I'll keep this simple. Ask to see real evidence of any claims made by that individual. Question the evidence itself.

You don't have to believe anything you don't want to.

In fact, *take everything that is not a part of your direct experience with a big grain of salt.* It is not necessary for you to believe everything you hear in order to enjoy a presentation. But be careful with what you accept as "real." The same goes for "channeling." I'm not saying these aren't authentic experiences and modalities. I'm saying that *some of the people using them* might not be sincere or ethically-minded. Use your discretion.

Sean McNamara

Spotting trouble AFTER joining a group

Here are signs to watch out for:

- A large portion of the group's energy is focused on the teacher's personal dramas or emotional flare-ups.

- Unspoken group tension following rumors of conflict.

- Individuals quietly leave the group without giving notice or explanation, as if escaping.

- Members are kicked out, then welcomed back in with a gross overexpression of acceptance and love, called "love bombing," from the teacher or other group members.

- The teacher speaks about students or others when they are not in the room, making examples out of them or explaining "their" side of things.

- You feel tense or uneasy during lectures, meditations, or ceremonies (trust your gut).

- You discover there are "hoops" you must go through to reach the next "level." These hoops come with an exorbitant fee, a requirement of some kind of service, or statement of personal commitment.

- You begin to determine your self-worth by *how much* attention, or the *quality of attention* you receive from the teacher and group members. This can include the pursuit of special titles or roles.

- You stop spending time with family or friends outside the organization, or feel awkward speaking with them about your group and teacher.

- The proceeds from special fundraisers or regular income are spent on things other than their stated purpose.

- The teacher projects a glorified, idealized, or oversexualized image of themselves on social media or other types of advertising.

- You become afraid of speaking openly, particularly when you have doubts, questions, or a need to challenge someone in a fair manner.

- You haven't made any progress responding to your unique, individual spiritual inquiry. Instead, your true path has been overshadowed or derailed by what their tradition says you "should" be focusing on instead.

ESSAY: The "100-Hour Telekinesis Challenge" for Students and Researchers

In May of 2019, I was invited to Portland to spend a few days with theoretical physicist George Weismann, PhD. and neuroscientist Mike Weliky, PhD., who wanted to do some telekinesis experiments together. We were joined by Nancy Du Tertre, author and psychic teacher. The primary goal was to see if we could successfully move the object inside of a vacuum-sealed container and settle the question about how this type of psychokinesis actually happens.

Nobody knows for certain what produces telekinesis. However, Dean Radin PhD from the Institute of Noetic Sciences and John Valentino from Princeton University both suggested to me that rather than moving the tinfoil (or other objects) directly, I might be causing the air molecules around it to move in such a way as to "push" on the object.

This involves using consciousness to change the state of the molecular movement from one of "randomness" or "entropy" to one of "coherence" or "syntropy." Personally, I believe they're correct.[30] This is why testing telekinesis in a vacuum would help determine the cause. If the object still moved even when there wasn't air inside the container, then there'd have to be another reason for its movement.

As part of the experiment, Mike and George wanted to make sure I wasn't simply "heating up" the air inside the container, and causing

---

[30] For a detailed explanation, find the related video link at www.RenegadeMysticBook.com/links

the air to move by convection. Mike placed a highly sensitive thermometer inside the container. It was connected to special software which made it possible to watch the moment-by-moment change in temperature on a graph, displayed on a nearby computer screen.

As I usually did, I placed my hands on the glass to begin moving the object. This is my way of "connecting" with it. Normally, I'd move my hands a couple inches away after a few minutes, then place them in my lap a little bit later, and after a while, I'd stand several feet away from the whole setup while keeping the object moving.

But now, we were able to see how quickly the temperature inside rose after I placed my hands on the glass. The temperature also rose when I merely put my hands very near the glass, not even touching it. As soon as we saw this, I came apart. I'd placed a lot of pressure on myself to do a good job for our group, and suddenly it looked like I wasn't actually doing telekinesis at all.

I have to admit my intimidation by their credentials as "PhDs," even though I'd already experienced them as kind, patient, enthusiastic and optimistic. Even with their support, I fell into a foul mood, fearing I'd unintentionally committed fraud all these years by telling people I was using psychic means to move the object. We had only a few days together, and I spent most of that time emotionally kicking myself, which had the effect of rendering me nearly useless.

It appeared that all this time, I'd fallen victim to what psychologists refer to as "confirmation bias." *It appeared* that anytime the object moved, I falsely confirmed the cause to be something psychic instead of physical.

I became frozen, stuck on the "heat issue," which kept us from moving on to focusing on the vacuum question.

Curiously, by the end of our time together, Nancy, George and Mike still believed psychokinesis was real. I was the only one who'd lost all faith, and was now ruminating about what kind of public detractions

Sean McNamara

I needed to make. If anything, this revealed how much of an ego I'd developed around telekinesis, and how fragile that ego was.

Unfortunately, it wasn't until I'd left Portland when I realized my error. On the return flight, I inserted my earbuds to enjoy some soothing music, eager to forget about the whole affair. After listening to several tracks, I became deeply relaxed, and allowed my mind to drift off. Eventually, I noticed a stream of thoughts entering my awareness, trying to get my attention. It was as if an old friend was trying to set me straight with a feeling of "Don't you remember?"

<u>"Don't you remember?"</u>

- When I was first learning telekinesis, I'd struggled for two and a half months before seeing *any* movement at all, even with my hands very close to the glass.

- With practice, I was able to *change which direction the object spun* on the needle, even from a distance, by altering my breathing pattern and how I focused my mind.

- Repeated sessions showed anytime I began to try *too hard*, which increased my level of physical and mental tension, the object would slow down or come to a halt. Then, by relaxing myself once more, the object would commence its prior state of motion. This occurred even when I was seated several feet away.

- I became more proficient the more I practiced. If the movement was solely due to heat, there would be no increase or change in how soon the object responded to me. The fact that my performance improved over time indicates this isn't random.

- When using the same object for an extended period of time, it became increasingly responsive to my intention. It started moving at the beginning of the session *faster than a fresh piece of tin foil or paper would*. Sometimes, it even responded to me just as I entered the room, *as if we had an established connection.* This didn't happen with brand new objects.

- When I placed three objects inside one container, they rarely moved at the same time. I could even focus on one of the objects and cause it to move without disturbing the others. Convection is too generalized for that kind of specificity.

- When I aligned three containers, each with one object inside, and with one closest to me and the third furthest away, the farthest object would often be the one to respond to me first. But this one was *least* susceptible to my body heat, so why should it move while the other sat still? At other times, the second object, in between the closest and farthest containers, would move first.

- Also, since heat is a natural byproduct, or correlate of molecular movement, wouldn't it be *impossible* to cause the air to move by psychic means without increasing the temperature in the process? Therefore, even though heat was present, *it didn't necessarily mean* it caused the movement.

- And, so what if heat was helpful in getting the object moving? Have you ever push-started a car whose battery had died? It might be the case that the psychic effect is only discernible after the object has been brought into motion by ordinary means.

Parapsychologists are well aware of cases where a placebo effect leads to a *real* outcome. For instance, when a shaman uses simple tricks to create the illusion of psychic healing, they produce objective, physical, and verifiable effects in a patient's body. To be absolutely clear, yes, I'm saying that fooling a person into *thinking* they are performing psychically can cause them to actualize their *real psychic ability.*

As an aside, perhaps this is the true purpose of rituals in religious traditions. Might they simply be placebos which at one point long ago, actually produced a result? Sadly, humans have a tendency to

Sean McNamara

continue rituals long after losing their efficacy, simply in the name of tradition. And as the popular phrase goes, "Tradition is just peer pressure from dead people."

It's also important to consider whether practicing a ritual imported from outside of one's natural culture limits its potential. Maybe something important really does get lost in translation. Of course, that's something each person needs to decide for themselves.

Let's return now, to the main topic at hand. When I teach telekinesis in a classroom, the sessions generally last just under two hours. In that time, everybody learns to successfully influence the movement of the object (usually tin foil, sometimes paper) while keeping their hands in their laps. A portion of the group can go further, standing up and moving several feet away while continuing to influence it.

Everyone begins the same way, by putting their hands directly on the glass, which is my instruction to help them "connect" to the object. And here's the problem. Who's to say that during the two-hour class, some of them haven't actually used telekinesis *even though they think they have.* How can we be sure they weren't falling for "confirmation bias," believing they were doing it when they really weren't?

Several times during the class, I make sure to ask them if they've noticed the object's movement responding to their level of tension and relaxation. I also ask if any of them can control the direction and speed of the object by following the training instructions.[31] In most cases, they say they can. But still, how can they be so sure?

The Challenge

The 100-hour challenge is a way for telekinesis students to immerse themselves in the experience and to confirm, to a high degree of

---

[31] These instructions are in the book "Defy Your Limits: The Telekinesis Training Method" and in my online video course.

312

confidence, that they can willfully influence the movement of the object.

Simply keep a practice journal, and log at least 100 clock hours of practicing telekinesis before deciding whether or not one is truly doing TK. Until then, one should remain an "open-minded skeptic," which means avoiding coming to conclusions either way, while focusing on collecting more data, direct experience in this case.

Why 100 hours? Because in that length of time, a person will not only succeed at influencing a single object in a non-random manner, but they'll be able to experiment with influencing multiple objects in one container, then multiple containers, other kinds of objects, and from varying distances.

The 100 hours implies the person will do most, if not all, of their experiments alone and at home, which is the most relaxing type of environment they could find. Being given a few hours in a laboratory where observers are hovering while a camera is recording everything is like begging for the experiment to fail. The various levels of stress created by this kind of environment can have debilitating consequences.

The extended training period also increases the probability the practitioner will experience certain *anomalies*, such as a well-used object behaving as if it has a relationship with them. Other things might happen too, such as an increase in synchronicities, or the enhancement of other psychic abilities like clairvoyance or precognition.

Researchers and Pseudo-skeptics

Researchers and pseudo-skeptics (debunkers) should also be willing to undergo the 100-hour challenge when investigating telekinesis. As long as they follow the training instructions with *at least* a neutral attitude and a high level of fidelity, they'll realize there really is something to this. To give it a shot for one or two hours then give up while saying "it doesn't work" just isn't fair. It's not that "it" doesn't work, but rather, they *didn't do the work* themselves.

But that's common behavior for pseudo-skeptics. They come to conclusions without doing any actual research or considering any data which contradicts their beliefs. Even if they do, they're prone to another kind of bias which affects us all, called "the backfire effect." The backfire effect is the tendency for people who, having been shown facts which contradict their beliefs, respond by denying the facts even more vehemently and recommitting to their original stance.

Similarly, too many people are quick to become believers, and fall too easily for certain types of telekinesis demonstrations available on YouTube and other sites. It's difficult to tell whether the person in the video is attempting to fool the public on purpose, or if they actually believe they're doing authentic telekinesis.

To help new TK students understand what I'm talking about, I've recorded myself performing *fake* telekinesis, mimicking a couple of the demonstrations I've seen online. These videos are intended as illustrations of possible "confirmation bias" or outright fraud.[32]

---

[32] Find the videos at www.RenegadeMysticBook.com/videos

ESSAY: Free Will and the Varieties of Consciousness

I wrote this essay to clarify the use of the word "subconscious" in contemporary fields of spirituality and psychology. Doing so will hopefully assist you in better understanding what's at play during consciousness exploration and spiritual experiences.

Part 1: "Subconscious Mind" as Brain

On New Year's Eve, 2019, a smiling, elderly man walked through a crowded plaza in Italy, when suddenly a woman nearby reached out and grabbed his hand. She seemed genuinely happy to see him. He, on the other hand, was surprised, and even winced as she pulled him toward her, keeping his hand tightly gripped in hers. A moment later, he vigorously slapped her hand. A split second later, he went to slap it again, but she released her grip, causing him to miss. Video cameras showed him scowling sourly as he walked away.

Who was this man? Pope Francis.[33]

On the night of April 30th, 2019, three friends named Adam, Bradley, and Sabrina met inside their hotel to have a few drinks together. They were there to attend a conference the following day. By 3:00 am, they'd met up with another friend, William, and headed out to the local strip club together. Discovering it was closed, they decided to go to a nearby White Castle restaurant.

---

[33] Find the video and article at www.RenegadeMysticBook.com/links

Sean McNamara

William went inside to order food, while the others stayed out in the parking lot. Two guys cruised by in an SUV, and one of them shouted something at Sabrina. She decided to show the jerk her middle finger.

Unfortunately, the strangers decided to stop the car and get personal. Adam and Bradley ended up in a fist fight with the strangers, one of whom had a gun. He shot Adam and Bradley, then sped away with his buddy. Sabrina stood there, watching defenselessly. Adam and Bradley survived. Authorities determined their blood alcohol levels greatly exceeded Indiana's legal driving limit.

If only the White Castle had been closed, this might not have happened. Or if only the strip club had been open, this might not have happened. Or if the friends had stayed at the hotel, or decided not to get drunk the night before the convention, this might not have happened. Or if Sabrina hadn't taunted the strangers by "giving them the bird."

Were Sabrina, Adam, Bradley and William short-sighted college kids, or super aggressive stock brokers, or Hollywood types looking for some action? No. They were county judges, and were there to attend a special conference for judicial officers.

What did the Pope and these four judges have in common? Simply put, their willpower was drained, and they were unable to restrain the instinctive urges which emerged out of their brains' survival center. Let's call this part of the brain "the *physical* subconscious."

My guess is that in the Pope's case, he probably hadn't had a decent meal in several hours. On top of that, he was surrounded by hundreds of fans, each one vying for his attention while calling out to him as if he were a rock star. Obviously surrounded by TV cameras and bright lights, he was probably working hard to maintain his composure the whole time. It was night, so he'd already used up most of his willpower in the course of normal business earlier in the day.

The end result was that his brain was running low on glucose. Because of the shortage, all available fuel was assigned to the parts of his brain most necessary to his survival. This is the part of his brain which controls one's behavior, emotional response, and decision-making ability.

The four judges must've also been hungry since they were at a White Castle when Sabrina lost her temper. I suppose it's fair to say that at least one or two members of the party had been feeling horny since their primary mission was to get into a strip club. The first assault on the group's willpower came by starting off the night drinking a lot of alcohol.

Drunk and hungry, the "executive function" of their prefrontal cortex, which we can refer to as their *physical* consciousness, stood no chance against the basic instincts of physical and sexual aggression, which lurk inside the much older parts of the brain.

Was the Pope exhibiting "free will" when he slapped his innocent admirer's hand? I don't know how he'd answer that, but he did apologize the next day, saying "We lose patience many times. It happens to me too. I apologize for the bad example given yesterday." Instead of saying he lost his patience, we could say he lost control over the part of his brain that goes into "automatic pilot" whenever the higher levels of the brain go off-line due to a lack of fuel.

We could say the same for the judges. If they hadn't been drunk, hungry or sleepy, they would have had the mental option to choose another path that night.

Sabrina probably would've remembered that she was a judge, and decided against provoking a couple of locals into a confrontation. Likewise, Adam and Bradley may have chosen to walk away from a possible fight than risk being arrested for the charge of "misdemeanor battery." Instead, their caveman brains took over, leaving them no choice.

Sean McNamara

But the debate over whether or not humans have free will goes even deeper. In 1983, neuroscientist Benjamin Libet ran an experiment in which he asked his subjects to tap their fingers whenever they felt like it, or let's say, whenever they "chose" to. Yet, brain scans revealed that their brains had *already decided* when to tap each finger <u>before</u> a subject <u>consciously</u> decided to do so.

This result led some researchers to think that we're just pre-programmed creatures who only *think* we're in control of what we do next.

I think it's partly true. We know that when we learn a new skill, such as tying one's shoelaces, we have to use the conscious part of our mind to pay attention and move our fingers a certain way. But after doing it a dozen times, we've programmed the movement into our subconscious mind so we can do it automatically from that moment on, literally without thinking about it.

My meditation retreats include something called "walking meditation." In this practice, people walk around in a circle, at a slower-than-normal pace. Walking is a subconscious function for adults, since the only time we had to think about how to walk was when we were toddlers. But once we programmed it in through trial-and-error and some repetition, it became automatic.

The funny thing is, once in a while during walking meditation, I see someone roll their ankle or lose their balance, nearly falling down. It's so funny to watch, that it's almost impossible to burst out laughing. Unless, or course, I'm the one falling over. I do it too.

Why do meditators nearly collapse while slowly walking in a circle? Because they're trying to walk by relying on their conscious minds instead of leaving it to their subconscious programming.

And, they're doing it because they think this is what it means to be "mindful," a problematic catch-phrase in contemporary pop spirituality. In doing so, they prevent their natural programming from doing what it's supposed to do, and try to take over with their logical minds. And just like that, they've forgotten how to move their own feet.

So, when it comes to walking, tying one's shoes, swallowing food and falling asleep, we don't want to rely on "free will." Letting the pre-programmed, subconscious aspects of *our brains* manage those tasks is the smart thing to do.

Part 2: "Subconscious Mind" as Non-physical Consciousness

Earlier in the book, I mentioned the need to get my subconscious mind "on board" with allowing me to leave my body during an OBE. But in this case, I'm using the phrase "subconscious mind" to indicate something else, my *non-physical* consciousness. Some people might call it their "spirit," or "soul," or "higher self," etc.

We've already discussed that part of what makes us "us" is our survival instinct and pre-programmed behaviors. We're also composed of a more sophisticated mind, equipped with "executive functioning" which puts the brakes on our animalistic tendencies and allows for decision-making and long term planning. It's what makes us more complex and logical than other creatures on this planet.

I think most of our individualized personalities come from the combining of these two aspects. We've all heard about "nature vs. nurture" and I think it's generally safe to say that our personality is also shaped by our environment, social systems, and all the many good and bad things which happen to us as we grow up.

But as they say, "You can't take it with you." When a person dies, their brain dies too. The computer-like, animalistic programming is gone, as is our sophisticated, intelligent style of being in the physical world.

But there's a part of us which existed before we had a physical brain, and which exists after our brain's physical death. This is one's non-physical consciousness. And that's what I refer to when I say things like "getting in touch with the subconscious" when discussing spiritual or psychic matters.

Maybe our brain isn't really capable of experiencing free will at all, and we're 100% on automatic pilot. So, what? What if our non-physical self has only entered the body to temporarily join a "whole self," merely as a passenger on this crazy ride called "life?"

What if its only goal is to experience things on a physical plane, and to impose physical, flesh-based limits on itself as a prerequisite?

Perhaps some capacity for free will exists, and only manifests when our soul *really* wants us to move in another direction, make a different choice, or override our brain's "regularly scheduled programming."

What if the conscious mind, based in the brain, is in a *symbiotic relationship* with our spirit? Our brain can "be *and do* better" when listening to our soul's counsel, and our soul can grow by feeling life through our eyes and skin, and by receiving the lessons of our actions.

In the brain, "love" might be nothing more than the release of oxytocin, dopamine, and other neurotransmitters under the appropriate circumstances. But this physical experience might be analogous of a higher kind of love, a non-physical expression of awareness, not bound by time or space. As for other emotions or mind states related to a sense of "meaning," I'll leave that to you to ponder.

Part 3: Having a Physical Body Here on Earth is a Spiritual Experience of its Own

I often wonder if having an OBE or other psycho-spiritual experience is really a step forward, or if instead, it's like getting a "hall pass" in this universe's classroom. It certainly *feels* spiritual, and has granted me and countless others a wider perspective on reality.

But above anything else, and setting religion and spirituality aside, I believe that simply being born as a human or animal on this planet is a complete spiritual path in itself. Being born into a body is *an opportunity to grow* as an inherently conscious aspect of reality. By having our physical sense organs, nervous systems, modes of communication and culture, we are *already on a continuous path of learning* and experiencing.

We often think of spirituality as a way to transcend the vicissitudes of life and rise above it all. But, what if the point has always been to simply be alive, to feel, to suffer, to have compassion, to have pleasure and pain alike... Thinking this way, I don't believe anyone is inherently better than anybody else. I also think all "traditions of transcendence" might be missing the mark on some level. Show me a person who struggles day and night just to find food and shelter, and who lacks education and religion. And, I'll show you a *conscious being* who is gaining just as much experience and knowledge about this reality as we are, *if not more.*

Of course, it's only because I have certain privileges (income, health, education, race, freedom from societal hostility, etc.) that I can make this kind of statement, and it can seem extremely callous. So, to be clear, the fact that people who are suffering or in severe deprivation might be having a complete spiritual existence *doesn't excuse us* from doing what we can to help them.

Perhaps by helping people less fortunate than ourselves is the way privileged people can learn their particular lessons in this life. And who knows, maybe the tables will be turned the next time around?

The same goes for our treatment of this planet. Without it, our physical bodies will have nowhere to live. That means our non-physical consciousnesses won't have bodies to inhabit. Please be very careful if your knee-jerk response is "It's ok, there are plenty of other planets out there for us to live on."

In some ways, Mother Earth is as complicated a system as the brain. Who's to say she doesn't host her own non-physical consciousness? Perhaps Gaia really is consciously interacting with us, her children.

I think the best thing to do is stay humble, loving, and generous, and not force other people to adopt our beliefs. We could have it all wrong, after all. And in the end, we're all in this together.

Part 4: The Interchange of Physical and Non-Physical Experience

In 1848, just outside of Cavendish, Vermont, a railroad worker named Phineas Gage was preparing a blasting hole inside a rocky outcropping. He filled the hole with gunpowder, then used a long iron rod to tightly pack dirt and sand over it. Unfortunately, the rod caused a spark against the rock, causing an explosion which transformed the rod into a missile.

Phineas was standing right over the hole, allowing the rod to shoot up and enter his head just beneath his left cheek bone, piercing through his brain, then exiting out the top of his skull, landing 80 feet away.

Miraculously, Phineas survived. Or did he? His case became famous because of the distinct changes in personality his friends and coworkers noted as he recovered over the following years. Before the accident, he was polite, dependable, and easy to get along with. Afterward, he became aggressive, uncouth, and wishy-washy. To them, he seemed like a different person.

This event shed significant light on the fact that the physical brain has a great deal to do with one's personality. Many of us have personal experience with this through watching the effects of dementia on our loved ones. Previously genteel people can become physically and verbally aggressive as the disease progresses.

Severe depression also has a physical cause. The brain of a depressed person has problems modulating neurotransmitters such as dopamine, serotonin and norepinephrine.

Most commonly, we all undergo a brief personality change when we're unable to satisfy a basic addiction, such as sugar, caffeine, nicotine or alcohol. Recent research concerning our gut bacteria indicate these tiny organisms can also alter our moods through their own chemical processes.

People who don't believe in a non-physical existence or soul might see these facts as evidence that we're nothing more than our physical bodies. But if we consider the earlier part of this essay, we know this isn't necessarily the case.

If one's spiritual consciousness is a sort of passenger or witness inhabiting the body, then a brain-trauma-related personality change will simply change the kind of experience one's spiritual consciousness receives. If we regard the brain as a radio, and the non-physical consciousness as the signal, all that's happened is that the radio's been altered in some way. The signal remains the same.[34]

Granted, if the signal wants to influence the radio (the spirit influencing the mind), it might face a greater challenge if the damage is too great.

Most importantly, that deeper part of us, or of our loved ones, is *still in there*, experiencing, learning, and growing.

The interchange of physical mind and non-physical consciousness really comes into play during meditation, OBE's, and other altered states of awareness. These are times in our life when the communication lines are fully open. We shift our perception to receive information from "the other side" then bring that experience back with us into our day-to-day, physical experience. Our personalities change, and we increase our knowledge of reality by this process.

I'm not a neuroscientist, but I'll suggest the idea of "neuroplasticity" is at work here. The brain integrates our non-physical experiences by creating or changing its neural network. I suspect my process of learning telekinesis over many weeks had the effect of rewiring my brain until it was sufficiently "tuned" to produce the mind-over-

---

[34] I don't mean to imply consciousness is a radio signal, or *any* kind of wavelength, for that matter. I only intend it as an analogy here.

Sean McNamara

matter effect. I've also heard of research into the brains of UFO contactees, where brain scans reveal certain physical changes in the aftermath.

The modern challenge of daily life is to defend ourselves from the onslaught of undesirable influences upon our brain and consciousness. Meditation can change our brains for the better, and enrich our experience of *this* life in the process. But how much time do we actually dedicate to our spiritual practices compared to hours spent watching television or absorbing social media?

And still, this is all a choice, and I don't think there's a wrong answer. Even if a person chooses to spend the next sixty years binge-watching TV shows while eating chicken-and-donut sandwiches and chain smoking in the basement, *they are still having a fully spiritual experience.* Their non-physical consciousness is still learning and growing from everything their physical reality has to teach, no matter what our personal opinions of their choices may be. They still deserve respect for having had a human life.

A final point. There exists the risk that a spiritually-inclined person's brain can fool them into believing they're perceiving reality from a transcendent viewpoint, when they really aren't. Worse, this kind of person might believe societal rules, customs and laws no longer pertain to them.

We must always remember that as long as we inhabit a physical body and lives among other people, regardless of our level of "spiritual attainment," we must respect others, and follow our society's rules and cultural norms, so long as they're benevolent.[35]

---

[35] Societies and political leaders haven't always upheld virtuous principles in governing themselves or their neighbors. Sometimes, ethics have mandated resistance or even revolution.

ESSAY: The Importance of Meditation and Retreat Practice

Note: I've written this section under the assumption you've already read the previous essay, "Free Will and the Varieties of Consciousness."

Meditation is like the mind itself, you can use it for anything you want. Today, "mindfulness" is a popular phrase, and the practice is attributed to reduced stress levels, an increased ability to be "present," and improved performance in a variety of settings, from athletic competitions to corporate board rooms.

In today's anxiety-filled, overstimulating and invasive environment, mindfulness training offers an effective, accessible, and affordable (it's free) option for supporting one's mental, emotional and physical wellbeing.

I think it's fair to suggest this kind of meditation works on one's *physical* mind, located in the brain and nervous system. That's why some people use *conditioning* methods to help themselves feel better during meditation. They listen to soothing music, burn pleasant-smelling incense, and light candles. Conditioning techniques are rituals in themselves. They change the meditator's environmental experience, to which their nervous system responds positively.

But there is a more profound type of meditation. Its ultimate goal isn't to simply reduce one's stress levels. Rather, it has to do with reconnecting with, or re-experiencing one's *non-physical* mind, the part of us that was there before our body was born, and which will still be there after our body's demise.

Sean McNamara

Essentially, this deeper mode of meditation requires us to disconnect or disassociate ourselves from our physical nature, namely our bodies and the surrounding physical environment. To do so, two things are crucial.

First, we must relax our bodies in order to reduce the amount of neurological "input" streaming through the conscious and subconscious part of the physical brain. Some traditions teach people to do this sitting up, while others do it lying down.

Secondly, we must turn our interest away from any stimulation originating from a physical source. That is to say, when we're vigilant about every ache, itch, tickle, or every memory, thought, or emotion processed by our brain, it keeps us "locked in" to our physicality. Therefore, these kinds of meditators typically anchor their attention by placing it on a single thing, like one's breath, or a particular chakra, mantra, or a visualization.

Conditioning methods such as listening to music or smelling incense can't take one very far for this level of meditation, and the meditator must let go of their reliance on those kinds of physical stimulation after a certain point.

This is because staying attentive to physical inputs will prevent the meditator from completely transferring their point of perception into a non-physical state.

Once the meditator has transferred to a non-physical perspective, they won't even be able to perceive the sounds, smells, and sensations their physical body would normally be aware of.[36]

This is called the "unconditioned state." It's the state when one's awareness and sense of self is uninfluenced by physical input, yet capable of perceiving a world which is *invisible to the eyes*.

---

[36] Various meditative traditions refer to this state as "absorption" or "samadhi." I recognize that the phrase "the unconditioned state" might be defined differently in certain traditions. This is a matter of semantics and context, which is outside the scope of this book.

326

If the meditator is unable to transfer their point of awareness, or their sense of "self," to a non-physical perspective, they simply fall asleep after sufficient relaxation.

But, if they manage to "hold on" long enough, while any remaining physical signaling falls away into the background, they'll be able perceive reality from a non-physical perspective.

After entering, or reconnecting with, their non-physical awareness, a meditator can gain information about the past, present or future, communicate with other non-physical beings, and gain a deeper understanding about the meaning of life. This is a common theme across the world's religions.

It might sound like I'm talking specifically about training to have an out-of-body experience, but I'm not. I'm certain this kind of meditation can happen in a variety of ways, including traditional or religious contexts, such as a Buddhist or contemplative Christian retreat.

In January of 2020, I led a three-night retreat at a mountain home in the foothills of Colorado. I was joined by four meditation friends, Kathy, Stacy, Jill and Dawn. I don't lead large public retreats anymore, largely because I realized how much better it was to do retreats with a very small number of experienced meditators, especially whom I'd known a long time and cared deeply about.

These four have been meditating with me since way back when I was a teacher in the old organization, and I'm grateful that we've maintained our connection up to today.

Our daily schedule is on the next page.

Sean McNamara

This was our daily retreat schedule:

7:00 am - 8:00 am **Meditation**
8:00 am - 9:00 am Breakfast
9:00 am - Noon **Meditation**
Noon - 2:00 pm Lunch and rest period
2:00 pm - 5:00 pm **Meditation**
5:00 pm - 5:30 pm Tea/Afternoon snack
5:30 pm - 7:00 pm **Meditation**
7:00 pm - 8:00 pm Dinner
8:00 pm - 9:00 pm **Meditation**

With Dawn Kirkwood, Kathy Bruce, Stacy Linrud and Jill Lowy,
marking the end of another retreat together.
These are precious memories I'll cherish for years to come.

We maintained silence (no talking) about 90% of the time. I didn't give any lectures or instructions, and the only ritual we used was to ring a gong in order to signal the start and end of each meditation period. No chanting, no shrines, no altars, no offerings and no candles. Nothing. No *conditioning*.

Each person had their unique goal for that weekend, and used whatever technique they chose for themselves. *Conformity* during group practices can stifle genuine experiences from happening, so my only significant role as the group leader was to watch the clock.

328

Near the end of the weekend, Dawn approached me immediately after I'd rung the bell to mark the end of the meditation period. She needed to tell me something that had just happened to her.

Amazingly and *unintentionally*, she'd disassociated from her body, and had an illuminating personal experience. The simple process of meditating in silence, hour after hour, for several days in a row, was enough to draw her out of her physical reality and into something much vaster. Dawn had a genuinely mystical experience.

Meditation as Initiation: The Essential Instructions

Here are the core instructions[37], which I believe are at the root of many meditative traditions from around the world. If you strip away the rituals, the dogma, and the religious symbolism, it comes down to these:

Choose something to leash your mental attention to, such as the feeling of your inhalation and exhalation, a candle's flame, your heart center, or a visualized image.

Relax your body while resting your attention on your object of attention. Sit in a posture which doesn't cause undue strain or soreness over time. It's *not* necessary to sit cross-legged on the floor. A chair works just as well.

Anytime your mind drifts off, or pays attention to anything else, gently bring it back to your object of attention.

In time, perhaps 5, 10, 20 or 40 minutes of doing this, you are likely to experience an assault of sensory inputs from your brain. These could be thoughts like worries, fantasies, or fears. You could be overcome by new or strange emotions, including sadness, regret,

---

[37] If you are new to meditation, you might start by getting my free video courses "Guided Meditation Journeys" and "Vagus Nerve Stimulation" from www.MindPossible.com to follow along with. They offer a variety of techniques and useful support to support your individual needs.

Sean McNamara

anger, or even joy, gratitude, or spiritual inspiration. Let's refer to this assault as "hitting the wall."

Be especially vigilant of tricky emotions like boredom, or the sudden impulse to end the session and go do something else. These are also aspects of hitting the wall.

Hitting the wall is a precious opportunity because it clearly defines the part of your "self" associated with the physical brain. All these sensations, thoughts and emotions are coming from your nervous system. In other words, these come from your *physical existence*.

But you are also a non-physical being, with a non-physical consciousness. In time, you'll realize that part of the awareness witnessing your meditation is associated with your *non-physical self*. It's there in the background, silently watching the "physical you" hitting the wall.

Upon hitting the wall, you must stay put. Don't give undue attention to the storm inside your mind. Don't try to calm it down, and don't try to improve it.

If you're angry, don't try to make the anger go away by "positive thinking" or anything like that. The same goes for any other emotion. If you're stuck in a cycle of rumination, don't try to slow it down or stop it. Just let it run its course. It may or may not come to a stop in due time, but it doesn't matter. Let your physical aspect "be and do" just as it is.

If you stick with it long enough, one of two things will happen, if not both. First, the storm will calm down on its own, and you'll find yourself more able to rest your mind on your object of attention.

Second, you'll realize that your point of presence has shifted away from being the recipient of the emotional and cognitive turmoil, the victim of the storm. Instead, you've become an *outside witness* to it all. In New Age terms, you'll realize you *are* your own "higher self," watching your experience from a deeper perspective.

330

And that part of you is always at peace, unmoving, undisturbed, and timeless as it watches.

Once you surpass the wall, and the mental storm subsides, you'll experience some degree of peace for a while. There are two kinds of peace.

Physical peace comes from your brain calming down, reducing the number of signals being sent into your experience of self. This is the level of basic "mindfulness."

The second, and more profound level of peace, comes when your perspective shifts more deeply into your non-physical consciousness, your higher self. You're still awake inside your body, but you are identified with your non-physical mind, your soul, instead of with your brain.

The interesting thing about the second level of peace is, over months and years of meditation training, you'll be able to tune in to your deeper self *even when your physical self is suffering*. Remember, this takes repeated practice, it's not a one-time thing.

If you give up, get bored, or get distracted, or if you quit as soon as you hit the wall, you won't be able to make the shift into your deeper self.

This is the crucial point. If you're meditating simply to calm down a little bit, doing it for twenty minutes a day is fine. But if you want to achieve a profound shift of identity and of perspective, you must sit long enough to hit that wall, then to surpass it.

Many people ask "how long should I meditate?" The answer isn't a matter of counting minutes. It's however long it takes to hit that wall, endure the storm, and experience the peace waiting on the other side.

Once you feel that, you can end your session. This is the process of initiation, and it only happens when you're willing to endure the struggle.

Sean McNamara

Physical sensations will become intensified, such as aches, pains, or itches that beg to be scratched. Some traditions, for example Zen, give the instruction to not move an inch to make yourself feel better, and simply ride it out. I think there are pros and cons to this approach, but I won't go into them here.

In my culture, and for the kinds of people I meditate with, I think the more efficacious instruction is to go ahead and shift your body or scratch that itch if it's truly too much to bear. This will allow you to continue your process of relaxing even more deeply, which will eventually result in experiencing profound levels of consciousness.

Whatever you do, don't end your session prematurely. All you have to do to succeed in meditation is *not give up.*

Doing it every day will lead to progress sooner than doing it once or twice a week will. But it's up to you, and what your lifestyle allows. It's a personal choice, and you shouldn't compare yourself to what other people do. It's not a value judgement. For most people, it comes down to priorities and externally imposed demands on your daily schedule.

It's also about opting against easy sources of pleasure, like watching TV for three hours. How badly do you want to experience what meditation might have to offer you? If you'd rather not meditate, it's ok. There's no need to beat yourself up for not doing it. As I wrote before, just the fact that you have this physical body is a spiritual experience in itself. Go out there and live!

On Solitary Retreat

My first solitary retreat was 10 days long. I rented a tiny stone cabin at a Buddhist center in the southern mountains of Colorado. It was a one-room structure, with an outhouse situated a dozen yards away. I used propane gas to cook, and hand-pumped fresh water from a nearby well.

This outhouse didn't even have a door. But that wasn't a problem, since the situation was such that I wouldn't see another living person for the duration of my time there. Since there were no mirrors in the cabin, I wouldn't even be able to look at myself.

Can you imagine that? Especially in this day and age when many people can't pass a single day without posting a "selfie" or making themselves heard on social media?

That's the power of solitary retreat. It's not really about what particular style or technique you use during your meditation. Being in retreat *is* the practice.

It builds a certain kind of character. There wasn't a phone, or radio, or TV, much less a computer inside my cabin. When I wasn't going inward in meditation, the best I could do was try to entertain myself by fixing myself a snack, feeding bird seed to the local nuthatches, and chopping wood for the stove, which was the only way to heat the cabin.

In solitary retreat, one has no choice but to experience one's own mind. Every. Single. Moment. Without external distractions, it's only a matter of time before "unfinished business" and unresolved memories come to the forefront of your awareness. You have no choice but to look at yourself.

There's no escape. You can't even "meditate it away." The strange, habitual, painful and even pleasurable mental states which arise become the objects of meditation themselves. This is the complete opposite of what we do in daily life.

Anytime we feel uncomfortable, or something deep down inside starts rising to the surface, we distract ourselves. We open our social media apps, turn on the TV, eat some sugar, get high or have a beer. We overwork ourselves at the office, or over-train in the gym. The list goes on.

But in solitary retreat, there is no list, there are no options. You have to live your real life, and see the real you. You "be." Out of that, comes wisdom.

It also opens the doors to entering non-physical realms and experiencing non-ordinary states of consciousness. Especially at night.

I highly recommend going on solitary retreat at least once in your life. I think ten days was too extreme for me, and five or seven days would have been kinder. Then you can do longer retreats after assimilating the experience of the shorter one. Keep in mind, assimilation can take months, even years.

Nevertheless, even if you can only get away for two or three nights, you might get a taste of what I'm talking about here.

My first solitary retreat cabin

Here are some guidelines for solitary retreat. Get a place where you are guaranteed to not see another person. Leave your phone, laptop and all your books at home. I also recommend abstaining from journaling, since writing down your thoughts can be a form of entertainment. All you need is food, a first-aid kit (just in case), toilet paper, toothbrush, and the like.

Write down your daily practice schedule, perhaps something similar to the one above, and stick to it. Go easy on your first and last days, perhaps meditating for an hour or two on your arrival day, and an hour the morning of your departure. You want to ease into retreat, then on your way out, ease back into ordinary life.

There will be many times when you'd like to go for a walk in the forest instead of sitting down to meditate. Save the walks, or other forms of exercise such as yoga or Tai Chi for your retreat's designated break times. If you meditate for 45 minute blocks, the 15 minutes in between can be times for doing walking meditation outdoors, or just enjoying the sunshine in silence. Listen to Mother Nature, she might have things to tell you.

Above all, stick to your schedule.

Finally, and most importantly, you must commit to *not* leaving retreat early. As Winston Churchill said, "If you're going through hell, keep going."

If the notion of solitary retreat is too daunting, consider putting together a group retreat with some friends *who match your level of commitment*. You can rent an Airbnb together at a remote location. It'll likely be an affordable option because it should be pretty basic, with as few amenities to entertain and distract you as possible.

If there's a big screen TV or a computer in the living room, throw a blanket over it. Cover the bathroom mirrors with cloth.

Set some ground rules for the group, and designate someone who will call everyone in when it's time to do another meditation session, and keep their eye on the clock during the session. They can use a bell or any other device to mark the start and stop times.

A word of caution, though. If you suffer from depression, anxiety, unresolved trauma, a dissociative disorder, or if you are vulnerable to other mental conditions, intensive meditation both in and out of retreat can do much more harm than good.

Sean McNamara

At the very least, you should speak with an experienced mentor, therapist, or counselor before undergoing any kind of meditation intensive.

Do not force children to meditate. Their brains are growing in such a way that forcing them to concentrate their minds this way could be damaging to them. Besides, they're already more open than us adults. In some ways, we need to be more like them, not the other way around.

ESSAY: Rhymes with "God"

Alternately titled "Everything is Information"

Part 1: Information in Mind-Over-Matter Experiments

Let's begin by reviewing the process of telekinesis. Imagine someone sitting several feet away from a closed container, modulating their mind and body in such a way as to get the piece of tin foil inside to spin, then changing its direction by will. As I wrote earlier, a hypothesis I've heard and lean toward, is that the person's mind isn't moving the tin foil directly. Rather, it's causing the air molecules inside the container to change from moving randomly into a more organized pattern, pushing on the tin foil to make it move.

Let's regard a molecule or an atom as nothing more than a bit of information. Indeed, the closer we look at subatomic particles, the more we're reminded there's nothing, as in no "thing," really there, except the "arising of an experience," which I'll refer to as "information."

However, this information has two aspects. Before the telekinesis experiment began, the molecules were *projecting* their current state of information by moving in a certain way. When the person set an intention and paid attention to their goal of moving the tin foil, the molecules received, or *perceived* the person's mental influence and responded by projecting a different state of information. This caused them to move differently, more coherently, to be precise.

The informational qualities of projecting and perceiving are no different from how our own minds operate. Every moment, we perceive our internal and external worlds and behave, or project, accordingly for our survival and fulfillment.

A curious issue lies in the fact that the person was focusing on the tin foil, not on the air surrounding it. This implies that either a subconscious aspect of the person's mind, or another type of awareness was, for lack of better words, "helping out" by influencing the molecules to produce the desired effect.

If we see telekinesis as having two active subjects, the person and the tin foil, or the person and the air molecules, we might be wrong. I believe there's a *third* participant involved in the experiment.

Whatever the third participant is, it perceives what the person is trying to achieve, then projects itself onto the air molecules *on the person's behalf.* The molecules perceive the third participant's intention and project a new behavior accordingly.

If we understand this example, then it's not difficult to apply it toward things like spoon bending or other types of psychokinesis, including healing a person with the use of intention and energy. Earlier, I mentioned how tying one's shoes or the act of walking is an automated event controlled by the brain's subconscious mechanism. We don't need to know which specific muscles are involved, or to tell them precisely how to move. Some other part of us takes care of those details.

During mind over matter experiments, the third participant might be a *non-physical analog* to our brain's subconscious system. While we focus on our desired outcome, something or someone else takes care of the details for us and makes it so.

Part 2: Information in Out of Body Experiences

As you recall from my OBE journal entries, there were times when what I perceived in the non-physical state differed considerably from what the physical world looked like. Take the instance when I looked back upon my body lying on the couch, seeing it was facing a particular direction and wearing a white shirt. But upon my return, I realized my body had actually been facing the other direction and I was wearing a dark shirt instead. How could this be?

The issue lies in the fact that when a person leaves their body, they no longer have eyes, or ears, or skin with which to perceive their world. This would explain why I'm often "blind" the first few moments after separating from my body. When I try to "see" or "open my eyes," I'm basically asking my non-physical consciousness to produce an experience which mimics my physical experience, producing "sight." It's the result of being conditioned to "see" from the day I was born until now.

During an OBE, the mind *translates* information about the physical world into something I can perceive in my non-physical state[38]. And maybe it doesn't get it right all the time. An interesting question is, "Who is doing the translating?" Is it my own, personal consciousness? Or is a *third participant* involved?

Could some greater, unified field of consciousness be involved? Something we're inherently a part of, but which we partially separate from in order to have unique, distinct experiences during one's current lifetime?

I've learned that when initiating separation at the start of an OBE, the best results can come from letting go of control and intentionally handing the reins over to my "higher self," allowing it to decide where I should travel. I wonder if my "higher self "is the same thing as this "third participant."

I often wonder why I don't have greater control during an OBE, or access to deeper knowledge than what I've already experienced. Surely there's much more to see, and know. After all, there's an entire universe out there, spanning all time and space. I think it's

---

[38] In fact, the mind is translating not only information about the physical plane, but non-physical or non-Earthly planes as well. *Everything* is being translated all the time, there's no such thing as objective reality (as a hypothesis, at least).

Sean McNamara

simply because during an OBE, a significant portion of one's consciousness stays "in" the body while another portion goes "out."

This limits how much one can do and perceive during an OBE. The other limitation is how much information the "physical filter of experience," our *physical brain*, allows to seep into our conscious awareness after we return. The filtration could serve a valuable purpose, though. If the physical world, with all its limitations, is a classroom, and living a physical life is the lesson, the experience of becoming omniscient would be akin to cheating by finding the answers at the back of the book.

I question whether we actually go anywhere during an OBE. Here's the same question from a different angle. Is my non-physical consciousness really some sort of energetic *thing* which leaves the body and floats away? Or is that experience a mental *representation* of something entirely different? What if the experience of separation is merely a mental interpretation of one's *change of perspective*?

It could be that my consciousness is simply tuning itself to perceive non-physical information, revealing a whole other world. I've heard people say that the afterlife is *right here*, all around us, just out of reach from our ordinary senses. Still, it's just close enough that a modest shift of consciousness allows a person to communicate with that world. Based on my experiences, I tend to agree with them.

Are animals only physical beings, or do they have a non-physical aspect as well? Do they have a soul? I think most dog, cat, and horse owners don't need anyone to tell them the answer to that question. I think a more significant question is if an animal's consciousness is more or less evolved than a human's. I think many assume that animals are lower on the ladder of development than people, but I'm not quite so sure.

I dare say that humans only appear to be more complex than animals because of the physical capacity of their brains. If you left your body right now and entered the body of a worm, you'd still *be* the deepest aspect of "you."

However, you wouldn't have the same "equipment" to work with as when you were in a human body. Obviously, you'd lack the advantages of having a prefrontal cortex a pair of thumbs, and a larynx designed for speech. Your experience of being alive would be completely different, and quite limited.

Have you ever heard of animals of two different species behaving like companions in utter contradiction of their natural instinct? Could it be that their non-physical consciousnesses are somehow influencing or even overriding their neural programming?

Or have you ever known a human being who behaved almost exclusively on animal instinct, highly aggressive and short-sighted, and lacking empathy? I wouldn't suggest there are cases of soulless zombies walking among us. But, we might all know someone who seems tragically disconnected from their soul, or who is hypersensitive to their base impulses.

There is also the spiritual extreme of thinking we can override our base instincts by making a mental commitment regarding our behavior. Taking a vow of celibacy doesn't turn off a person's natural sex drive, perhaps the most powerful drive there is. A person with a naturally reduced drive, because of age, injury or hormone levels, might do fine with such a vow. But everyone else has their limits.

Essentially, a person must find a workable balance between being a physical organism, "hard-wired" to act certain ways, and a spiritual being, capable of ascending the peaks of consciousness.

Thankfully, the universe seems to be eternal, or long-lasting at least. Therefore, everyone, human, animal, or other, has plenty of time to learn. Day after day, life after life.

Part 3: Information in Clairvoyance/Remote Viewing

During a remote viewing session, the viewer sets their intention to *perceive* information concerning a specific "target," be it a person,

Sean McNamara

place, event, or thing. After a period of time, thoughts, emotions, images, etc. enters the viewer's conscious awareness, at which point they write it down.

After comparing their notes to the actual target by going there in person, or being shown a picture of the target, they find they've indeed perceived the target with their mind.

Still, nobody knows how this really works. Here are three possibilities to consider, although I'm sure there are many others:

- The viewer shifts their perspective to their non-physical state, travels to the target to perceive it, then returns and transmits the information to the physical brain.

- The viewer sets their intention, which is akin to making a request, and a *third participant* acts as mediator by retrieving the information from the target and projecting it into the viewer's consciousness.

- The viewer's non-physical consciousness is *already* embedded into the universal fabric of reality, at a level where spatial and temporal distance does not exist. Since the target is also an inherent aspect of reality, the subject and object are *already* in direct perception and projection of each other.[39]

The passage of time from when the viewer sets their intention to when they "receive" psychic information might have to do more with taking time to adjust their brain functioning so they can consciously perceive the already-present information. People do it by relaxing, meditating, or doing what remote viewers call "cooling down." Some people can adjust faster than others.

---

[39] This means no kind of "wave" or other signal transfer is involved. This will sound familiar to those who've learned about "entanglement" in quantum theory, and the idea that everything in the universe has been entangled since the Big Bang.

In the book "Everybody's Guide to Natural ESP," Ingo Swann described how he believed the psychic perception happens. He thought that psychic information first enters through the subconscious mind, then moves "up" into the conscious awareness. The viewer's challenge of course, is telling the difference between target information and all the other unrelated thoughts and feelings mixed up in it.

Children are said to be particularly open, and perhaps it's because their physical brains haven't yet changed in such a way to limit their psychic abilities. Perhaps it has to do with changes in the prefrontal cortex.[40]

Luckily, because of neuroplasticity, I believe adults can train in such a way as to rewire their brains to be more like children again, at least regarding the ability to perceive information psychically, if only to a minor degree. Having done several solitary meditation retreats, including one lasting 30 days[41], I can tell you that one's mental functioning does change with practice, if only temporarily.

Part 4: Catching Fleas with a Butterfly Net

Researchers have tried unsuccessfully to determine the actual mechanism behind psychic functioning. Decades ago, one line of inquiry had to do with determining whether a psychic signal was transmitted to and from people's brains via some kind of electromagnetic wave, perhaps an ELF, an "extremely low frequency" wave. As far as I know, the idea has since dried up.

---

[40] If you are interested in this topic, an online search using the terms "prefrontal cortex child development" will get you started.

[41] I'm not bragging here, especially because 30 days is nothing compared to meditators in the Himalayas and even here in the U.S. who commit to months and even years of living in retreat. But to do that, one must abandon their worldly life completely. For myself, I'm here to *be here*, *in* this world, *in* this life, at least this time around.

Sean McNamara

I think the problem is that using *physical* scientific equipment to measure the *cause* of psychic phenomena is like trying to catch fleas with a butterfly net. The equipment is inherently wrong for the job.

Of course, we can use empiricism to score and verify instances of clairvoyance. And we can use equipment such as random number generators, lasers, and simple video cameras to record and measure psychokinetic *effects*. But I'm not talking about effects here. I'm talking about detecting and identifying the *causal mechanism*.

It's not about "What happened?" anymore. Enough studies have shown that psychic phenomena are real. We need to get over it and move on, focusing more on *"How* did it happen?"

That fact that we don't yet have technology to identify the cause should give us a new appreciation for the brain, nervous system, and whatever other parts of the physical body are sensitive to psychic inputs. Somehow, the three pounds of flesh bobbing around inside our skulls is able to do what no electronic equipment can.

Specifically, the brain can *interface* with non-physical consciousness and exchange information with it.

This brings to mind a concept called "state-specific sciences," developed by Charles Tart, PhD. As he writes on his website[42], state-specific sciences are a means practicing science within various altered states of consciousness.

Recall the OBE I wrote about earlier in which I found myself in a room, holding a mysterious device to my chest. The man in front of me did something to activate it, which knocked me down and sent me sliding backward across the room, forcing my OBE to end. Could it be that he was practicing state-specific research, albeit in a questionable manner?

---

[42] https://blog.paradigm-sys.com/state-specific-sciences-altered-state-origin-of-the-proposal/

There is no way for me to know with 100% certainty whether he was an actual person also in the out of body state, or if he was just a "thought form," a subjective figure produced by my own mind. But I only mean to use him here as an illustration of what state-specific science might look like in the future. In 2015, Tart wrote that this idea seems to be ahead of its time. That could be the case, but it doesn't' have to be.

The obvious bottleneck is people's unwillingness to actively pursue this type of research. It's probably also a lack of funding, and the fact that any scientist who dares publicize their involvement with it would be committing a "CLM," a career-limiting move. Until society evolves enough to support the idea of state-specific sciences, researchers will continue to use the wrong kind of equipment when studying the cause of these phenomenon.

The good news is, I do know of one extraordinary team of scientists who have incorporated state-specific science in their research, which I'll discuss in the next essay, "Energy Healing."

ESSAY: Energy Healing

You might be reading this book from the perspective of an energy worker. And, you might already be a Reiki healer or medical Qigong practitioner, or have participated in a prayer circle. I thought it would be good to share my experiences as an energy healer here, especially for anybody considering becoming one themselves.

Earlier, I described information as having two aspects, as a perceiver and as a projector, or influencer. If a person's consciousness is a *locus of information*, and the world around them is a separate or distinct locus of information, then what we call "experience" itself is simply various loci of information perceiving and/or projecting onto each other in various ways. It's how a person can affect an object through psychokinesis, or gain information using clairvoyance, precognition, or through dreams. It's also how we go about our ordinary, physical lives.

And, it's how a healer brings about beneficial changes in another person's physical, emotional, or energetic experience, which we call "healing."

After several years as a massage therapist, I noticed that once in a while, my hands would spontaneously feel significantly warmer than usual during a session. Sometimes, a client would remark on the heat even before I'd noticed it myself. Their observations usually included a remark about how much better they were feeling at that point of the session.

There were also times when I'd spontaneously receive an insight about that person's life, or feel like someone or something else was

346

occupying the room with us. Instances like these are not uncommon among various types of therapists and wellness workers.

In the spring of 2019, Joyce Anastasia[43] invited me to participate in a healing energy study being conducted at IONS[44], the Institute of Noetic Sciences, at the Earthrise campus in Petaluma, California. Joyce was the research management consultant for the team headed by Garret (Gary) Yount, PhD[45].

In her process of inviting me, she asked me to send her a description of my healing modality. This is what I sent her:

> Modality: "Loving attention with positive expectation"
>
> My protocol is a blend of three ways of being present with the client. First, I direct subtle *energy* toward the whole person as well as to specific body parts in need of healing, with the *intention* of supporting the healing process. Second, I arouse and expand the feeling of *unconditional love* for this person and their circumstances. This is not a personal type of love, but rather the view that the whole universe loves this person already, and that it is an active participant in this person's life. Third, I *envision the person in their post-healing state*, moving his or her body in ways that they will be able to once the healing is fulfilled, and expressing emotions such as happiness and confidence.

Essentially, I was describing a combination of lessons I'd learned from three sources. First, my experiences in massage therapy. Second, telekinesis. Third, what I'd read in Lynne McTaggart's book "The Power of Eight," which I then applied in my own group intention experiments at Mayu Sanctuary in Denver.

I told Joyce I was hesitant because I didn't feel like I had substantial "work experience" as an energy healer, and that I couldn't

---

[43] Learn about Joyce Anastasia at www.LeadByWisdom.com.

[44] www.noetic.org

[45] Learn about Garret Yount at noetic.org/profile/Garret-Yount/

Sean McNamara

guarantee results. For some reason, Joyce was accepting of me and encouraged me to come anyway.

I fell in love with the Earthrise campus as soon as I set foot on the land. Several miles distant from town, and surrounded by rolling hills and nothing but clear sky above, I felt like I'd arrived at some heavenly domain.

I was initially afraid I'd encounter a scientifically cold and restrained atmosphere, but nothing could be further from the truth. Every single person I met there, whether they worked in the lab, registration office, or in the kitchen, was warm, friendly, curious, and open minded.

Every day during the study, I'd have either one, two, or three healing sessions with volunteer clients, depending on their availability. The sessions occurred inside of a small room lined with metal and other materials with the purpose of blocking out any kind of electromagnetic influence. The room was a large Faraday cage.

Three people participated during the session. The client, me, and a person who was designated as the "seer." The seer was Dee Merz[46], a healer herself, and senior teacher at the Academy of Intuition Medicine in Sausalito. As the seer, her role was simply to observe the session on both the physical and non-physical planes. As a highly intuitive person, Dee would be able to see any kind of energetic exchange taking place, as well as whether or not any other entities were involved.

By assigning Dee the role of "seer," Garret, Joyce and the rest of their team were engaging in what Charles Tart refers to as *state-specific sciences*.[47] Dee was obtaining empirical evidence by entering an altered state of consciousness to see what was happening between me and the client.

---

[46] Learn about Dee Merz at www.DeeMerzEnergy.com

[47] See the previous essay.

348

Knowing this kind of seer would be watching me while I worked made me a bit nervous. I was still far from having a stable level of confidence in myself in the healing arena, and now there was somebody who'd be watching to see if anything was actually happening beyond what the physical eyes can see.

Luckily, Dee was just as optimistic and supportive as Joyce was, and by the end of the week, I realized how lucky I was to share the experience with her. Soon enough, I'd see that Dee was able to perceive some of the very same non-physical experiences I was having or intending upon the client during our sessions. The confidence I gained from sharing this time with Dee is invaluable.

I journaled my experiences, and will share three selections here, edited to protect client privacy. Instead of explaining my process afterward, I hope the journal entries will offer valuable guidance by themselves, as a starting point.

Some things to note at the start:

- Joyce would time each session, signaling when to start and end by ringing a bell from outside the room. Only the client, the seer, and I were inside.
- The volunteer clients were there primarily for issues pertaining to carpal tunnel syndrome, which is why I refer to their wrist at points in the journal entries.
- The clients reclined in an easy chair. I began each session seated next to them, but would usually get up and move around the room, stand behind them, or kneel at their sides or by their feet. Dee was seated in a corner, silently observing while taking notes.
- The room was quiet, and no music or other sounds were played.

Sean McNamara

Client #1:

<u>Before the starting bell</u>

I asked the client which wrist hurt, and "What kind of sports or other activities would you do if it didn't hurt?" She replied "golf."

I suggested that she imagine herself playing golf without pain, or that she could fall asleep, or simply relax and daydream during our session.

<u>During the first 6 minutes</u>

I brought her whole person to my attention in a broad manner - seeing her, feeling her. Periodically glanced at her wrists. Also, visualized her playing golf joyfully and painlessly.

I then invited non-physical beings (Ezekiel and any other guides in my life) to come and do their work. I also reached out to Edgar Mitchell (Apollo astronaut and the founder of IONS, who passed away in 2016) in case he had a team "up there" supporting our efforts.

Then, I generated a feeling of love to serve as a pathway for "energy flow."

<u>Main period</u>

I saw a white flicker over the top and to the side of the client, near the ceiling. It was about the shape of a napkin, angular, and looked physical. It lasted only a moment.

Continued sending and generating love, visualizing her playing golf, and checking in with "my team."

Added the visualization of her moving her arms, wrists and hands like a hula dancer. Graceful, painless, happy.

Stood behind her, lowered my hands over her energy field until I felt a boundary. Felt/joined with her energy there while continuing to send love and doing the visualization.

Lowered my hands further only when her energy allowed it, and when prompted by my deeper self, and/or "my team."

Sensing it was time to get specific, I moved to her right side (she has reported that her right-side pain was greater than left-side). Placed my right hand just over her wrist. Felt her energy there, then began sending my energy into it.

Brought my left hand up near her left shoulder, intending to increase energy flow along the length of her arm.

Eventually, I moved my right hand from over her wrist to just off her knuckles in order to include her hand and fingers in the process.

When I felt an increase in the flow through her arm, I stood up and moved to face her. Sensing/feeling her whole person again. Generating more love.

Extended my forearms, hands, and fingers to send more energy into her whole field. Felt the "nudge" to turn my hands for better flow. Nudge, from who? The team? Deeper self? Both? Doesn't matter in the moment. My job is to listen, feel, follow, *then let go.*

Time to work on left wrist, moved to chair (located to her left). Moved my hands over her wrist and shoulder as before.

<u>During the final 6 minutes</u>

Spent the time sending more love and visualizing her happily playing golf.

Sean McNamara

<u>Other notes</u>

Early on, I could tell she was relaxing, breathing more deeply. While standing in front of her and in the final 6 minutes, I saw her fingers twitch, and her wrists roll once in a while. Good signs.

Standing in front, hands and fingers extended, I could feel strands of energy flowing from my fingers toward the client.

Periodically distracted, wondering about results, data, and what the seer was perceiving. Realizing each moment of distraction, I returned my attention to the client as quickly as possible.

Overall, this method is effortless and relaxing, and heart-opening. Feeling, listening, allowing, then letting go.

Client #2:

<u>Before the starting bell</u>

I noticed the client had a lovely field of energy around him, and came to like him easily after we discovered we shared the same taste in music.

<u>During the first 6 minutes</u>

Had a sense to just wait and "be" with the client. It felt like once the main session began, things would really happen, and now was just a time for a buildup of some kind.

<u>Main period</u>

I stood to face him. Raising my arms to feel the boundary, I needed to take a step back - BIG energy around him. Could periodically see the field as a soft white glow around his head and shoulders.

Knelt to focus on his right wrist. His arms and hands were under a blanket, but that didn't matter. After a few minutes, my hands were "pulled" from over his wrist to move closer to his heart area. My hands opened, fingers extended toward his chest.

His heart space felt empty, hollow, shallow, weakened, as if needing support or additional energy. It felt like a disconnect between his heart and the rest of his being.

I returned to the chair to focus on his left wrist.

Both wrists felt like they were blocked, but energy seemed to start flowing better after the "specific" work.

Returning to broader work, when I'd try to imagine him working out and doing other things without pain. I got the hint, from my guides perhaps, to instead imagine him as a baby or toddler, and to focus on his "purity" at that age - his health and happiness before all the *stuff* that happens to all of us later in life.

Feeling the energy around his head, my right hand had to move far behind him. I sensed some deep preoccupation, or "lots going on" way in the back of his mind.

Final 6 minutes

Continued seeing him as a child, and otherwise simply being present with him.

Client #3:

First 6 minutes

As I looked at her to begin cultivating a loving feeling, I had a strong sense that some of her departed friends and family were coming in. Images of them kissing her on the top of her head, spontaneously came to mind.

Sean McNamara

Main period

I felt a spontaneous urge to sit at her feet and apply energy there. As I started working, I saw that there were surgical scars on the top ankle (her ankles were crossed). The work near her feet was intended to flow into her whole body.

Then, I stood up and remained facing her. As I felt her field with my hands, I felt a weak area over her lower abdomen and pelvis. I lined up my hands, one over the other, palms aimed at that area, and sent energy there.

Sat down to focus on the left wrist. Her whole arm felt weak, the energy was flat. Could not discern any change by the time I decided to move on.

Moved to focus on her right wrist. Also felt flat. The bell rang so I had to return to the chair. From the chair, my hands extended toward her right wrist, sending it what energy I could in the remaining time.

Final 6 minutes

As I gazed at her, I saw she was deeply relaxed. I suddenly got tired, as if I could have dropped into a deep sleep in this space with the client. I wondered if I was being called to "get out of the way" so other things could happen, but I'm really not sure. Or was I simply relaxed from the work? Or somehow drained?

Other notes

After the last client, Joyce, who'd been outside the room watching the clock, mentioned hearing music during the session, although she couldn't locate the source. Was this an instance of telepathy?

I'd been mentally "blasting" highly evocative songs inside my head, replaying them in my imagination during each session. The songs serve to provoke visceral sensations of love and inspiration (pleasant and tingly feelings in my chest, spine and head), which I then project

354

to the client. I often link those feelings to the positive visualization I hold during the session. Had Joyce psychically "heard" the music playing inside my mind?

******

I was only one of 17 healers who participated in the study, and I cannot take credit for its overall results, and don't want to risk misrepresenting myself. Therefore, I won't mention what the clients said to me as they left the room.

A publicly available report on the study, written by Steven Swanson can be found by doing an online search using the terms "IONS phase one of energy healing study."[48] Three sentences from the report stand out to me:

"The majority of clients reported a reduction in pain from before to after the session..."

"...heart rate variability and synchrony increased, indicating greater coherence between healer and subject as the session progressed."

[Measurements taken using a device called a Quantum Number Generator indicated that] "the healing sessions caused *entropic ripples in spacetime*."

I hope sharing this with you, the reader, serves to support your interest in energy work, or inspires you to engage in the kind of cutting-edge science being done at the Institute of Noetic Sciences. If you ever get the chance to go there, for any reason at all, go.[49]

---

[48] https://noetic.org/blog/phase-1-energy-healing-study-success/

[49] See photos from my visit there at www.RenegadeMysticBook.com/pictures

ESSAY: UFOs, Extraterrestrials and Dakinis

I'd like to begin by recalling Verse 22 from the Book of Ezekiel in the Bible, "Spread out above the heads of the living creatures was what looked something like a *vault*, sparkling like *crystal*, and awesome."

The mention of a vault, sparkling like crystal reminded me of the biography of an 11th century Tibetan saint named Milarepa. He had a tragic childhood, then met his teacher, and went on to live the rest of his life alone inside various mountain caves. As a side effect of his meditation, he became proficient with various psychic abilities. He is most remembered for his ability to fly through the sky.

After reading about Ezekiel's vision, I pulled out my old copy of Lobsang P. Lhalungpa's "The Life of Milarepa," and opened to where I knew I'd make the connection. It was Part 2, chapter 9, "Nirvana." The chapter describes Milarepa's death and cremation, and the strange events which followed.

At one point, Milarepa's main disciple, Rechungpa, is mourning aloud and calling out to his dead teacher. A "sky-goer," the Tibetan word being "dakini," appeared in the sky, holding something in her hand which "projected a stream of light in five colors." Later, "the light then split in two, one part becoming a lion throne…" From the other part, "…a crystal stupa took shape…and came to rest upon the throne."

The rest of the chapter is filled with descriptions of variously colored dakinis floating in the sky, emanating different kinds of light, and various kinds of structures moving through the air.

356

I see a lot of similarities between Milarepa's story and Ezekiel's vision. Obviously, they're reminiscent of UFO encounters. Many fans of the movie "Close Encounters of the Third Kind" aren't aware of the fact the scenes of colorful spaceships, big and small, appearing as one, then as many, are inspired by *actual witness accounts*. I would encourage anyone to watch the movie, then read the Book of Ezekiel followed by the last chapter of "The Life of Milarepa."

Now, to draw on another kind of experience. For this, I suggest you do a YouTube video search for "modern apparitions of Mary." I refer you specifically to the following videos:

- "Virgin Mary Appears over Ivory Coast"[50]
- "Virgin Mary appears in Egypt and Spain - Eye Witnesses Confirm"
- "SAINT MARY Appearing in Church in Cairo. Egypt 16/12/2009"

I think the similarities between what was captured on camera and what is described in ancient texts is noteworthy. As an aside, I have no way of knowing if what is depicted in these videos is authentic or not, but I try to keep an open mind. The thing is, what shows up is astounding, but also vague enough to be interpreted in whatever way a person pleases. The Catholics saw Mary in the sky. But the nebulous blob, surrounded by blinding light could've been *anything*.

There's a personal element for me here. The Buddhist deity who I referred to earlier, Vajrayogini, is herself regarded as a "dakini," a sky-goer. In the context of the ritualized meditation practice I'd been initiated into, she is regarded as a symbolic representation of enlightenment.

But, for many devotees throughout history, dakinis are much more than symbolic images. They are real. Ancient lore is filled with stories of dakinis appearing in near-humanoid form to interact with humans in various ways. They have acted as teachers, as oracles, as lovers…

---

[50] Links to these three videos are at www.RenegadeMysticBook/links

Sean McNamara

In these ancient accounts, could it be that these apparitions from the Tibetan Buddhist pantheon were really extraterrestrials, or something else entirely? Who did I have my otherworldly sexual encounter with?[51] Was she a dakini? Or an E.T.? Are they the same thing? And what was the purpose of having such an experience?

Or was the whole thing, including the resultant surge of energy up my spine, a figment of my imagination?

Regardless, I'm certain these apparitions and midnight encounters are connected to many of the other anomalies which I and countless other people throughout history have experienced. I think it's a part of our evolution, and even more awaits us in the future.

Whether we can ever accept and incorporate these phenomena into our society, especially without projecting our religious biases onto them, waits to be seen.

---

[51] See journal entry from May 10, 2018

CONCISE INSTRUCTIONS FOR LUCID DREAMING

INTRODUCTION

The instructions in this chapter and the next are *concise*, meaning "brief," "to the point," "pithy," and "compact." There are many books dedicated to teaching you how to have lucid dreams and OBEs. What you will find in these two chapters are many of the same instructions, but stripped bare of any fluff, conversation, definitions, or anecdotes.

I earnestly believe that if you follow the advice written here, and don't give up, you will eventually succeed. Simply reading these instructions won't do anything for you. You must apply these methods every day (as appropriate), for as long as it takes, until you achieve success.

Many, if not all, of the questions that arise during your training will answer themselves as you continue the practice and reach new milestones along the way.

Sean McNamara

Lucid Dream Instruction #1: Modify Your Sleep Habits

Dreaming happens while you're in the REM (random eye movement) stage of sleep. Your brain cycles through various stages of sleep every night, each with different levels of brain wave activity, approximately every 90-110 minutes. Most importantly, every new cycle contains progressively longer periods of REM activity.

Your first four hours of sleep are mostly Delta-wave level sleep, or deep (and dreamless) sleep. This is when your brain and body are concerned with physical recovery and healing. After seven or eight hours, the sleep cycles contain the most REM activity. This is why most people report long and vivid dreams just before waking up.

This means you need to shift your nighttime behavior to get as much sleep as you can. Specifically, do what you can to ensure eight or more hours of sleep, if possible. If you can alter your schedule so you can wake up without your sleep being cut short by an alarm, that's great!

Consider going to bed earlier, and avoid screen time after dinner. Replace it with meditation, reading, yoga, a hot bath or shower, or other peaceful activities that are good for the mind.

Keep in mind that your *greatest opportunity* to become lucid during a dream will happen after seven to eight hours of sleep. If you're serious about lucid dreaming, then you need to be serious about sleeping for as long as you can each night.

Lucid Dream Instruction #2: Keep a Dream Journal

The act of recording your dreams as soon as you wake up will increase your capacity to remember your dreams, and eventually, to realize that you are dreaming *while the dream is happening.*

Choose a blank notebook with a cover that is attractive or symbolic to you. As you'll discover, symbolism in the waking world is as important as symbolism in the dream state.

360

Resolve to *only* place your dream journal near your bed on the nights you commit to recording your dreams. Otherwise, if you keep it there and don't use it, it will literally gather dust while it loses its symbolic power. Using a dream journal is a ritual. It's only effective when you do it with proper intention and commitment.

Sometimes you'll go to bed knowing you won't have time in the morning to write down your dreams. That's alright. Simply put your journal somewhere else, like a bookcase in another room. Then, the next time you know you will be using your journal, the act of laying it at your bedside will be a subconscious signal to yourself, priming your mind to become lucid that night.

Record any dreams you have as soon as you wake up. If you happen to wake up at 3:00 am because you need to use the bathroom, and you remember the dream you were just having, record that dream as soon as you return from the bathroom, before falling back asleep. If you sleep straight through the night, record your dreams first thing in the morning after waking up, ideally while you're still in bed.

A journal has two main components to it:

1. The individual journal entries, which make up the majority of the journal.

2. A list of "dream signs" (defined below). Start making your list on the last page of your journal, and work your way backward in the pages as needed.

What to Include in Journal Entries:

1. The date and time you went to bed (write this down just before you turn out the light).

2. The time of your dream. This would be the time you woke up to write the entry, whether it was in the middle of the night or in the morning.

Sean McNamara

The purpose of recording the time of a middle-of-the-night dream is to determine your ideal time to apply the "Wake, Back to Bed" Method (WBTB), discussed later.

3. A description of the dream in **words**. Include as many details as you can. Write as if telling a story, leaving nothing out. After finishing the story, write down how it made you feel, or how you interpret or understand any symbolic meaning to it.
4. A description of the dream with **drawings**. Drawing a scene is a powerful way to capture a lot of information quickly. People, animals, buildings, vehicles, symbols and scenes are easily depicted through art.

5. Any *dream signs* which appear: These are people, animals, scenes, places, or other things which occur in more than one dream. Perhaps they show up on a regular basis. Naturally, you'll record their appearance in your journal entry every time you dream of them.

Be sure to also add them to your *list of dream signs* which you started on the very last page of your empty journal.

When you reach the point where you're recording several dreams each night, you can be confident that you're closer than ever to having your first (or next) lucid dream.

Lucid Dream Instruction #3: Set Your Intention

Before going to sleep, and after returning from any midnight bathroom trips, set a strong intention to become lucid the next time you're in the dream state.

Here are three different ways to do this:

1. Have any of your *dream signs* been showing up a lot lately? Repeat to yourself, over and over, with energy and emotion, "If [dream sign] shows up in my dream tonight, I will realize I'm dreaming." You can repeat this mentally, or even better, write it down over and over, filling a whole page in order to condition your mind.

362

2. You can also repeat a more basic intention (verbally or in writing), such as "The next time I'm dreaming, I will *become aware* that I'm dreaming." Or choose words that resonate better with you.

3. Do you often see a physical part of yourself when you dream, like your hands or feet? If so, set the intention "The next time I see my hands, I will become aware that I'm dreaming." You might even look at your own hands while setting this intention to prime your mind for dreamtime recognition.

Even if you don't have a lucid dream right away, you will notice that setting these intentions increases the number of dreams you remember in the morning. These are all aspects of the MILD technique, mnemonic-induced lucid dreaming.

"Mnemonic" refers to memory, and this type of intention-setting helps you remember to become aware during the dream state.

Lucid Dream Instruction #4: Re-Enter Your Dream

Why is it that you often have vivid recall of a dream when you wake up in the middle of the night for a bathroom break? It's because the sleep cycle you were in contained substantial REM activity.

After five hours of sleep, REM activity becomes so substantial, in fact, that when you go back to sleep, your mind can return to the REM stage it was in when your bladder started to bother you.

Therefore, you have the fantastic opportunity to become lucid by recalling the dream you were just having, and setting the intention to return to that same dream, this time with full lucidity.

To do this, recreate the dream you were just having by remembering every detail. While your body drifts off to sleep, consciously engage your dream by actively participating in it. Enjoy it! Fight off any mental fogginess or drowsiness, as much as you can.

As your body falls asleep, your mind will also want to fall asleep. Don't let it! While you imagine yourself in the dream you were just

Sean McNamara

having, say to yourself, "I know that I'm dreaming right now! I will stay awake within my dream!" Anytime you start to lose the slightest bit of consciousness, repeat these words while rousing your awareness.

Ideally, your recreated dream will transform into an actual dream, yet you'll be *lucid*, completely aware and awake inside the dream. Alternately, your mind may fade into the darkness of sleep for a short period of time, yet re-enter the REM stage, where you'll suddenly become aware that you're dreaming.

Holding onto your awareness as your body falls asleep is called the WILD technique, wake-initiated lucid dreaming.

Other ways of using WILD include:

- focusing on your heartbeat while you drift off to sleep

- focusing on your breathing while you drift off to sleep

- mentally counting back from 100 to 1, slowly, asking yourself in between counts, "Am I dreaming?" rousing your awareness as you do so in order to keep from blacking out

Lucid Dream Instruction #5: Utilize Your REM Window

The WBTB (Wake, Back to Bed) method is done by setting your alarm for a time in the middle of the night when you know you tend to have long REM periods.

How do you know what time of night is best for you? Remember your dream journal, and the instruction to write down what time you woke up to record your dream?

If you look back over several weeks of journaling, you'll start to see your personal pattern of sleeping and dreaming. For example, if many entries are written down between 3:00 am and 3:30 am, then that's a great time to set your alarm. If your bladder is as dependable (schedule-wise) as your alarm, you can rely on that instead!

The point is, by interrupting your sleep and then applying an intention-setting technique as you fall back asleep, you're tapping into a rich opportunity to become lucid. You can also try this when you wake up later in the morning, before starting your day, by falling back to sleep one more time. Remember, the later it is in the morning, the longer and more fruitful the REM period becomes.

Lucid Dream Instruction #6: State Checking

If you do a certain behavior multiple times a day, chances are you'll also do that behavior during a dream. *State checking* is a wonderful technique for training yourself into realizing you're dreaming.

If you were to jump up into the air right now, you'd be back on the ground in an instant. Gravity, right? Or, if you pressed your right index finger into your left palm, nothing more would happen than perhaps leaving an indentation in your skin from your fingernail.

But in a dream, if you were to jump up into the air, you'd very likely float upward and even fly away. Or, if you press a finger into your palm, you would like poke a hole in it. Those are great cues to make you realize you're dreaming!

State checks combine a physical ritual with a mental intention for initiating lucidity. Let's say you choose the jumping state check. Several times each day, you'll ask yourself, "Am I dreaming right now?" and then you'll jump up into the air. Naturally, you will land back on the ground immediately.

But what if you don't? What if you start to float up into the sky? If you've been training with state checks you will have asked the question "Am I dreaming?" which *switches on* your self-awareness, allowing you to realize you're in the middle of a dream.

Here's an important point. While you're asking yourself (again, several times each day), "Am I dreaming right now?" it's important to pay attention to your mind. Really look at yourself, and notice your surroundings. If you don't, the words will become meaningless and the technique will become rote.

Sean McNamara

I often hear from hopeful lucid dreamers that they performed a state check within their dream, asking the question and jumping, yet answered themselves with "Nope, I'm wide awake." Meanwhile the dream continued without their awareness.

So, *every single time* you perform your state check, do it with full awareness. Pay attention!

Another method is to pull one of your fingers. In the dream state, it might stretch out like rubber, or come off completely. If you wear a digital watch, you could check the time while asking yourself "Am I dreaming?" In the dream state, the numbers might appear scrambled, and if you notice it, you'll become lucid.

How can you remember to do your state check many times each day? You should use both "scheduled" and "unscheduled" state check techniques.

Scheduled state checks are planned. An easy way to schedule your state checks is to set an alarm on your watch or phone for every hour of your waking day. When the alarm goes off, do your state check no matter where you are or what you're doing. Pushing a finger into your palm or pulling on a finger are easy to do even during a business lunch or when hanging out with friends.
You can also coordinate your state checks with predictable, daily events such as every time you enter an elevator or get in your car.

Unscheduled state checks are random. An unscheduled state check happens when something unexpected or odd occurs during the daytime. If you're at work and see a clown walk through the office holding balloons, do your state check at that very moment.

Doing a state check anytime something strange happens in real life is wonderful because *strange things happen in dreams, all the time*! The problem is, you usually don't notice the oddness of dreams because you haven't trained your awareness.

Until now. By paying attention to unusual occurrences in everyday life and combining them with state-checking, you'll soon become lucid while you're dreaming.

A Note About Sleep Paralysis

Sleep paralysis is when you wake up yet are unable to move. It is normal, and nothing to be afraid of. Sometimes, in the moments after waking up, your brain is slow to activate your muscles. It's a good thing your brain deactivates them during the REM state, otherwise you might hurt yourself by sleepwalking or otherwise acting out your dream. If you wake up and feel paralyzed, simply relax and wait it out, or try wiggling a finger to get things moving again.

There is nothing mysterious, supernatural, or paranormal about sleep paralysis, no matter what you read on social media. But if you become anxious, avoid conjuring up images or stores about paralysis. Doing so, particularly in this half-awake state, can easily lead to hallucinations such as someone holding you down, which will only escalate your anxiety.

So just breathe, relax, and wait a few moments, and everything will be fine.

Summary of Lucid Dream Training

- Modify your sleep habits/schedule

- Use a dream journal regularly

- Set your intention every time you fall asleep

- Practice dream re-entry, and the WILD technique

- Utilize your REM window, waking up in the middle of the night

- Perform state checks every day

There are more techniques out there, but these six provide a solid foundation. If you do these techniques well, you won't need any others. If you don't have the self-discipline to do these six on a regular basis, you won't have the self-discipline to do any others, either.

For some, lucid dreaming happens easily and quickly. For others, it can take months or years. But even if it takes years, people generally find that they make incredible discoveries about themselves throughout the process, regardless of their lucid dreaming success.

Whether or not you become fully lucid, you can still develop more presence in your dreams. Everything inside a dream is a part of you, it's all your mind! And the information that is revealed is meant for you to receive, and to enrich your life with.

CONCISE INSTRUCTIONS FOR OUT-OF-BODY EXPERIENCES

OBE Guideline #1: Use an OBE journal

Journaling your OBEs is similar to journaling your dreams. I record both my OBE training and dream work in the same book. Essentially, you should track three things:

1. Dreams and Lucid Dreams

2. Your daytime OBE training schedule, and any sensations, insights, or other significant occurrences that occur during the training sessions

3. Your nighttime OBE experiences, regardless of whether or not you separate from your body. Events when you feel like you're "getting close" to separating are especially important to record. This includes the very subtle and strange sensations you'll feel while you practice your visualizations, such as twitching, temperature changes, pressure in the head and chest, the sensation of falling or floating, and more.

Remember, using a journal faithfully tells your deeper self that *you are committed* to making this happen.

Sean McNamara

OBE Guideline #2: Choose One Technique

* Specific *techniques* are described in the section following Guideline #14

It's important to choose a technique that appeals to you the most, and to stick with it for a significant period of time. "Appeals to you" doesn't necessarily mean a technique which you're instantly good at performing. Proficiency comes with regular practice and its ensuing familiarity.

It's most important to be driven by your curiosity and your passion. Forcing yourself into a technique that doesn't inspire you won't produce results, primarily because you'll stop training altogether, unless you find a new way to fuel your heart's desire.

For many people, results come slower than they prefer. Keep in mind that the experience of separating your conscious self from your physical body requires the cooperation of your subconscious self, as well as any other hidden aspects which make you whole.

If words like "spirit," "soul," "higher self," "deeper self," "guides" or "God/deity" help you, incorporate them into your understanding of reality, and their role in your progress, as you see fit.

Ultimately, this is a process of inner transformation which takes time to achieve. As you practice with your chosen method, day after day, night after night, you'll experience periods when it seems like nothing is happening. Please consider that changes may be occurring very deep inside your psyche or soul, and that these changes may be imperceptible to your rational, conscious mind.

There will also be periods when a lot of development seems to be happening. You might experience a greater frequency of both ordinary and lucid dreams. Or you may begin to feel energetic shifts while you're doing an afternoon visualization practice, or start to have separation signals while drifting off to sleep at night.

Whatever the case may be, take it all in stride, and continue training in steady fashion.

Finally, if you do get the strong sense that a technique truly isn't for you, then it's time to move on and choose a different one.

OBE Guideline #3: Be Prepared for Unusual Phenomena

It's important to know about *separation signals*, also known as the *vibrational state*, from the very beginning.

There is a particular state of consciousness on the edge of falling asleep, known as the hypnagogic state. When your brain is shifting its level of awareness, drawing ever closer to the razor's edge of sleep, it tends to produce random phenomena, primarily auditory and tactile hallucinations.

You might hear strange sounds, such as a person saying your name, or footsteps in the room, loud roaring, or even the sound of a gunshot. The sounds can be delicate and sweet as well, like tinkling bells or angelic melodies.

You might also feel someone touching your arms or legs, or feel pressure inside your skull, chest, or belly.

Sometimes these unexpected experiences can provoke a fear response inside your mind. Or, your mind may create a dream or hallucination based from that sensation. For example, if you feel pressure in your chest and become afraid, your brain may produce the image of some frightful creature sitting on top of you.

If you've ever fallen asleep in front of the TV and realized your dream incorporated the sounds from the program you were watching, then you know what I'm talking about. The mind can incorporate and confuse the information it's receiving while awake, as well as asleep.

These things can also happen while waking up. In that case, they're referred to as hypnopompic hallucinations.

There is an immense amount of misinformation on social media concerning these phenomena, typically centered on fear-based religious beliefs. I urge you to avoid and ignore these kinds of messages, particularly because your own beliefs (including those you unknowingly absorb from the internet) have a great deal of influence over how you respond to these sensations and sounds when they occur.

Instead, I encourage you to take any strange occurrence as a positive sign. If you are conscious enough to perceive any of these phenomena while you're on the fine line between being asleep and awake, then you're ever so close to consciously separating from your body.

Therefore, you might look forward to experiencing these things, instead of fearing them when they occur.

Here is an exercise to help you become relaxed and comfortable with hypnagogic phenomena. First, lie down in a room where you can be alone. Doing this in the darkness and quiet of nighttime is ideal.

Take a few minutes to relax, whether you're lying down on the couch, in bed, or on the floor.

Then, spend some time pretending that an invisible person is gently brushing or poking your arms and legs, pulling your toes, or twirling your hair. You'll likely notice your heart rate increase, and you might have other feelings of anxiety. First, remember that you're creating all of this. Second, breathe deeply while continuing to imagine the sensations, reminding yourself that you're perfectly safe. Continue doing this until your heart rate has returned to normal, and your body and mind feel completely relaxed, and peaceful.

Then, perhaps the next day, repeat the exercise, but imagine that you can hear noises in the room all around you. Listen for creaking sounds in the floor, walls, and windows. Notice any anxious responses to this scenario, and stay with them while taking deep breaths. Again, continue until you feel totally at ease, and even completely bored. Boredom is a sure sign that you're relaxed.

Doing these exercises a few times will prepare you to remain calm and steady when you have actual hypnogogic or hypnopompic hallucinations, or when you experience the famous "vibrational state."

OBE Guideline #4: The Vibrational State

The vibrational state was made famous in the modern era when Robert Monroe described his spontaneous OBEs in the now classic *Journeys Out of the Body*. However, this experience has been described in many other texts as well.

Whereas hypnogogic and hypnopompic hallucinations mark the ripe opportunity to separate from one's body (the time when the body is asleep but the mind remains conscious), the vibrational state is regarded as the hallmark of an impending separation from the body.

Imagine quietly lying in bed, or in your OBE training area, when suddenly you feel waves, swirls, lines or pulses of energy flowing up and down your body, from your feet to the top of your head and back again.

Imagine that your entire body, and even your bed, are trembling and shaking as if an earthquake were happening.

Along with those sensations, imagine a loud buzzing, like the sizzle of electricity, or a loud roar, like from an engine or a tornado, filling your ears.

These are just a few of the many ways you might experience the vibrational state. Being aware of it now will help you remain calm and relaxed when you experience it in the course of your training.

Sean McNamara

Just know that the vibrational state, along with hypnogogic and hypnopompic sensations *are all good news*. They're all signs you're doing a great job of maintaining awareness on the edge of sleep.

Are these vibrations required in order to leave one's body? No. While some people experience them regularly, others never or rarely do. Some report their vibrational state has diminished or disappeared entirely over time.

Some people have OBEs without ever going through any vibrational state.

This is where it's extremely important to avoid turning my, or anybody else's instructions, into dogma or a set of rules. Take what I write as simple guidance and suggestions. It's a starting point. Your vibrational state may feel or sound completely different than what I describe.

So be open, and don't be swayed by people who say, "This is how it is. This is the one and only way." They may not have ever had an experience for themselves.

OBE Guideline #5: Separation is Primed, Not Forced

It is easy to assume that the vibrational state is something one does directly, like turning something on, or willing it to happen on command.

Please don't make that mistake. In my experience, the vibrational state, and also the actual separation from the body, happen naturally as a result of something that came before. What is that "something?" It's your specific technique.

To put it simply, you do your technique, and the vibrational state *happens on its own afterward*, as a natural result of applying your technique as your body falls asleep.

Your technique may be a visualization, or repeating an affirmation, or doing a meditation, or listening to special music, etc. Whatever

374

you choose, focus on that. When the time and conditions are right, and when you're mentally and emotionally ready for it, the vibrations will happen on their own, and separation may or may not follow immediately afterward.

OBE Guideline #6: Two Potential Moments

From this point forward, I'll use the term "separation signals" to include both the classic vibrational state as well hypnagogic phenomena.

Imagine that you've been lying in bed, doing a particular visualization for a while. In addition to simply falling asleep with nothing happening, two other outcomes are possible:

- You immediately experience one or more separation signals

- You fall asleep, but later that night, you become spontaneously conscious of separation signals. Your mind has "woken up," but your physical body is still asleep.

Almost all of my own OBEs have occurred the second way, after a brief "blackout" following a period of visualization or repeating affirmations. It's helpful for you to be aware of both possibilities so you can respond without surprise when they occur.

OBE Guideline #7: Allow and Direct Your Separation

There are two mistakes to avoid when you experience separation signals:

- Becoming overly excited and trying to force yourself out of your body too soon

- Doing nothing or waiting too long, and losing the opportunity to leave your body

I've made the first mistake many times, which was a great way to learn to relax, appreciate, and even enjoy the separation signals as

Sean McNamara

they occurred. I believe they have value in and of themselves, and are part of a process which must be completed before separating from the body.

I've also made the second mistake many times. I may have even been detached from my body, yet didn't leave it. It's as if I'd released the brakes, but didn't bother to step on the gas. Again, these times were great opportunities to learn how to navigate the separation process.

The best advice I've ever found has come from William Buhlman in his book *Adventures Beyond the Body*. He suggests that when the moment is right, to direct your mental attention anywhere other than your own body.

For example, when you feel ready to "leave," *point your mind* at your bedroom door, or the front door of your home. While keeping your attention on the door, *intend* to be there, at that exact spot.

Don't look at the door with your physical eyes. Don't move your head, or any other part of your body. Rather, simply generate the *desire* to be there.

Keep your intention steady, and you'll eventually feel separation taking place. Don't worry, you'll know it when it happens. It's unlike anything you've ever felt while you were physically awake.

OBE Guideline #8: Where Attention Goes, Energy Flows

Guideline #7 brings up another crucial piece of advice. When the separation signals occur, we tend to be focused on our body (whether it's the energetic, mental, or physical body doesn't really matter).

However, it's very important to ignore your bodily sensations, or anything else that keeps your attention on your physical identity. That's why pointing your attention at the door or anywhere else far from your body is important. If you keep your attention on where your body is lying, or on the body itself, that's where you'll stay.

So, point your mind somewhere away from your body and all its accompanying sensations to allow the non-physical "you" to follow.

This can be particularly difficult if annoying sensations like itchy pinpricks on the nose or face happen, or if your body feels extremely heavy. No matter what, don't move a muscle. Activating your physical body is the fastest way to sabotage a potential separation.

OBE Guideline #9: Keep Calm, Be Cool

In addition to focusing on your physical body, feeling fear is the surest way to end a separation in progress. Not only fear, though. *Any* extreme emotion, including positive excitement, has the capacity to stop the process. Therefore, remember that while an OBE is unfolding, it's important to stay emotionally calm the whole way through.

The truth is, fear and other intense emotions are almost completely unavoidable, and par for the course during OBE training. In my learning process, I realized that I could only get to a certain stage, and would have to wear out my fear and excitement over and over again before being able to progress to the next stage.

Contradictory as it sounds, you'll want to become bored with the process, at whatever stage you're in. Once you're bored, it means you're no longer afraid or overexcited, and the emotional barrier to the next stage will evaporate.

OBE Guideline #10: Awkward Departures

So many books and videos depict an OBE as a person floating straight up out of their body, as though they're being carried away by a cloud. That can happen, but there are many other possible modes of departure.

It's good for you to be aware of them ahead of time so you're not surprised when they happen:

- You might sink backwards through your mattress, then through the floor

- Your legs might lift straight up to the ceiling, so that you dive headfirst into (and through) the floor

- You might rise up into standing position

- You might just sit up, as if sitting on the edge of your bed, and simply walk away

- You might feel a rush of speed, as if moving through space, and "arrive" at a familiar or unknown location

- You might *instantly* find yourself at another location, without any sense of distance traversed

You don't need to worry about how to walk, fly, or teleport once you've left your body. You'll instinctively know what to do.

This image is an artistic depiction of being separated, yet still in the local environment. This is just one of numerous ways a person may experience the first moments after leaving their body.

OBE Guideline #11: Your OBE "body"

During OBEs, I've experienced my sense of self in many ways. None were by choice. I have no idea why or how these experiences arose. While out of the body my sense of "being me" has included:

- formless consciousness, just "mind" in space
- a dark body, with bright lights shining through "me" and with arms and legs that felt as physical and real as my biological limbs
- a large blob, stretching across the floor
- a normal human body (just like my biological body)

Some readers may have heard about "the silver cord," and been surprised when, after leaving their body, they don't see one anywhere! I personally believe the silver cord is a subjective and symbolic "thought form," a mental projection which is perceived as existent in the out of body state.

If a person has read books saying the silver cord is real, or been told that by someone they regard as an authority figure, they're likely to project the cord into their experience. Why do I think it's subjective? Some people have reported the cord as being attached to their lower back, others to the back of the skull, and others yet, to their navel! If it's an objective reality, how can it be attached to different parts of different people?

OBE Guideline #12: Control or Surrender?

Once you've separated from your body, you have a choice. You can try to control what happens next ("I want to go visit my friend"), or you can surrender to your deeper self, a higher power, or the like.

At a certain point, I realized that OBEs were easier and far more rich with meaning when I surrendered control after leaving my body. By evoking an attitude of "Ok, take me somewhere which will help me grow," I found myself in places I could never imagine.

Sean McNamara

The times I tried to maintain control usually found me doing meaningless things like walking through my apartment or down the street outside. Like everything else OBE-related, giving up control came through repeated trial and error.

OBE Guideline #13: Train Regularly

During the many weeks that I practiced before my first OBE, I took the training very seriously. Fortunately, I had a job which didn't require me to be at an office all day. Therefore, I often had multiple training opportunities each day.

I would typically practice first in the mid-afternoon, when I could be at home for a while. I used my living room as my training area (don't use your own bed, that's where you're conditioned to lose consciousness every night). I would lie down on the floor or the couch, and use a visualization until I either drifted off into a nice nap, or had to get up and go back to work.

My second training opportunity took place when I went to bed each night, usually around 10:30. As I drifted off to sleep I repeated the same visualization I'd practiced earlier that afternoon.

My third practice opportunity happened in the middle of the night, much like the "Wake, Back to Bed" technique borrowed from lucid dreaming.

One difference, however, is that instead of returning to bed, I'd lie down in my training area in the living room and do my technique there.

Whether it was unplanned (bathroom break), or planned (with my alarm), I would always practice the visualization as I drifted back to sleep. Some people might read this and wonder if an OBE produced with the WBTB method is actually a dream, since the REM stage is likely occurring in the brain at that time.

In my experience, OBEs, regular dreams, and lucid dreams each have distinct qualities, both in how they're initiated, and in what I encounter during each one.

Another reason I don't think a 3:00 am OBE is just a dream is because I've had dreams and OBEs *at the same time*, and could tell them apart. It was as if my non-physical mind was perceiving what the physical brain was going through in the REM stage. It was a little like walking around with a "heads-up display" projecting onto the field in front of me.

The point is, practicing for an OBE can be part of your daytime meditation, as well as something you do when you go to bed, and again whenever you get up in the middle of the night.

In fact, there's no rule that says you can't have an OBE while the sun is up. Many people succeed by returning to bed after waking up in the morning, and letting themselves drift off while practicing their visualization or affirmation.

OBE Guideline #14: Know When to Let Go

Some people fall asleep naturally while reciting affirmations or doing a visualization. Others tend to focus too hard, which keeps them awake. If this describes you, remember that sometimes it's good to be gentle with a technique.

At other times, it's best to just stop the technique completely after a few minutes, to *let go*, and to allow yourself to drift off, trusting that your investment will pay off in time. That time may be a few minutes after blacking out, or after an hour, or at a later date.

Sean McNamara

OBE TECHNIQUES

OBE Technique #1: Affirmations

This is just like Lucid Dream Instruction #3. Select a phrase which resonates with you, such as "I will leave my body," or "Tonight, I separate," or "Now I'm out of body."

You'll simply repeat it mentally as you feel your physical body falling asleep, or take a few minutes to write your chosen phrase down over and over again on a blank piece of paper.

Be sure to *feel your intention and desire* with every line that you write. Simply going through the act without the feeling won't produce any effects.

OBE Technique #2: Separation Rehearsal

Go to your practice area during the day, and lie down. Then, slowly sit up, and eventually stand up, feeling the floor beneath your feet. Walk toward the door, memorizing how your visual perspective of the room changes as you move forward. As you reach for the doorknob, memorize how it looks, and how it feels in your hand. Memorize how it feels to pull the door open, then walk through it.

Carry on this way, as you memorize how it feels to open doors and walk through your home and out the main door, continuing down the sidewalk and away from the building. Memorize all the steps you take. If you use an elevator in your building, memorizing the sensation of ascending and descending can be especially potent for initiating an OBE.

Do this routine regularly in order to maintain a clear and steady memory of what it's like to rise up from your training area and to walk away from it.

Once you've established a clear visualization, you can replay it in your mind while you drift off to sleep after lying down in bed. You

382

can also replay it as part of your afternoon training session, or as part of your WBTB method in the middle of the night.

OBE Technique #3: The Target Technique

I learned this from *Adventures Beyond the Body* by William Buhlman. Think of two or three physical objects which are easy for you to visualize, objects that you personally know very well, and which are small enough to carry.

Take those objects to a room in your home, far away from the bedroom or your OBE training area. Spend some time lifting them, holding them, and feeling their textures with your hand. Memorize exactly how they feel, as well as where you've positioned them in that room (on a specific table, for instance).

As you fall asleep, visualize yourself being inside that room, walking toward one of the objects, then spending time lifting, holding, touching, and looking at it. After a while, return the object to its proper place and repeat the process with the other objects, one at a time. The point is to do this with such presence of mind that you truly feel as if you were in that room, and as if you were physically touching those objects.

Like Technique #2, this visualization serves to *compel* your sense of self to travel to a location away from the physical body.

However, you should always allow that a subsequent OBE can take you somewhere *other* than the room you're using for your visualization.

For better effect, you might consider placing your objects in someone else's home, in a room you're familiar with. The increased distance from your bedroom or training area will be helpful.

OBE Technique #4: The Magic Ladder

To perform this visualization, first lie down in your training area. Then, look up at your ceiling and imagine a hole appearing, and

383

that a special ladder drops down from the heavens. The bottom rung hangs within easy reach of your arms.

To strengthen this visualization, physically raise your arms as if you were actually reaching for a ladder. Then, pretend that you're able to pull your body up the ladder using only your arms. Raising one arm after the other, feel your muscles working as you see yourself climbing higher and higher up the ladder, into the night sky above.

Do this for several minutes, memorizing what it feels like to move your arms like this. Also, memorize how you imagine rising up higher and higher along this ladder and into the night sky. Is there a breeze blowing outside? Is the air warm, or cool? Is it a full moon? What do the stars look like?

After going through this process several times, use this visualization while falling asleep, and during any other training period. Begin by moving your arms, then lay them down while you continue imagining them in motion.

If you'd like, you could replace the imagined ladder with a simple rope.

OBE Technique #5: Transforming a Lucid Dream

When you're having a lucid dream, you're much more in touch with your subconscious mind than when you're awake. You can ask questions, explore your creativity, activate your healing potential, and release your attachment to the physical body.

For this reason, when you find yourself completely lucid within a dream, you can command or request to have an OBE. Simply and firmly state something like "I separate from my body now!" or "Now I have an OBE!" Create a powerful phrase that works best for you.

If successful, your dream imagery will fade out, and different things can occur. You might become conscious of lying in bed and feeling the separation signals. Or, you might find yourself already transported to an entirely different location, or standing next to your bed while your body remains asleep. Other variations are possible as well.

OBE Technique #6: Asking for Help

Are you in touch with your guides, angels, deceased friends and family, or other non-physical beings? Why not ask them for help? Making earnest and repeated supplications while you fall asleep can be a powerful means for initiating the separation process.

When successful, you may simply become aware of the separation signals on your own. Or, you might be contacted by a non-physical being in a dream, who then assists you with leaving your body. Anything is possible.

As I wrote in the introduction to these instructions, you'll answer many of your own questions in the course of your training, and after having full-blown lucid dreams and OBEs.

Allowing people to find their own truth instead of telling them what I or others believe to be true is the best way to prevent a dogmatic attitude from prevailing in this field of consciousness exploration.

RECOMMENDED RESOURCES

The following resources have been grouped by topic. You can find clickable links to all of them at:

www.RenegadeMysticBook.com/links

Books by Sean McNamara

Defy Your Limits: The Telekinesis Training Method. McNamara, Sean. (2017). Mind Possible.

Signal and Noise: Advanced Psychic Development for Remote Viewing, Clairvoyance, and ESP. McNamara, Sean. (2020). Mind Possible.

Meditation X: Telekinesis: The Mindfulness Practice of Moving Matter with Subtle Energy and Intention. McNamara, Sean. CreateSpace Independent Publishing.

Online Video Courses by Sean McNamara
from www.MindPossible.com

*Get 10% off with code "Renegade"
- Lucid Dreaming & the Out-of-Body Experience
- Remote Viewing: A Course in Practical Psychic Perception
- Telekinesis Video Course
- Guided Meditation Journeys & Vagus Nerve Stimulation

Develop Your Own Psychic Perception

The Essential Guide to Remote Viewing: The Secret Military Remote Perception Skill Anyone Can Learn. Smith, Paul H. (2015) Intentional Press.

Everybody's Guide to Natural ESP: Unlocking the Extrasensory Power of Your Mind. Swann, Ingo. (2018). Swann-Ryder Productions, LLC.

Extraordinary Psychic: Proven Techniques to Master Your Natural Psychic Abilities. Katz, Debra Lynn. (2014). Living Dreams Press.

Mental Radio: Studies in Consciousness (Illustrated). Sinclair, Upton. (2008). CreateSpace Independent Publishing.

The Premonition Code: The Science of Precognition, How Sensing the Future Can Change Your Life. Cheung, Theresa & Mossbridge, Julia. (2018). Watkins Publishing.

Psychic Intuition: Everything You Ever Wanted to Ask but Were Afraid to Know. Du Tertre, Nancy. (2012). Weiser.

Remote Viewing Secrets: A Handbook. McMoneagle, J. (2000). Hampton Roads Pub Co.

If you want to Have an Out-of-Body Experience

Adventures Beyond the Body: How to Experience Out-of-Body Travel. Buhlman, William. (1996) HarperOne.

Explorations in Consciousness: A New Approach to Out-of-Body Experiences. Aardema, Frederick. (2012). Mount Royal Publishing.

Sean McNamara

How to Have an Out of Body Experience: Transcend the Limits of Physical Form and Accelerate Your Spiritual Evolution. [Audio Program]. Buhlman, William. (2010). Sounds True.

Hypnagogia: The Unique State of Consciousness Between Wakefulness and Sleep. Mavromatis, Andreas. (2010). Thyrsos Press.[52]

Journeys Out of the Body: The Classic Work on Out-of-Body Experience. Monroe, Robert. (1992). Broadway Books.

Navigating the Out-of-Body Experience: Radical New Techniques. Nicholls, Graham. (2012). Llewellyn Publications.

Out-of-Body Experiences: How to Have Them and What to Expect. Peterson, Robert. (2013). Hampton Roads Publishing.

Projection of the Astral Body. Muldoon, Sylvan J. (2011). Read Books.

If you want to Have a Lucid Dream

Exploring the World of Lucid Dreaming. Laberge, Stephen & Rheingold, Howard. (1991) Ballantine Books.

A Field Guide to Lucid Dreaming: Mastering the Art of Oneironautics. Tuccillo, Dylan, et al. (2013). Workman Publishing Company.

Lucid Dreaming, Plain and Simple: Tips and Techniques for Insight, Creativity, and Personal Growth. Waggoner, Robert & McCready, Caroline. (2015) Red Wheel.

---

[52] Everyone who practices any kind of night time explorations should read "Hypnagogia" by Andreas Mavromatis. It's a "must have."

Parapsychology & Scientific Research

Beyond Telepathy. Puharich, Andrija. (1973). Anchor Press.

The End of Materialism: How Evidence of the Paranormal Is Bringing Science and Spirit Together. Tart, Charles. (2009) New Harbinger Publications.

The Limits of Influence. Braude, Stephen E. (1996). University Press of America.

Mind to Mind. Warcollier, Rene. (2001). Hampton Roads Publishing.

Phenomena: The Secret History of the U.S. Government's Investigations into Extrasensory Perception and Psychokinesis. Jacobsen, Annie. (2018). Back Bay Books.

The Reality of ESP: A Physicist's Proof of Psychic Abilities. Targ, Russell. (2012) Quest Books.

Real Magic: Ancient Wisdom, Modern Science, and a Guide to the Secret Power of the Universe. Radin, Dean. (2018). Harmony.

The Selection Effect: How Consciousness Shapes Reality. Mertz, Herb. (2020). Penn Wolcott Press.

Synchronized Universe: New Science of the Paranormal. Swanson, Claude. (2003). Poseidia Press.

Supernormal: Science, Yoga, and the Evidence for Extraordinary Psychic Abilities. Radin, Dean. (2013). Deepak Chopra.

Sean McNamara

Energy Healing & Intentional Healing

The Biology of Belief: Unleashing the Power of Consciousness, Matter and Miracles. Lipton, Bruce. (2005). Authors Pub Corp

The Energy Cure: Unraveling the Mystery of Hands-On Healing. Bengston, William & Fraser, Sylvia. (2010). Sound True.

The Power of Eight: Harnessing the Miraculous Energies of a Small Group to Heal Others, Your Life, and the World. McTaggart, Lynne. (2018). Atria Books.

Books About Extraordinarily Psychic People[53]

China's Super Psychics. Dong, Paul & Raffill, Thomas E. (1997). Da Capo Press.

The PK Man: A True Story of Mind Over Matter. Mishlove, Jeffrey & Mack, John. (2000). Hampton Roads Publishing.

Psychic Discoveries Behind the Iron Curtain. Ostrander, Sheila & Schroeder, Lynn. (1971). Bantam.

Uri: A Journal of the Mystery of Uri Geller. Puharich, Andrija. (1974). Anchor Press.

Uri Geller, My Story. Geller, Uri. (1975). Praeger.

---

[53] Many people aren't aware that Uri Geller has had encounters with extraterrestrials since childhood. And E.T.s were integral to Ted Owens's (the "The PK Man.") abilities. There is much left to learn about the relationship between extraordinary powers and the influence of E.T.s and UFOs.

How to Meditate

The Experience of Samadhi: An In-depth Exploration of Buddhist Meditation. Shankman, Richard. (2008). Shambhala.

Mindfulness: A Practical Guide to Awakening. Goldstein, Joseph. (2016). Sounds True.

Moving Dhamma Volume 1: The Path and Progress of Meditation using the Earliest Buddhist Suttas from the Majjhima Nikaya. Vimalaramsi, Bhante. (2012). Dhamma Sukha Publications.

Extraterrestrials, UFO's, Non-Human Contact

Contact from Planet Apu: Beings from the Future Among Us. Gonzalez, Ricardo. (2016). Luminous Moon Press, LLC.

Conversations with Colonel Corso: A Personal Memoir and Photo Album. Harris, Paola. (2017). Luminous Moon Press, LLC.

The Super Natural: Why the Unexplained Is Real. Strieber, Whitley & Kripal Jeffrey J. (2017). TarcherPerigee.[54]

Dealing with Skeptics

Randi's Prize: What Sceptics Say about the Paranormal, Why They Are Wrong and Why It Matters. McLuhan, Robert. (2010). Troubador Publishing Ltd.

---

[54] One could almost regard "The Super Natural" by Strieber and Kripal as an unofficial companion volume to this book. Very insightful regarding contact experiences with otherworldly beings.

Dakinis and Saints in the Tibetan Tradition

Dakini's Warm Breath: The Feminine Principle in Tibetan Buddhism. Simmer-Brown, Judith. (2002). Shambhala.

The Life of Milarepa: A New Translation from the Tibetan. Lhalungpa, Lobsang. P. (1992). Penguin.

Movies

Third Eye Spies. Mungia, Lance. (2019). Conscious Universe Films.

Our Home (Original Title: Nosso Lar/Astral City). De Assis, Wagner. (2010). Cinética Filmes e Produções.

Out on A Limb. Butler, Robert. (1987). ABC Circle Films.

Superhuman: The Invisible Made Visible. Cory, Caroline. (2019). Omnium Media.

Witness of Another World. Stivelman, Alan. (2018). Humano Films SA.

Have Experiences, Learn & Connect

Applied Precognition Project (annual conference)
www.AppliedPrecog.com

Arthur Findlay College (Essex, United Kingdom)
www.ArthurFindlayColleg.org

The Institute of Noetic Sciences
www.noetic.org

Have Experiences, Learn & Connect cont'd

International Association for Near Death Studies
www.IANDS.org

International Remote Viewing Association (annual conference)
www.IRVA.org & www.IRVAConference.org

The Monroe Institute
www.MonroeInstitute.org

Parapsychological Association
www.parapsych.org

Rhine Research Center - Research on the Frontier of Consciousness Science
www.Rhine.org

Society for Scientific Exploration (annual conference)
www.ScientificExploration.org

StarworksUSA (annual conference)
www.StarworksUSA.com

SyncCreation - Manifest Your Dreams & Live a Life of Abundance
www.SyncCreation.com

Trebor Seven - Telekinesis
www.TreborSeven.com

William Buhlman - OBEs
www.Astralinfo.org

Windbridge Research Center - Studying dying, death, and what comes next
www.Windbridge.org

Sean McNamara

Avoiding or Healing from High-Demand Groups/Cults

Dangerous Personalities: An FBI Profiler Shows You How to Identify and Protect Yourself from Harmful People. Navarro, Joe (2018). Rodale Books.

Take Back Your Life: Recovering from Cults and Abusive Relationships. Lalich, Janja. (2006). Bay Tree Publishing.

YouTube Channels (see www.RenegadeMysticBook.com/links)

New Thinking Allowed with Jeffrey Mishlove (parapsychology, paranormal, spirituality, science)

Regina Meredith (consciousness and spirituality)

Richard Dolan (UFO, extraterrestrials, government involvement)

Sean McNamara's channels (Consciousness & Telekinesis)

Trebor Seven (telekinesis)

We Don't Die Radio with Sandra Champlain (near death experiences, afterlife)

Whitley Strieber's Dreamland Radio, UnknownCountry.com

In Colorado (groups, locations, and individuals)

Aprylisa Snyder, healing in Boulder/Longmont
www.HealCreateThrive.com

Boulder chapter of the Society for Scientific Exploration
www.BoulderSSE.org

Boulder BEES and IANDS with Jacqueline Arnold
on Facebook

BoulderExo - Exoculture, Exoconsciousness, Exopolitics
www.BoulderExo.com

Full Moon Books Metaphysical Bookstore and Event Center
www.FullMoonBooks.com

Goddess Isis Books & Gifts
www.IsisBooks.com

Jude Starks - Evidential Medium and Teacher
www.JudeStarks.com

Mayu Sanctuary, founded by Cierra McNamara
www.MayuSanctuary.com

Paige Losen - Artist
instagram.com/paigerefresh & www.PaigeLosen.com

Paranormal Research Forum with Rick Nelson
www.ParanormalResearchForum.net

Shining Lotus Bookstore
www.ShiningLotus.com

Sonya Shannon - Spiritual Healer, Artist, and Reader
www.Sonya-Shannon.com

ABOUT THE AUTHOR

[From the first edition]

I live in Denver, Colorado with my wife Cierra. I ordinarily spend a lot of time at Mayu Sanctuary, teaching meditation. Also, I periodically offer psychic development classes at various locations.

I could say more, perhaps about my future plans and career aspirations, but it's mid-March, 2020. As I put the finishing touches on this manuscript, there's still no clear end in sight to the COVID-19 virus which has impacted the entire population of our planet. So, "about the author." This author is taking it one day at a time, with a heart full of appreciation for this precious, beautiful life.

May you live long, and prosper.

Made in the USA
Monee, IL
27 October 2023

45307724R00246